The Canterbury and York Society

GENERAL EDITOR: PROFESSOR R.L. STOREY

ISSN 0262–995X

DIOCESE OF EXETER

CANTERBURY AND YORK SOCIETY VOL. LXXXVII

The Register of

Walter Bronescombe

BISHOP OF EXETER

1258–1280

VOLUME II

EDITED BY

O.F. ROBINSON

READER IN LAW
UNIVERSITY OF GLASGOW

Canterbury and York Society

The Boydell Press
1999

First published 1999
A Canterbury and York Society publication
published by The Boydell Press
an imprint of Boydell & Brewer Ltd
PO Box 9, Woodbridge, Suffolk IP12 3DF, UK
and of Boydell & Brewer Inc.
PO Box 41026, Rochester, NY 14604–4126, USA
website: http://www.boydell.co.uk

ISBN 0 907239 57 9

A catalogue record for this book is available
from the British Library

Details of previous volumes available from Boydell & Brewer Ltd

This publication is printed on acid-free paper

Printed in Great Britain by
St Edmundsbury Press Ltd, Bury St Edmunds, Suffolk

CONTENTS

FOREWORD

This volume completes the main content of the Register. It consists of calendared entries, in particular of institutions of various kinds. They normally add: 'and he has letters', but this will not be mentioned. The turn of the folio is marked as accurately as is possible. Interesting phrases are given in the original Latin in brackets or in a footnote.

Entries translated here, which are transcribed in full in Volume III, are marked with an asterisk. Some of these are not strictly transcribed in full, because the heads and tails have been omitted as being common form. In all cases a quotation mark indicates where direct citation starts. There are also a few translations of entries printed elsewhere; this is indicated by a footnote, as opposed to an asterisk. Some of the entries are interesting not simply for their content but because they give the flavour of the bishop's – or his chancery's – style. There are other entries – not institutions, etc – where a paraphrase rather than a bare calendaring seems adequate and appropriate.

Because Volume I was a facing-page text and translation there has been no need to transcribe entries of common form; the exception is **489**, because it dates from Stephen Langton's archiepiscopate.

Translations are fairly literal, but the breaking up of extremely long sentences often involves some alteration of the sentence structure. Paragraphs are also used to make comprehension easier. Marginal headings will only be noted in this volume when they are unusual, or supply information not given in the entry itself. Dots . . . represent a blank space.

When the MS spelling of a place name differs from the modern (other than by inflection) it is given in italics within round brackets the first time it appears. Unidentified place names are given as spelled in the MS, in italics. As was explained in the Introduction, vol.1, p.xi, fn.10, some folios, specifically fo.35v and fo.91v as well as later ones, were used for writing in entries concerned with the diocese but not the Bronescombe's episcopate.

Family names are identified with places within the diocese where possible, because there does seem to be a general preference for local men. Christian names have been anglicized, but most family names are left as they stand, with the exception of a few well-known ones, such as Champernowne (*Campo Arnulphi*), Raleigh, St Aubyn (*S. Albino*) or Sackville (*Sicca Villa*). Occupation names are normally rendered as surnames, at least for the clergy. *Filius* has been translated as 'son' except where a 'fitz-' family is known. The Index will collect the variant spellings of personal names.

Volume III will consist of the Latin text of the asterisked entries, and also an Appendix containing the deeds stitched into the register which date from Bronescombe's time or earlier. Another Appendix will give the cathedral statutes of 1269 and 1278. There will also be the Indexes.

In addition to the Acknowledgements in Volume I, I owe thanks to a number of people, and particularly to Professor John Thomson of the University of

Glasgow and Professor Jim Brundage of the University of Kansas, who both
have read through the Latin text, guiding me towards which entries should be
translated. Jim Brundage, in a private communication, has given me much
other help, particularly on matters of canon law. Professor Nicholas Orme of the
University of Exeter has helped me with the identification of place-names. As I
said earlier, the late Rev. F.C. Hingeston-Randolph had a deep knowledge of his
subject. Where he is dealing with strictly diocesan matters, the burden of proof
seems to be on the one who would correct him; hence, where I have parted from
his identification of places, I have explained why. However, he was not
particularly interested in the many non-diocesan matters in this register, and
his edition is not at all user-friendly. Professor Robin Storey continues to be a
general editor to whom all contributors to the Canterbury and York series must
be grateful. I am grateful to the Isobel Thornley Bequest for its subvention.
Sebastian, my husband, has continued to be a tower of strength, checking all the
translations, and beginning to compile the Indexes.

Corrections to volume I:

24 is deanery of Lezant.
112 is Halwill.
118 could refer to St Issey (*Egloscruc*), or Crewkerne.
239 should read Thorncombe.
466 is Harford, not Harpford.

O.F. Robinson
18 December 1998

476 Inst. of Philip son of Henry, subdeacon, to St Tudy (*S. Tudi*); patron, Henry son of Henry junior. Dartford, 25 April 1263.

477 Nicholas, rector of St Dominick in Cornwall, furnished security under oath about obeying the commands of the Church, and concerning this he gave a bond, in that he had intruded into Dittisham (*Dydsaham*) church, and he obtained the benefit of absolution in the Church's form. [No place], 18 May 1263.

478 Brother Geoffrey . . . was admitted by the lord bishop to the rule of Tywardreath Priory at the presentation, through a proctor, of the abbot and convent of St Serge, Angers, on terms that from now on the prior is in no way to be removed without the assent and agreement of the same bishop or his successors. London, 22 May 1263.

479 Collation of Master John de Esse to the prebend of Crantock (*S. Carantoci*) which Master William de Treiagou had held. Faringdon, . . . 1263.

480 Inst. of Hamelin de Hopeton, chaplain, to the vicarage of St Gennys (*S. Genisii*); patrons, the prior and convent of Launceston. Paignton, 22 June² 1263.

481 Inst. of Robert, chaplain, of Cullompton (*Calumton*), to the vacant parsonage of Rame, with the right of accrual and of succeeding to the whole right after the death of Robert, vicar of the same church; patron, Fulk de Ferrars. Paignton, 22 June, 1263.

482 Inst. of Master Oliver de Tracy to Ilfracombe (*Aufricum*); patron (*ad presentationem alias factam*), Henry de Champernowne, knight. Exeter, 25 June 1263.

483 Inst. of Nicholas called Rufus, chaplain, to Willand (*ecc. de la Wydelond*); patrons, the prior and convent of Taunton. Dunkeswell, 27 June 1263.

484 Inst. of Peter de Weure, deacon, to the vicarage of Cadbury (*Chadebery*); patrons, the prior and convent of St Nicholas, Exeter. London, 6 July 1263.

485³ Richard de Almeton, chaplain, given custody of the vicarage of Kingsteignton (*Teinton Regis*), until the bishop should come to the Devon area (*ad partes Devon'*); patron, the precentor of Salisbury, through his proctor, Master Walter de Sine Muro. London, 6 July 1263.

---

¹ It is possible that a new registrar started here, since the previous page was not fully used, and this entry is formally dated by the (continuing) year of the bishop's consecration.
² MS has *x kal. Junii*, ie 23 May, but if the bishop has reached Paignton *x kal Julii* is surely more likely.
³ See **503**, where Richard is called de Allempton.

486 Inst. of Sampson de Huxham, chaplain, to Poltimore (*Pultymore*), saving any other claim (*salvo iure cuiuslibet*); patron, Richard de Poltimore. Exeter, 16 August 1263.

487 Inst. of Payne de Liskeard, clerk, to Michaelstow (*S. Michaelis de Hellesbery*); patron, the king of Germany [Richard, earl of Cornwall]. Lawhitton, 23 August 1263.

488[4] SUBMISSION OF PLYMPTON. Letters patent of Walter called le Hostiler, canon of Plympton, proctor of the subprior and convent of Plympton, concerning the dispute between the bishop and the priory over the right of patronage to and the custody of the conventual church of Plympton (*Plimpton*), which the bishop claimed in time of vacancy, [fo.27] and over the election of Brother Robert called Blund, and over certain sentences of excommunication by the bishop and his official, and other matters raised before various judges. The proctor of the convent now recognized the bishop's rights in a vacancy – to be used discreetly (*et ea pacifice utatur et quiete*) – and on behalf of the subprior and other obedientiaries (sacristan, precentor, cellarer, and steward) he promised obedience to the bishop and now begged for absolution, promising that those who had been excommunicated by name and certain others would appear in person, on a date to be set, before the bishop in Exeter cathedral. As to the other matters at issue, he submitted himself, the subprior and convent to the decision of the dean of Wells [Edward de la Knolle], Henry de Bracton, and the archdeacons of Exeter [Roger de Torridge] and Norfolk [Nicholas de Plympton], to be given before the next 14 September. He promised obedience to the decision on behalf of the convent, under penalty of 100 pounds of silver due from the party reneging to the party observing the settlement, unless a satisfactory compromise was reached. When the election of Robert Blund should have been renounced, the convent would obtain licence to elect from the bishop, and would then proceed to the election of Robert or another, to be submitted for the bishop's approval. The bishop promised to give a similar undertaking, and both parties appended their seals. Witnesses: Sirs Henry de Tracy, H[enry] de Bracton, Ralph de Doddiscombe, John de Weston, Masters John Noble, Robert Everard, John de Bradley, John Wyger, Gervase de Crediton, W. de Ralegh, W[illiam] de Capella, and others. Winkleigh, 21 August 1263.

489* EXAMPLE OF A DISPENSATION.[5] 'To all the sons of holy mother church Stephen [Langton], by divine permission archbishop of Canterbury [1207–28], primate of all England, and cardinal of the holy Roman church, health in the Lord. It is proper that at a suitable time special grace should be bestowed on those recommended by the probity of their morals and the honesty of their life so that they may validly obtain by the benefit of grace what is not granted them by ordinary rule of law [fo.27v]. Therefore, since our beloved and confidential

---

[4] Cf **475** and **495–6**.

[5] A Walter son of Peter was treasurer of Exeter in 1264; it is chronologically possible that this might explain an otherwise strange entry. The only appearance in the *Acta* of Archbishop Langton (C & Y Society, vol.50) of Walter son of Peter is as a witness in 1227.

assistant, Walter son of Peter, clerk, had, before the General Council [Lateran IV, 1215], obtained certain ecclesiastical benefices – more with cure of souls than he could hold without special grace – we, duly mindful of his nobility, virtue and knowledge, as is proper, by the authority which we have from the lord pope have thought fit to grant a dispensation to the said Walter validly to obtain, and to retain in accordance with our dispensation, a further benefice with cure of souls, together with those he already has. In testimony whereof we have thought fit to grant these our letters patent, sealed with our seal, to the said Walter. Witnessed by: Masters S., archdeacon of Canterbury, Walter de Sumercote, Richard de St Edmund, Richard de Watlington, Robert de Schotindon; Bernard de Garing, Geoffrey de Otterford, laymen; Sir Robert de Mucegros, Richard de Wyke, Peter de Camera, and others.' No date.

490 As above, but varied by a specific reference to the papal delegation of the dispensing power, allowing Langton to dispense many of his clerks, among whom was the aforesaid Walter, for pluralism.

491 Admission of Brother Geoffrey de Swansea as prior of Minster (*Talchar*); presented by Reginald de Bottreaux and Geoffrey, prior of Tywardreath (*Thiwardrat*), as proctor for the abbot and convent of St Serge, Angers. Pawton, 26 August 1263.

492 Inst. of Roger de St Constantine to Lanreath (*Lanreython*); patron, William de Cerisy. Mere, 11 August 1263.

493 Collation of Stephen Haym, clerk, to the prebend at Crantock vacant through the voluntary resignation of Geoffrey [de Bisimano], archdeacon of Cornwall. Liskeard, 28 August 1263.

494 Collation of Michael de Northampton, clerk of Richard, king of the Romans, to the prebend at Crantock vacant through the resignation of Stephen Haym. Liskeard, 28 August 1263.

495 READING OUT OF A DEED. On the 30 August the bishop was a guest (*hospitatus est*) at Plympton Priory; the following day a matter which had conditionally been referred to arbitration was settled. The sub-prior and convent acknowledged, in their own chapter and before many clerks and laymen, that they were bound to keep two canons constantly in residence at St Kew (*Lanho*), and they promised to send them there immediately. Witnesses: Sirs Walter de Bath, John de Weston, Ralph de Chaluns, knights, Masters R[obert] Everard, J[ohn] de Blakedon, J[ohn] Wyger, R[obert] de Polamford, W[illiam] de Capella, Matthew de Egloshayle, William, chaplain, Hugh Splot, and a great crowd of people.[6] They also, on account of the sequestered churches of Dean Prior (*Dene*) and St Kew, their own transgressions and the bishop's expenses and losses, promised, in sealed letters patent, to pay him 100 marks. Plympton, 31 August 1263.

---

[6] The list of witnesses was written at the bottom of the page with signs to indicate where it should be inserted.

[fo.28] **496**[7]   Walter, called le Hostiler, made proctor, on 20 August 1264, of Thomas, the subprior, and convent of Plympton for negotiating a final settlement between themselves and the bishop, quoting letters patent to this effect; the proctorship was exhibited at Winkleigh on 21 August. Plympton, 23 August 1263.

497   Inst. of John de Langford, clerk, to Cornwood (*Cornwode*), vacant through the said John's previous voluntary resignation; patron, Walter de Bath, knight. Winkleigh, 21 August 1263.

498   Collation of Master John de Blakedon to Paignton, with the duty of making a settlement (*cum onere compositionis ineunde*). Ashburton, 1 September 1263.

499   Inst. of Richard de Hydon, clerk, to the entire rectory of Meshaw (*Mausard*), consolidating the portion which Juvenal, priest, formerly held with the parsonage or portion of two shillings; patrons, Rose, widow of Rogo son of Simon, and Simon, son of the same Rogo. Exeter, 3 September 1263.

500   Inst. of Master Godfrey Giffard[8], through a proctor, to Holcombe Burnell (*Holecumb Bernard*), which was annexed to a prebend of Wells; patron, the bishop of Bath. Exeter, 3 September 1263.

501   Inst. of Michael called Archdeacon to the vacant pension of two [marks] in Offwell (*Offewell*) church, to be paid by the vicar of the same, on terms that it should not prejudice him as regards another benefice before he should gain the entire church; patron, Sir John de Courtenay. 4 September 1263.

502   Inst. of Henry de Tiverton, chaplain, to the vicarage of Dunkeswell (*Dunkewell*); patron, the abbot of Dunkeswell. 4 September 1263.

503   Master R. Everard, the bishop's official, made (in writing) the bishop's commissary for the purpose of instituting Richard de Allempton, priest, to the vicarage of Kingsteignton (*Teynton Regis*);[9] patron, the precentor of Salisbury through his proctor, Master Walter de Sine Muro. 4 September 1263.

[fo.28v] **504**   The bishop held an ordination, and there ordained John de Leigh and Laurence de Aure to the subdiaconate. Horsley, 22 September 1263.

505   Inst. of the aforesaid John, subdeacon, to Southleigh (*Suthleg*); patron, John de Leigh. Horsley, 22 September 1263.

506   Inst. of Nicholas de Hyliun, subdeacon, to Whitestone [or Whitstone?] (*Witteston*); patron, Andrew de Powderham. Chidham, 25 September 1263.

---

[7]   In the margin beside this entry is written: Turn back to the bottom of folio 26, ie **475**; see also **488**.
[8]   Later bishop of Worcester, 1268–1302.
[9]   Cf **485**, where Richard is called de Almeton.

507   Collation of Master Robert de Polamford, clerk, to Meavy (*Mewy*), vacant through the resignation of Richard de Braundsworthy; patron, the bishop, by reason of his administration and right of patronage during a vacancy at Plympton Priory. Faringdon, 4 October 1263.

508   Election of Brother Robert, called Blund, as prior of Plympton confirmed, and (under letters close) to be installed by the archdeacon of Totnes. By letters patent the bishop commanded the obedience of the subprior and convent to him as their prior; he also commanded Master Robert de Polamford, clerk, who had custody of the priory during the vacancy, to hand over the temporalities, etc. to the prior. Horsley, 1 November 1263.

509   Inst. of Payne de Liskeard, clerk, to the portion of St Endellion (*Endeliente*) which Richard de Hemerdon had held; patron, Roger de Bodrigan. Farringdon, 24 November 1263.

510   Collation by the dean of Exeter [William de Stanway], at the bishop's command, of Master Robert Everard to the prebend of Exeter cathedral which Elias de Combe had held. Exeter, 30 November 1263.

511   The bishop approved and ratified the dean's collation, making good any defect in form there might have been, and collated anew Master Robert to the same prebend at the chancel steps in the presence of the clergy (*ad cancelliam in presentia clericorum*). Farringdon, 5 December 1263.

512   Ordination held in the collegiate church of Tiverton. Tiverton, 22 December 1263.

513   Collation of Hugh, called Splot, clerk, to Lawhitton (*Lawyton*). Tiverton, 22 December 1263.

514   Inst. of Gilbert de Yetminster, priest, to the vicarage of South Tawton (*Suthtauton*); patron, Nicholas Longespee, the rector. Exeter, 24 December 1263.

515   Collation of William Poylen, subdeacon, to East Anstey (*Estanesty*); patron, Robert de Cruwys, knight. Exeter, 25 December 1263.

516   At the order of the bishop, the official,[10] R. Rogers, the steward, and William de Capella audited the accounts of Master John de Esse; he has letters of quittance, but not in accordance with William's knowledge (*preter conscientiam Willelmi*). Chudleigh, 28 December 1263.

517   Collation of Master John Noble to the prebend at Exeter which the archdeacon of Totnes had held. London, 10 January 1264.

---

[10] Perhaps, 'At the order of the bishop's official, R Rogers, . . .'; the Latin is ambiguous: *de precepto domini episcopi officialis, R. Rogers, seneschallus, et W. de Capella* . . . . John de Esse may have been the official-peculiar.

518   Collation, by lapse, of Master Robert de Polamford to Feniton (*Feneton*). London, 10 January 1264.

[fo.29] **519**   Collation of Master John de Bradley to the treasurership of Crediton. London, 11 January 1264.

520   Collation of Roger de Dartford, clerk, to the prebend at Bosham which the archdeacon of Totnes had held. London, 11 January 1264.

521   Collation of Master Alan de Rockland to the prebend of six marks at Crediton which Roger de Dartford had held. London, 11 January 1264.

522   Collation of Master Walter de Pembroke to the archdeaconry of Totnes. London, 11 January 1264.

523   Inst. of Martin Pypard, priest, to the vicarage of Liskeard; patrons, the prior and convent of Launceston (*Lanceston*). Horsley, 17 January 1264.

524   Collation of Sir Henry de Bracton to the archdeaconry of Barnstaple. Horsley, 21 January 1264.

525   Collation of Adam de Ilchester to the Crediton (*Cryditon*) prebend which the archdeacon of Totnes had held. Horsley, 21 January 1264.

526   ORDINANCE AND INSTITUTION. The bishop issued letters patent concerning the rectory of Thorverton which had recently become vacant through the resignation of Richard de Chippestaple, and to which Richard de Bamfeld had been presented by the proctor of the abbot and convent of St Martin's, Tours; Master Edward de la Knolle, dean of Wells, had been appointed to bring about a settlement between these parties. He ordained that, during Richard de Chippestaple's lifetime, Richard de Bamfeld should take a half-mark of silver annually from the church, with the right of accrual to the whole church. The bishop, out of charity, admitted Richard de Bamfeld to the parsonage and instituted him rector, on terms that after the departure or death of Richard de Chippestaple he would be allowed to enter the whole church and its appurtenances, except that Richard de Chippestable should retain the occasional offerings as long as he should live. Since Richard de Chippestable was broken down by old age and weakened by various illnesses, and could not adequately manage himself and his own affairs (*senio confractus et egritudinibus variis debilitatus, se et sua competenter regere non potest*), he was given into the guardianship of Richard de Bamfeld, who was also to have the administration of the church. Horsley, 25 January 1264.

527   Inst. of Nicholas, called de Ponte, to the vicarage of Brampford Speke (*Bramford*); patrons, the prior and convent of St Nicholas, Exeter. Horsley, 27 January 1264.

[fo.29v] **528**   The bishop by special grace (*ex speciali gratia*) committed the custody of Tregony Priory, until Easter, to Brother Geoffrey de Algia, canon of

Ste Marie du Val in Normandy and proctor in England of the said abbot and convent, on terms that no right should accrue to him from this commission, nor should he claim any other right in the priory. Horsley, 27 January 1264.

529 The bishop by special grace committed the custody of Woolfardisworthy (*Wolfardesworthi*),[11] until Easter, to William de Heathfield, priest, saving any other claim, on terms that no right should accrue to him from this commission, nor should he claim any other right in the church, and that no other person with any claim be prejudiced. William still alleges that that his presentation was made on 5 January at Exeter in the presence of his patron; on behalf of the other presentee it was asserted to the contrary, and alleged that the patron had not been present.[12] Horsley, 27 January 1264.

530 Inst. of Hugh, called Splot, clerk, to the rectory of Meavy, vacant through the resignation of Master Robert de Polamford; patrons, the prior and convent of Plympton. Horsley, 28 January 1264.

531* FORMULA. The bishop wrote to Master R[obert] Everard, his official. 'Since the duty of our office summons us to follow closely in the steps of the holy fathers, and since in the council very recently held in London[13] it was for our salvation decreed that nobody's executor be permitted to dispose of or administer the testator's estate unless an inventory had already been drawn up of all the goods of the deceased and presented to the local ordinary; further, after the will has been proved before the ordinary, the execution or administration of the deceased's estate is not permitted except to such persons as can give a competent account of their administration when duly interrogated on the subject, and who show themselves to claimants as responsible persons with at least the resources to meet [any claim]; we command you, firmly enjoining you in virtue of your obedience, that you forbid the executors of the will of the late Thomas [Pincerna], formerly archdeacon of Totnes, any administration of the estate until the will has been proved before us, an inventory – fortified with the seals of the executors – accurately made of all his property and formally shown to you, and, further, adequate security furnished in writing by the executors for rendering the accounts of their administration when requested, and for responding to any claimants. You are to inform us by your letters patent how you have executed our command, keeping safe the security given in respect of the foregoing by subjecting – if there be need – the goods of the deceased to our sequestration until such time as those matters which are expressly set out above have run their due course. By the authority of the Council, we desire and command that this procedure be observed in the wills of other men.' Horsley, 28 January 1264.

[11] In the deanery of Molton and the hundred of Witheridge; the Woolfardisworthy in the hundred of Hartland was only a chapel.
[12] See **550**.
[13] This presumably means c.20 of the Lambeth Council of 1261, *Councils and Synods* II 1, 681–2, which required the taking of an inventory, but the MS clearly says 'London'; perhaps in Devon, Lambeth was London.

532　(Custody) The bishop reserved the vacant church of Lawhitton (*Lawytton*) for John le Rus of Modbury (*Mouber'*) and collated it to him if he should be in Holy Orders by 24 June, but otherwise no right should accrue to him. Faringdon, 14 February 1264.

533[14]　Inst. of Master Thomas called Payn, deacon, to the rectory of Marwood (*Merwode*); patron, Sir Henry de Tracy. Paignton, 16 March 1264.

534　Inst. of Roger de Respren, chaplain, to the rectory of Huntsham (*Honesham*); patron, Sir William de Punchardon. [No place], 23 March 1264.

[fo.30] **535**　The bishop by special grace committed, at his pleasure, to Thomas de Bosco, chaplain, the custody of Eggesford (*Egenesford*) church. [No place], 25 March 1264.

536* COLLATION WITH FORMULA. Inst. of Roger de St Constantine, clerk, to a parson's benefice of two marks in the church of Newlyn (*S Neuline*), with the right of accrual; patron, [Richard, earl of Cornwall,] the king of Germany. The bishop issued letters patent. 'Be it known that we repeatedly, both in our own person and through our officials, have had summoned those clerks of the diocese of Exeter who are holding in plurality benefices with cure of souls in order that they show their dispensations, if they have them, and, finally, we have issued a demand that they should show them on the appointed day or otherwise be deprived of the benefices with cure of souls after the receipt of which they received other benefices with a similar cure. Among these Sir Alan de Nymet had frequently been summoned in the aforesaid terms, since, after receiving a pension of two marks in the church of Newlyn together with the right of accrual, he accepted another church with cure of souls. The aforesaid Alan has been summoned by our official to our presence, beyond what is required, to show his privilege, if he should have one, but he did not trouble to do so, to the prejudice of our beloved son R[oger] de St Constantine, who has been presented to the same pension of two marks by the illustrious lord Richard, King of the Romans, and to the peril of his own soul. Therefore, not wishing to neglect the cure of souls – as indeed we should not – or to drag out the present business further to the detriment of both parties to the presentation, at the instance of the presenter we have admitted, and instituted as rector in the same, the same R[oger] to the aforesaid pension with the right of accrual to all rights in the aforesaid church after the death of [the incumbent] Sir H[enry de Cirencester] , precentor of Crediton. We do not desire, however, that any prejudice should arise to the aforesaid Sir Henry during his lifetime from this our admission and institution to the same church.' *Wytemers* (?Wytham, Berks), 1 March 1264.

537　Inst. of Benedict de St Wenn, subdeacon, to the rectory of St Michael Penkivel; patron, Sir John de Treiagu. Bishopsteignton, 5 April 1264.

---

[14] A marginal sign indicates that this entry should follow **536**.

538   Collation of Master Robert de Tefford[15] to the archdeaconry of Cornwall, vacant through the voluntary resignation of Sir Geoffrey de Bisimano. [Exeter,] 3 April 1264.

539   Collation of Sir Geoffrey de Bysimano to the prebend at Bosham vacant through the voluntary resignation of Master Robert de Tefford. [Exeter,] 3 April 1264.

540   Collation of Sir William de Bysimano the younger to the prebend at Crediton vacant through the voluntary resignation of Master Robert de Tefford. [Exeter,] 3 April 1264.

541*   FORMULA.[16] With the consent of the dean and chapter of Exeter, the bishop handed over in farm all his land at Arwennack[17] (*Arwennech*) to Richard, rector of St Columb Major, with letters patent. [fo.30v] 'Let all know that we, with the common consent of the dean and chapter of Exeter cathedral, have granted and delivered to Richard de Lanherne, rector of St Columb Major, for the term of his life all our land at Arwennack with all appurtenances, and the common pasture in our uncultivated land on the southern side, between the house of John de Arwennack and the sea, for an annual rent of 30 shillings, payable to us and our successors in equal instalments each 1 May and All Saints' Day, in return for all service, action, plaints, claims, and suit of court, except that the said Richard must attend, in person or through an attorney, the Michaelmas and Easter meetings of our court at Penryn. If the said Richard or his attorney should incur a fine, he is to be fined in accordance with the degree of the offence according to the view of his peers. After the departure[18] of Richard all the said land of Arwennack and its appurtenances is to revert to us or our successors without any objection, save for his growing crops and any of his moveables on the said land. Furthermore, it is lawful for the said Richard, whenever he chooses, to remove, bequeath, alienate or assign to anyone he wishes, without challenge, his moveable goods which are on the said land, provided that the aforesaid rent be paid annually to us or our successors by him or by someone else. Further, the aforesaid Richard must improve the aforesaid land, so that it may return to us or our successors in better heart than he received it. For the securing of this, we have thought fit to append our seal, together with the common seal of the dean and chapter, to the present letters, indentured in the style of a chirograph, and one part, sealed with Richard's seal, remains with us.' Exeter, 3 April 1264.

542   Collation by lapse of John, called Rufus, of the rectory of Little Hempston (*Hemeston Minor*). [No place,] 13 April 1264.

---

[15] The former official, not the chancellor.
[16] J.A. Brundage suggests that the clerks in the bishop's chancery wished to provide a model form for a lease.
[17] Near Penryn; the site of the Killigrew mansion.
[18] *recessum* in MS; this presumably includes his death.

543 Collation of Warinus, called the Breton, chaplain, of the vicarage of Talland (*Tallan*), 'at the special and express wish of the prior and convent of Launceston'. [No place,] 17 April 1264.

544 Collation of William Poyntz to the prebend at Crediton which Master Hugh Poynaunt had held. [Exeter,] 19 April 1264.

545 The bishop held an ordination. Exeter, 19 April 1264.

546 In sealed letters patent, the bishop committed the wardship of the lands in his manor of Lawhitton which had been held by Richard de Trekarl, now dead, to Matthew, called Bacon, until Richard's heirs should come of age. Crediton, 24 April 1264.

547 Collation of Sir H[enry] de Bracton to the chancellorship of Exeter. Bishop's Tawton, 18 May 1264.

548 Collation of Sir Richard, called Blund, to the archdeaconry of Barnstaple, vacant through the resignation of Sir Henry de Bracton. Also collation of Master Roger de Torridge to the prebend at Bosham vacant through the resignation of Richard Blund. [No place,] 25 May 1264.

549 Collation of Sir John de Exeter to the prebend at Crediton which Master Roger de Torridge had held. [fo.31] Also collation of William de St Martin, chaplain, to the prebend at Crediton which John de Exeter had held. [No place,] 25 May 1264.

550 Inst. of William de Heathfield, chaplain, to the rectory of Woolfardis-worthy[19] (*Wolfardisworthi*); patron, Richard le Dispenser. [No place,] 5 June 1264.

551 Inst. of Gilbert de Plympton, priest, to the vicarage of Maker (*Macre*); patrons, the prior and convent of Plympton. [No place,] 6 June 1264.

552 Inst. of Michael de Lodeford, chaplain, to the vicarage of Bishop's Nympton (*Nemeton*); patron, Sir Walter son of Peter, treasurer of Exeter. The vicarage was allegedly taxed by the archbishop of Canterbury but the bishop reserved his right to tax. When the archbishop's taxation came to light, the bishop released in perpetuity the vicar from the payment of 20 shillings mentioned in it.[20] [No place,] 6 June 1264.

553 Consecration of Brian as abbot of Torre (*Tore*). Barlinch, 8 June 1264.

554[21] Collation of William de St Martin, priest, to the precentorship of Crediton, and of Master Constantine [de Mildenhall] to the prebend there which William had held. [No place,] 24 June 1264.

---

[19] Cf **529**.
[20] This last sentence was added in the margin.
[21] This entry and the next are marked respectively with *b* and *a*.

555 Resignation of Sir Henry de Cirencester as precentor of Crediton, in the presence of many, and the next day, at the prompting of charity, the bishop collated him by special grace [to a prebend] in the same. Dunkeswell, 13 June 1264.

556 Collation of William de Bracton, chaplain, to the prebend at Crantock which Master Constantine [de Mildenhall] had resigned. [No place,] 24 June 1264.

557 [Intended entry invalidated, with a *va . . .cat.*] London, 2 July 1264.

558 Collation by lapse of John de Anagni, clerk, to the rectory of Feock (*S Feoce*); patrons, the lady Joan de Rouen and Noel de Trevelle. [London,] 2 July 1264.

559 Collation by lapse of Master William de Stanway, dean of Exeter, to the rectory of Alphington (*Alfinton*). [London,] 2 July 1264.

560 Collation of Master Henry de Bollegh to the prebend of St Buryan (*S Berian*) which Sir Henry de Cirencester had held. [No place,] 29 July 1264.

561 Collation of Master Robert de la More to the vicarage of Breage (*S Breace*), devolved to the bishop's collation *de iure*. Lambourne, 30 July 1264.

562* Collation, by papal authority, of Master Luke de Paignton, or of Walter called Curdet, to the rectory of Antony (*Auntton*) in Cornwall; patrons, the abbot and convent of Tavistock. In sealed letters patent the bishop announced: 'We have some time ago received a mandate from the lord pope that we should make provision by papal authority for Master Luke de Paignton to an ecclesiastical benefice of which the presentation belongs to one of the religious houses in our diocese; by the authority of which mandate we have indeed, on numerous past occasions, suspended all the religious of our diocese from any collation or presentation to benefices until provision was effectively made for the same Master [Luke] by the aforesaid authority to an ecclesiastical benefice. But because the said Master [Luke] from the aforesaid mandate had so far received nothing satisfactory, we, desiring as is fitting to obey the command of the supreme pontiff − In the Name of the Father and of the Son and of the Holy Spirit, Amen − have thought fit to provide the same Master Luke by the foregoing authority to the vacant church of Antony in Cornwall, whose patronage belongs to the religious men, the abbot and convent of Tavistock, and we have collated him to the same, with all its appurtenances, by the papal authority which we enjoy in this matter, on condition that the same Master [Luke] or his proctor is willing to accept this provision. Otherwise, having a similar apostolic mandate addressed to us, we have by papal authority provided Master Walter, called Curdet, to the same church with its appurtenances and collated him to the same, and we inhibit [fo.31v] by the authority committed to us the same abbot and convent of Tavistock, or any other person whatsoever, under pain of excommunication and suspension to be incurred *ipso facto* if they should dare to attempt anything contrary to the foregoing, that they may not presume to disturb or hinder in any manner what we have done in this regard; nevertheless, we decree that anything which may be attempted by the same abbot and convent, or by any other persons, against any or all of the foregoing is null and void, reserving to ourselves the power committed to us by the aforesaid authority to take more severe measures against them or any others who disobey.' Faringdon, 31 July 1264.

563[22]   LETTER FOR THE COMMON BENEFIT OF THE CHURCH AND REALM OF ENGLAND. 'In the same year, following the decision of the greater part of the prelates of the province of Canterbury, who had met together in London, on the common defence of the church and realm of England, certain letters were sent out to each diocese; and the bishop of Exeter wrote in this form: Walter, by divine mercy bishop of Exeter, to our beloved son, Master R. Everard, our official, health, grace and benediction. Since many things may be forbidden which, in other times, for the sake of expediency and in time of urgent necessity, would be permitted, your mind ought not to be disturbed if certain things are perhaps decreed which in the judgment of some people may smack of harshness or severity. It is for this reason that, since both the realm and the ecclesiastical community already stand wounded and disturbed in various ways from the various turns of affairs, and since fear and rumour of a graver wound and a more violent disturbance, to wit, the hostile arrival of foreigners to the overthrow of the realm and undoing of the constitution, has already invaded the hearts of true-born Englishmen, as you have heard, [we] having weighed and bent [our] minds to the dangers and threats which encompass the realm and all its inhabitants – unless it be protected by the Lord [our] gracious defender – it ought not to be reckoned as prejudicial or troublesome if in some way ecclesiastical persons may contribute from their spiritualities to the succour of the estate of the English church, which has been brought unusually low in many respects both in itself and in its privileges, and to the defence of the motherland, to which the bond of nature binds and summons each one of us. Since therefore, just as we have said above, in order that the church may be succoured and that it may be possible to resist with stern fortitude the hostile invasions of foreigners who, rejecting conditions of any kind, would spare neither place nor person, it has been ordained and appointed by the authority and counsel of the bishops and prelates of the realm and of the clergy recently met together in London that all ecclesiastical, religious and other persons should contribute from their ecclesiastical properties a tenth part in accordance with the normal form of taxation, any excuse to the contrary being utterly rejected. [W]e [therefore], exciting by these present [letters] their devotion to the common weal and their own advantage, with rather weighty consultation, command that you assign a tenth part of all ecclesiastical revenues to certain reliable persons, who shall be deputed by us by our authority to giving very prompt effect to the aforesaid, rejecting all obstruction or subterfuge. Besides, since time waits for no man and the threat of enemy invasion is imminent, which must to be resisted with all due preparedness, it is expedient – just as has been appointed – that half of the

---

[22] Printed in *Councils and Synods* II 1, 698–9. For the circumstances of the battle of Lewes and its aftermath, see F.M. Powicke, *Henry III and the Lord Edward* (OUP, 1947) 466ff.

aforesaid tenth be paid before the feast of the Beheading of John the Baptist [29 August].' Tandridge, 11 August 1264.

564 Inst. of Master William de la Stane to the vicarage of Southtown (*Suthton*);[23] patrons, the prior and convent of Plympton. [No place,] 16 October 1264.

565 Inst. of John de Henley, priest, to the vicarage of South Tawton; patron, Sir Nicholas Longespee. [No place,] 18 October 1264.

566 Master Stephen de Arbore given custody of the vicarage of Breage, devolved to the bishop's collation *de iure*. Horsley, 19 October 1264.

567 Herbert de Pyne resigned any right which he had in the church of Upton Pyne (*Opeton*), in the presence of Masters Constantine [de Mildenhall] and J. Bradley, Robert de Polamford, Hugh Splot, Matthew de Egloshayle, Richard de Grangiis, and others. Horsley, 20 October 1264.

[fo.32] **568** AMICABLE RECONCILIATION. An agreement was made at Newenham on 8 November 1264 between the abbot and convent of Newenham and Master Nicholas de Honiton, rector of Axminster, after each party had taken an oath, to accept the bishop's ruling over various contentions and suits between them. In letters patent the bishop decreed that Nicholas was to be a faithful friend to the abbot and convent, who were to give him four marks; any further dispute was to be brought at once for arbitration to the bishop or his official; only failing a peaceful settlement could some other jurisdiction be invoked. Exeter, 14 November 1264.

569 Resignation in letters patent by Sir Geoffrey de Bisimano of the prebend of Walton (*Waleton*) in the church of Bosham. Crediton, 20 November 1264.

570 Collation of the same [Geoffrey de Bisimano] to the precentorship of Crediton which Sir William de St Martin had resigned. Crediton, 20 November 1264.

571 Collation of Roger de Dartford, clerk, to the prebend of Walton in the church of Bosham. [No place,] 21 November 1264.

572 Collation of Master Robert Everard to the parochial prebend of the church of Bosham which Roger de Dartford had held. [No place,] 21 November 1264.

573 PROCTORSHIP FOR PARLIAMENT. In a letter addressed to H[enry de Sandwich], bishop of London, and to the other bishops of the provinces of Canterbury and York and to the whole community of the lower clergy, the bishop appointed proctors for the parliament to be held at St Albans on 7 December. Because of poor bodily health, weakening of powers (*virium*

---

[23] Since absorbed into Plymouth, which did not then yet exist.

imbecillitate), and other blows of fortune, the bishop was unable to be present, so he appointed Masters John Wyger and J[ohn] de Bradley his proctors, jointly and severally, to negotiate, accept and ratify on his behalf whatever they, communally in that meeting, should think fit to decree, ordain or do, to the honour of God, the advantage of the Church, the promised word of the king, and the profit of the realm. Bishop's Nympton, 23 November 1264.

[fo.32v] **574**   The bishop, at the prompting of charity, gave to Sir Geoffrey de Bisimano a pension from his private purse (*de camera sua*) of twenty marks a year, until he should provide Geoffrey with a benefice, without cure of souls, of equivalent value. Crediton, 20 November 1264.

575   Inst. of Geoffrey de Santon, subdeacon, to the rectory of Stoodleigh (*Stouleg'*); patron, Sir Roger fitzPayne. Bishop's Nympton, 24 November 1264.

576   Walter de Bratton, clerk, of the diocese of Exeter, resigned to the bishop the church of Newton St Cyres (*Nyweton iuxta Exon*) and any rights he had by reason of his *de facto* provision to it. On the same day he was ordained subdeacon with title to the vicarage of Dean Prior and instituted perpetual vicar of the same. Launceston, 20 December 1264.

577   The bishop held an ordination. Launceston, 20 December 1264.

578   Collation, at the prompting of charity, of Roger de St Mabyn, chaplain, to the rectory of Little Petherick (*Nansfunten*); patron, the bishop. [No place,] 25 December 1264.

579   Resignation by Master Gervase de Crediton of all his right in the church of Budock (*ecclesia S. Budoci*) in Cornwall; on the same day, collation, at the prompting of charity, of him to Calstock (*Calestok*), devolved to the bishop's collation *de iure*. Exeter, 12 January 1265.

580   Collation, at the prompting of charity, of Gilbert de Molton, chaplain, to the vicarage of Ashford (*Esford*), devolved to the bishop's collation *de iure*. Exeter, 12 January 1265.

581[24]   Inst. of Walwyn, priest, to the vicarage of Buckfastleigh (*Buffestr'*); patrons, the abbot and convent of Buckfast. Exeter, 12 January 1265.

582   Inst. of Geoffrey de Tottescumbe, priest, to the rectory of Trentishoe (*Trendeleho*); patron, Richard de Trentishoe. Farringdon, 19 January 1265.

583   The bishop held an ordination. Branscombe, 26 February 1265.

584   Inst. of John de la Combe, subdeacon, to the rectory of Stowford (*Stafford*); patron, the lady Alice de Huish. Salcombe, 26 February 1265.

---

[24] In this and the next entry no mention is made of the patron actually making a presentation.

585 Collation by lapse of John de Belsal, subdeacon, to the rectory of Truro (*Tryueru*). Salcombe, 26 February 1265.

586 Resignation by Master Robert de Paignton of his portion in the church of Budock, in the presence of Brian, abbot of Torre, the priors of Bodmin and Totnes, and many others. Chudleigh, 15 March 1265.

587 Collation, at the prompting of charity, of Master R[obert de Paignton] to the rectory of Lawhitton; patron, the bishop. Chudleigh, 15 March 1265.

588 Master William de la Stane, perpetual vicar of Southtown, and Simon le Bonda, who had been presented to the rectory of Moreleigh (*Morleg'*), submitted themselves to the bishop at Plympton on 19 March. Three days later he laid down that Simon should be admitted as rector while paying 100 shillings to William for his expenses and damages; both parties had letters. St Germans, 20 March[25] 1265.

589 Inst. of Richard de Bamfeld to the rectory of Thorverton, to which he had previously been admitted as custodian, *ut patet supra in quarto folio* [ie **526**]. Penryn, 26 March 1265.

[fo.33] **590** Walter, called le Prior, given custody, at the bishop's pleasure, of the vicarage of Padstow (*Lalestou*) and all its property. Pawton, 29 March 1265.

591 Inst. of James de S Victore, clerk, to the rectory of Morebath (*Morba*); patron, Sir Warren de Bassingburn. Pawton, 29 March 1265.

592 The bishop held an ordination. St Germans, 4 April 1265.

593 Inst. of Robert de Stormy, subdeacon, to the rectory of Manaccan (*Menst'*); patron, the lady Joan Bozon. St Germans, 4 April 1265.

594 Inst. of Sir Stephen Haym to Kea (*Landege*) and Kenwyn (*Kenwen*), with letters dated 24 June 1264. [No place,] 12 April 1265.

595 CUSTODY OF THE SEQUESTERED CHURCHES OF TAVISTOCK ABBEY.[26] In letters patent the bishop committed to Robert, rector of Monk Okehampton (*Monkochmenton*), the sequestration of the churches belonging to Tavistock Abbey. The abbot and convent had been summoned to appear before the bishop on 24 April in Pilton (*Pelton*) church to show their titles for the appropriation to their own use of the parish churches of Tavistock, Lamerton (*Lamberton*), Milton Abbot (*Midelton*), Brentor (*Brintetor*), Abbotsham (*Albedesham*), North Petherwin (*Nordpydrewyn*) and Hatherleigh (*Hatherleg*), the chapel of Monk Okehampton (*Monchocmenton*), and certain annual pensions from the churches of Burrington (*Burninton*), Werrington (*Wlfrinton*), Denbury (*Defnebery*) and Antony, as well as

---

[25] *Die Iovis proxima, videlicet die S Chutberti* [sic]; the Thursday is actually 19 March.
[26] For the other side of the story, see H.R.P. Finberg, *Tavistock Abbey* (CUP, 1951), 23.

the annual tithes in the parishes of Sheviock (*Seviech*) and Rame. The abbot and convent did not appear on the appointed day to answer for their titles but contumaciously absented themselves, and squandered the fruits and incomes of the said churches, chapel, etc. The bishop therefore sequestered all the churches, chapel, etc. and gave their custody to Robert, or to anyone he should think fit to appoint for this purpose, with power on the bishop's authority to excommunicate or suspend those who objected or rebelled. Bishop's Tawton, 24 April 1265.

596 FORM OF INSTITUTION OF THE PRIOR OF BARNSTAPLE. The bishop admitted Brother Simon de Gurneye as prior of St Mary Magdalen, Barnstaple, at the presentation of the prior and convent of St Martin des Champs, Paris. Brother Simon swore canonical obedience, and promised that Barnstaple Priory's income would be devoted to its own needs, except for the customary pension of 20 shillings due to the mother house. He also also promised not to give up the rule of the priory without the bishop's permission. He gave his letters patent to the bishop as evidence of all this, adding that he would ratify, as far as in him lay, the judgment given by papal authority that a full community of thirteen monks was to be maintained in the aforesaid monastery of Barnstaple, promising on his word as a priest to give effective obedience to the said judgment as soon as he could find suitable persons for this purpose. Chudleigh, 20 August 1265.

[fo.33v] **597** Inst. of Vivian, chaplain, to the rectory of St Edmund's super Pontem, Exeter; patrons, the mayor and citizens of the city of Exeter. [No place,] 25 August 1265.

598 Inst. of John de St Probus, deacon, to the vicarage of St Wenn; patrons, the abbot and convent of Tewkesbury. Faringdon, 2 September 1265.

599 Collation of Gilbert de Tyting, clerk, to the rectory of Cheriton Bishop (*Cheriton*), devolved to the bishop's collation. [No place,] 21 October 1265.

600 Inst. of Master Martin de . . . to the vicarage of St Neot; patron, the prior of Montacute. [No place,] 22 October 1265.

601 Collation of Richard Blund to the archdeaconry of Totnes. Canterbury, 1 November 1265.

602 Collation of Master Constantine de Mildenhall to the prebend of Exeter cathedral which Sir Walter de Pembroke had held; on the same day, collation of Sir John de Kirkby to the prebend of six marks in Crediton which Constantine had held. [No place,] 6 November 1265.

603 Collation of Master Godfrey Giffard to the archdeaconry of Barnstaple, resigned by Sir Richard called Blund. [No place,] 8 November 1265.

604 Collation of Walter de Exeter, chaplain, to Huxham (*Hukesham*), devolved to the bishop's collation. [No place,] 18 November 1265.

605   Inst. of Master Vincent de Loders to the vicarage of Axmouth (*Axemue*), vacant through the resignation of Vivian; patron, the prior of Loders (*Lodres*). Horsley, 24 November 1265.

606   SETTLEMENT.[27] Sir Michael de Fiennes, canon of Thérouanne (*Morinensis*) [near Boulogne], resigned by letters patent his whole right in the church of Paignton, and, at the prompting of charity, the bishop, by sealed letters patent, granted him for life 40 marks a year from his private purse (*de camera sua*) to be paid to Michael, or his alternate, at New Temple, London, on the feast of Pentecost. The grant was to be confirmed by the Exeter chapter when the bishop should arrive in Devon, and Michael would receive a charter. The payment would cease if Michael became either a bishop or a monk. Witnesses: Masters G. Giffard, archdeacon of Barnstaple, William de la Cornere, John Noble, John Sackville, Robert of Poitou[28], John de Esse, W. de Wacre, and others. London, 6 December 1265.

607*   RELEASE FROM DEBT.[29] The bishop issued letters patent: 'Let all know that the prior and convent of Plympton were obliged to us under their letters patent for the sum of 100 marks sterling – of which we have received 50 – on account of various injuries, contumacies and offences. But we, on consideration of the standing of the same monastery, have respited demanding or seeking the payment to us of the remainder of the said 100 marks on request during our lifetime [fo.34]; on condition indeed that, if we should chance to die before the said remainder has been either paid or demanded, the said prior and convent are to be quit of the same remainder which we remit as from that time, while the aforesaid letters of obligation, in whatever place and in the possession of whatever persons they are found, are totally invalidated.' Crediton, 6 January 1266 (*Domini anni presentis*).

608   Inst. of Roger de Merwood (*Merwode*), priest, to the vicarage of Bovey Tracey (*Bovy*); patrons, the master and brothers of the hospital of [St John the Baptist] Bridgewater (*Bruges*). [No place,] 5 January 1266.

609   Collation, at the prompting of charity, of Achimus de Crediton, chaplain, to the prebend of six marks in Crediton church which Richard Blund had held, vacant by Richard's voluntary resignation. Crediton, 6 January 1266.

610   Consolidation of the vacant vicarage of Washfield (*Wesfeld*) with the benefice of two marks from it that William de Berkeley was accustomed to take. Exeter, 10 January 1266.

[27] See **247**.
[28] This member of the bishop's household could be a relation of the Robert le Poitevin who was sheriff of Devon in 1258.
[29] See **488, 495**.

611   Inst. of Gilbert de Rye, priest, to the vicarage of Cullompton (*Columpton*); patrons, the prior and convent of St Nicholas', Exeter. Faringdon, 26 January[30] 1266.

612   Inst. of Walter de Bletchworth, priest, to Landcross (*Lancars*); patron, Sir Richard de Beauchamp. Faringdon, 26 January 1266.

613   The bishop held an ordination in his London chapel (*in capella sua London*). The same day he gave Master Jordan de Pacheall, subdeacon, custody of . . ., to which church, he alleged, he had been presented by Sir William de Raleigh. London, 20 February 1266.

614   Inst. of Adam de Stratton, clerk, through his proctor, Ralph de Stratton, clerk, who had a special mandate to take oath for him and to swear canonical obedience to the bishop,[31] to Poltimore (*Pultimore*); patron, Sir Richard de Poltimore. Leigh (*Ley in Dorsett'*), 28 February 1266.

615   Inst. of Richard . . ., priest, to the vicarage of Monkleigh (*Monckeleg'*); patrons, the prior and convent of Montacute (*Montis Acuti*). [Bishop's] Clyst, 6 March 1266.

616   The bishop held an ordination. The same day . . . was admitted to the vicarage of Seaton (*Seyton*); patrons, the abbot and convent of Sherborne (*Syreburn'*). Totnes, 13 March 1266.[32]

617   Inst. of John de Dundon to Mamhead (*Mammehesd'*); patron, Sir Nicholas son of Martin, by reason of his wife's dowry (*ratione dotis uxoris sue*). Plympton, 14 March 1266.

618   Inst. of Roger de Warleggon, priest, to the vicarage of St Mabyn (*ecc. S. Mabene in Cornub'*), which was to be taxed; patron, Sir Thomas de Tracy, by reason of his wife's dowry. [Bishop's] Tawton, 28 March 1266.

[fo.34v] **619**   Collation, at the prompting of charity, of Achimus[33], priest, to the prebend of Crediton which Serlo le Tyes had held. Crediton, 31 March 1266.

620   Inst. of Robert de St Austell, priest, to the vicarage of St Anthony in Meneage (*vicariam S. Antonini*), which was to be taxed; patron, the prior of Tywardreath. [Bishop's] Clyst, 4 April 1266.

---

[30] The Latin is inconsistent: *die lune in crastino Convertionis S Pauli*, but the feast itself fell on the Monday.

[31] The name and functions were added in the margin.

[32] In the ninth year of the bishop's consecration.

[33] Is this the same man as Achimus de Crediton, chaplain, who was collated to Richard Blund's prebend in January – **609**? Presumably also the Thomas Achym who is recorded as dead in **948**.

621 Collation of William, rector of Worplesdon (*Werpesdon in Surr'*), to a prebend of six marks in the church of Crediton. Horsley, 11 April 1266.

622 Inst. of Stephen Haym to the deanery of St Buryan (*ecc. S. Beriane*); patron, the king of Germany. Windsor, 26 May 1266.

623 The bishop held an ordination, ordaining two priests, two deacons, and five subdeacons; the bishop held their titles (*quorum tituli remanent penes episcopum*). New Temple, London, 22 May 1266.

624 Inst. of William Porteroye to the vicarage of St Keverne (*vicariam S. Kerani*), which was to be taxed; patrons, the abbot and convent of Beaulieu. London, 10 June 1266.

625 Inst. of Walter, called le Prior, to the vicarage of St Issey (*Egloscruc*), which was to be taxed; patrons, the dean and chapter of Exeter. London, 10 June 1266.

626 Inst. of Henry de Esse, clerk, to Musbury (*Musbery*); patron, Sir John de Courtenay. London, 10 June 1266.

627 Inst. of Master Matthias de Cellis to Stoke [Climsland] (*Stok'*); patron, the king of Germany. London, 10 June 1266.

628 Inst. of Roger de . . ., chaplain, to Blisland (*Bleston*); patron, the king of Germany. London, 10 June 1266.

629 Inst. of Richard de Cirencester to a prebend of Chulmleigh; patron, Sir John de Courtenay. Northampton, 15 June 1266.[34]

630 INSTITUTION. The bishop gave to Master Roger, called Barat, custody of the portion of St Teath (*ecc. S. Thetthe*) which William de Bisimano junior had held. London, 7 July 1266.

631 Collation, by legatine authority as well as his own, of Master Philip de Exeter to Stockleigh [Pomeroy] (*Stokkeleg'*). Oxford, 13 July 1266.

632 Commendation of Roger de Dartford to St Columb Major (*ecc. S. Columbe*); patron, as was known (*ad quem tunc ius patronatus ecclesie pertinere dignoscebatur*), Sir Ralph de Arundel. Pawton, 14 August 1266.

633 Inst. of R. de Inneswork, priest, to the vicarage of Marystow (*ecc. S. Marie Stou*); patrons, the prior and convent of Plympton. Pawton, 15 August 1266.

634 Commendation of Walter Peverel to Boconnoc (*Boskenech*); patron, Sir Thomas de Kent. Pawton, 15 August 1266.

---

[34] Shortly afterwards the bishop signed the Dictum of Kenilworth.

635 The bishop ordained William de Mules subdeacon, and inst. of the same William to Exbourne (*Hecesburn'*); patron, Sir John de Mules. Faringdon, 18 September 1266.

636 The bishop gave to William de Cartaret, monk, custody of Otterton (*Ottrinton*) Priory at the bishop's pleasure, and to William de Pratellis custody of the Priory of St Michael's Mount (*prior. S. Michaelis in Cornub'*) in the same form. Dorchester [on Thames], 23 September 1266.

637 Inst. of Robert de Dun to Tedburn (*Tettesburn*); patron, Thomas de Tedburn. Islip, near Oxford, 24 September 1266.

638 Inst. of Master Odo, called Tureth, to the vicarage of Padstow (*Allestou*); patrons, the prior and convent of Bodmin. Brightwell, 14 October 1266.

[fo.35] **639** The bishop gave to Master Adam de Belstede custody of Helston at the bishop's pleasure; patron, the king of Germany. Brightwell, 14 October 1266.

640 Collation, at the prompting of charity, of Isaac de Blakedon, priest, to the vicarage of Broadhempston (*ecc. de Hemeston Maioris*); patronage devolved by authority of the Council to the bishop. Northampton, 27 October 1266.

641 Inst. of Hugh de Plympton to Ugborough (*Huggeburn'*); patrons, the prior and convent of Plympton. Iffley, [October/November] 1266.

642 Inst. of Master Roger de Torridge to Bridestowe (*Brydestou*); patrons, the prior and convent of Plympton. Iffley, [October/November] 1266.

643 Inst. of Adam, called Poylen, to Blackawton (*Aueton*), vacant by the voluntary resignation of Master Roger de Torridge; patrons, the prior and convent of Plympton. Also of William de Sackville to Meavy (*Mewy*), vacant by the voluntary resignation of Hugh de Plympton. Iffley, [October/November] 1266.

644 Collation of Master John de Bradley to the prebend of Exeter – together with a stall in the choir and a seat in the chapterhouse (*et stallum in choro et locum in capitulo*) – vacant by the death of Master Nicholas de Plympton. London, 23 November 1266.

645 PROXY FOR THE ROMAN CURIA. In sealed letters patent the bishop made Richard de Honiton, clerk, his proctor, on showing these letters, for requesting, challenging or accepting a judge, and gave him power to appoint or substitute other proctors in his place when expedient, as long as it was with the advice of one or both of those prudent men, Masters Berardus of Naples, papal chaplain and notary, and Philip de Cancellis, papal subdeacon and chaplain, and also to fix a salary for such a proctor or proctors, in accordance with the customs of the court, on the advice of the same. The bishop would ratify whatever Richard or his substitutes did in his name. He also revoked all earlier proxies and alternates, in whatsoever names. London, 1 December 1266.

646[35] [repeats **637**, but Robert is called subdeacon, and the date is given as 25 September.]

647 [repeats **638**.]

648 [repeats **639**.]

649 [repeats **640**.]

650 Inst. of William de Pratellis as prior of Otterton; patron, the abbot of Mont St Michel (*S Michaelis in periculo maris*). Also of Ralph de Cartaret as prior of St Michael's Mount. London, 21 December 1266.

651 Inst. of Robert de Landrake, priest, to the vicarage of Fowey; patrons, the prior and convent of Tywardreath. Horsley, 6 January 1267.

652 Collation of Sir Bogo de Clare to the prebend of Exeter which Ralph de Ilsington, precentor of Exeter, had held. Horsley, 30 January 1267.

[fo.36] **653** Inst. of Robert Basset, subdeacon, to Eggesford; patron, Sir W. de Meavy. Plympton, 2 April 1267.

654* The bishop granted absolution in the following terms. 'Robert de Meledon, Roger de la Stane, Nicholas de Foley, Richard Osmund, and Richard de la More, parishioners of Okehampton, appeared on behalf of themselves, and of the other parishioners of Okehampton, as they alleged, before the said lord bishop in the chapel of the Blessed Thomas, Martyr, at Kingswear,[36] in the presence of the abbot of Torre and Brother Ralph, canon of the same house, Masters John de Blakedon, canon of Exeter, John de Esse, Robert de Paignton, William de Capella, Walter de Laking, Roger de Dartford, clerks, William de St Martin, Peter de Guildford, chaplains, Hugh de Plympton, Richard de Grangiis, Nicholas de Stoke, clerks, Walerand de Cirencester, steward of Sir John de Courtenay, and others. They sought the benefit of absolution from the sentence of excommunication which they had incurred inasmuch as they had deprived their parish church of its customary burial fees by their own audacity and had mutually conspired, having taken an oath, to keep the fruits of such deprivation. On account of these and other lawful grounds the said church was placed under ecclesiastical interdict, and meanwhile, as the crown of their wrongdoing, the said men withheld other rights from the said church. Having taken an oath to abide by the commands of the church and to submit themselves totally to the ordinance of the said lord bishop, they obtained the benefit of absolution in legal form, in the presence there of Adam, perpetual vicar of Okehampton, who submitted himself in similar terms to the ordinance of the same lord bishop, and promised that he would observe it on his word as a priest. The same lord bishop, therefore, taking account of the passage of time and the

---

[35] This and the next three entries were repeated on fo.35, and crossed out with a huge X.
[36] Ie in the bishop's audience court.

long duration of the interdict, and on the advice imparted by his legal advisers, ordered, in virtue of the oath they had taken, that they should render within three days the burial fee customarily falling due to the church, whereof they had deprived it, under the will of Robert de Oke, which had been for long the subject of litigation between the parties, and then the other dues as they occurred, and should restore before next Easter the rights which had meanwhile been withheld, saving to them any petitionary action they might wish to bring in legal form. Also, at the order of the said lord bishop, they gave one hundred shillings sterling as pledge to the said vicar for his losses and expenses, the payment of which he ordered to remain suspended to await their future conduct, on condition that if thereafter they should ever, without a court judgment, deprive their church of any right which it possessed, they should *ipso facto* be liable to pay the whole sum to the said vicar before any litigation was begun. They also pledged to the said lord bishop of his grace 60 marks sterling for their contempt and for having borne his interdict in this contempt for so long, concerning which he would declare his pleasure when he wished. They also promised, under a similar duty, that they would in good faith and as far as in them lay reconcile the absent parishioners, their accomplices and fellow-conspirators, to the terms of such an agreement, and that they would never in future join with them in this matter or in any similar plot, and that they would doggedly avoid contumacious persons, and inform the lord bishop of their names.' Kingswear, 6 April 1267.

655 Collation of Master J. de Bradley to the archdeaconry of Barnstaple, vacant by the voluntary resignation of Master Godfrey Giffard. Clerkenwell, 24 May 1267.

656 Inst. of Peter de Plymstock, priest, to the vicarage of Dean Prior; patrons, the prior and convent of Plympton. [Bishop's] Clyst, 25 July 1267.

657 Inst. of Bartholomew de Totnes, priest, to the vicarage of Totnes; patrons, the prior and convent of Totnes. [Bishop's] Nympton, 7 August 1267.

658 Collation of Master Robert de Paignton to Ashprington; with the assent of the patrons, the prior and convent of Totnes. Crediton, 15 August 1267.

659 Collation of Master Richard Paz to Lawhitton (*Lawytton*), vacant by the voluntary resignation of the aforesaid Master Robert. Crediton, 15 August 1267.

660 Inst. of Walter le Fras to the vicarage of North Tawton[37]; presented by Osmund de Valle Torta, the rector. Crediton, 16 August 1267.

[fo.36v] **661** INSTITUTION THROUGH A PROCTOR. Institution, insofar as an absentee rector could be instituted according to the canons, by letters patent of Ottobuono, son of the noble Mazo de Fieschi, to Berry [Narbor] (*Bery*) through his lawful proctor, Master William de Capella, at the command of the

---

[37] South Tawton in the MS, but this must be wrong – see **1001**; also, N. de Longespee was rector of South Tawton from 1262 to 1278 or later – see **460–61, 514, 565, 1294**.

lord Ottobuono, cardinal deacon of St Adrian and papal legate; patrons, the prior and convent of Lewes. [Bishop's] Nympton, 18 September 1267.

662   Inst. of Master John de Yarcombe to Rackenford (*Rakeneford*); patron, Philip de Sideham. In letters patent the bishop declared that Michael de la Stane, clerk, had been presented by the patron, but he had been unable to admit him as of right because of defects of age and literacy;[38] however, on the departure or decease of John, Michael would be admitted as long as the said or any other canonical defects did not prevent it. [Bishop's] Clyst, 3 October 1267.

663   At the prompting of charity and at the bishop's order, Master John [de Yarcombe] granted to Michael de la Stane by letters patent a pension of five marks from Rackenford. [Bishop's] Clyst, 3 October 1257.

664   The bishop confirmed the gift of the advowson of St Feock (*ecc. S. Feoce*) by Walter Peverel, the patron, to the church of St Thomas, Glasney, and its canons. [Bishop's] Clyst, 10 October 1267.

665   The bishop confirmed his previous gift of the church of Sithney (*ecc. S. Sydnii*), of which he was patron, to the aforesaid church of St Thomas [Glasney] and its canons, on terms that, after the death of the rector, they could legally enter into possession of the aforesaid church and appropriate it with all its fruits and occasional offerings; an appropriate vicarage was to be assessed there, and a vicar appointed, whenever there was a vacancy, by the bishop of Exeter of the time. They had a letter patent [sic] concerning this. [Bishop's] Clyst, 10 October 1267.

666   Inst. of Robert de . . ., chaplain, to Luppitt (*Louepette*); patron, John de Mohun, proving his right of patronage through a royal writ in the king's court.[39] Horsley, 27 October 1267.

667   William son of Rogo ordained subdeacon, and instituted to High Bray (*Hautebraye*); patron, Richard le Fleming. Horsley, 17 December 1267.

668*   'By authority of the papal legate, the lord bishop dispensed the Lady Margaret de Morchard, nun of Polsloe (*Polslou*), from the defect of birth which she suffered, and on the same day he admitted her, as being canonically elected, to the administration of her house and instituted her as prioress in the aforesaid house.' Winchester, 24 December 1267.

669   Collation of Master William de la Cornere to the prebend of Exeter which Master Richard de St Gorran had held *de facto*, in the presence of Masters William de Capella, Roger Barat, Thomas de Buckland, William de Braddon and Peter de Guildford, priests, and Hugh de Plympton and Richard de

---

[38] The canonical age was 25 according to X 1.6.7 §2 (= Lateran III c.3), but dispensations were granted.

[39] *Dominus episcopus per breve domini regis ad presentationem Johannis de Moun evincentis ius patronatus ecclesie de Louepette in curia domini regis admisit . . .*

Grangiis, clerks. And he commanded in writing that a stall in the choir and a seat in the chapter should be assigned to the aforesaid Master William. Chidham, 31 December 1267.

670 At the presentation of Sir Walter Giffard, knight . . . . . . Cowick, 25 February 1268.

[fo.37] **671**⁴⁰ ESTABLISHMENT OF THE VICARAGE OF STAVERTON. Collation by lapse of Walter de Teignmouth, priest, to the vicarage of Staverton. In sealed letters the vicarage was assigned all the altarage, the mortuary fees, the tithes of apples, of hay, and of the mills, the glebe with its buildings, and certain lands belonging to the dean and chapter of which the value was formerly estimated at 25 shillings a year, viz. a meadow called *Pollismeede*, and *le Moore*, an enclosure called *le Lee*, reckoned at four acres, and an enclosure called *Maglond*, reckoned at four acres; the dean and chapter were to receive all the greater tithes. The vicar was to bear all the due and customary burdens. Ashburton, 16 September 1269.

[fo.37v] **672** Inst. of Henry Snellard, subdeacon, to Buckland Filleigh (*Suthbocland*); patron, Ermegarde de Saunton. Crediton, 5 April 1268.

673 Inspeximus of Pope Urban IV's letters of dispensation to Alan de Nymet.⁴¹ [Bishop's] Clyst, 11 April 1268.

674 Sealed letter issued on behalf of Stephen Haym. The bishop, following papal commands, had summoned all pluralists in the diocese to show their dispensations in accordance with the canons of the [Lateran] Council.⁴² Stephen Haym, rector of Lanteglos, had shown Pope Alexander IV's dispensation for holding Lanivet (*Lannived*) as well, and also Menheniot (*Mahyniet*) and the deanery of St Buryan, and so was permitted to retain these benefices. [No place,] 11 April 1268.

675 Inst. of Master Roger Barat to Newton St Cyres (*Nyweton*), saving Master William de Capella's right in the same church by papal provision, which would stay in force on the departure or decease of the aforesaid rector; patrons, the prior and convent of Plympton.⁴³ Exeter, 8 April 1268.

676 Inst. of Roger de Gonewardeby, subdeacon, to Stithians (*ecc. S. Stethyane in Cornubia*), vacant by the resignation of Robert de Kington; patron, the Lord Richard, king of Germany and Earl of Cornwall. London, 21 April 1268.

---

⁴⁰ This entry (identical with Dean and Chapter MS 1597), some eighteen months out of place, was copied into the register in a late sixteenth century hand. There follows a note of William Germyn, registrar, that Bishop John Wolton [1579–94] had handed the document over to be inserted by the hand of Sir Stephen Townsend, Dean, on 13 May 1585.

⁴¹ Their subject is not mentioned, but see **536**.

⁴² Lateran IV c.29 (= X 1.6.44); cf Lateran III c.3.

⁴³ . . . *salvo iure magistri W. de Capella quod per provisionem domini pape sibi adquiritur in eadem et in robore suo duraturo predicto rectore cedente vel decedente.*

677 Collation by lapse of Thomas de Perers, deacon, to Goodleigh (*Godeleg'*). London, 29 April 1268.

678 Collation by lapse of Richard de Braundsworthy, clerk, to Great Torrington (*Toriton*). London 29 April 1268. The collation was renewed and repeated (*innovavit et innovando iteravit*) on 10 June 1268 — at **686**.

679 The bishop sent a letter to the dean [William de Stanwey], confirming his collation of the prudent Peter de Vienne, dean of Sion, to the prebend at Exeter which the right reverend Master Godfrey Giffard, now bishop-elect of Worcester, had held, and commanding him to instal Peter or his vicar in the said prebend, assigning him a seat in chapter as was customary for absentees. London, 22 May 1268.

[fo.38] **680** By letters patent the bishop granted to Peter de Vienne, dean of Sion, the annual pension of twenty marks which Philip de Meluno, clerk, had formerly received from the vicar of St Merryn, but had resigned; it was to be paid by the vicar each 1 May. London, 2 June 1268.

681 At the same time all records (*instrumenta*) concerning the said dean [of Sion] were invalidated.

682 The bishop promised by letters patent that he would pay to the same dean [Peter de Vienne], as long as he lived, the said pension in London, and to his proctors at the due days. At the same time the same dean appointed by letters patent Brother Richard, canon of St Bernard Montjoux, Master of Hornchurch Hospital in the diocese of London, and Master William de Capella, clerk, or either of them, as his proctors for claiming, demanding, and receiving on his behalf. London, 2 June 1268.

683 Collation of Simon de Ponchardon, subdeacon, to West Buckland (*Westbocland*); patron, Emma de Huxham. London, 3 June 1268.

684 Inst. of John Modret, subdeacon, to the portion in the church of St Endellion which John Bozon had held; patron, Robert Modret. London, 3 June 1268.

685 The bishop ordained Master John de Anden — presented by Master G. de Naples — John Modret and Simon de Ponchardon as subdeacons, William called England as deacon, and Ralph de Bigbury as priest. London, 2 June 1268.

686[44] Renewal of collation to Great Torrington. London, 10 June 1268.

687 Inst. of John de Totnes, priest, to the parish church of Barnstaple (*Barnastap'*); patron, Sir Henry de Tracy. St Germans, 14 August 1268.

[44] See **678**.

688   Inst. of Master Simon de Lodge to East Allington (*Alynton*); patron, Sir Hugh de Treverbin. [Bishop's] Clyst, 23 August 1268.

689   Inst. of Master Laurence de Padstow to the vicarage of Phillack, presented by Master John called Rufus, the rector, with the consent of Sir Guy de Nonant.[45] [Bishop's] Clyst, 23 August 1268.

690   Inst. of Henry de Montfort to Pyworthy; patron, Sir Anselm Basset. [Bishop's] Clyst, 29 August 1268.

691   The bishop gave a quittance to Roger de Dartford, canon of Bosham, from the annual payment of twenty marks from his prebend to William de St Martin, priest, rector of Petrockstow (*Patricstouwe*).

692   Collation of Master Oliver de Tracy to the chancellorship of Exeter, with all its appurtenances, and he had letters of induction, assignation and institution in common form. [Bishop's] Clyst, 3 September 1268.

[fo.38v] **693**   Collation of Master G[ervase] de Crediton to the prebend of Crediton (*Cryditon*) which Master Oliver de Tracy had resigned. [Bishop's] Clyst, 3 September 1268.

694   Collation of Stephen de Salcombe, priest, to the vicarage of Paignton. [Bishop's] Clyst, 3 September 1268.

695   Collation of Henry de Sackville, rector of Dartington (*Dertinton*), to the prebend of Crediton which Master Gervase de Crediton had resigned. [Bishop's] Clyst, 3 September 1268.

696   Collation of William de St Martin, priest, to the prebend of Crediton which William de Bisimano junior had resigned. [Bishop's] Clyst, 3 September 1268.

697   Collation of Odo de Arundel to the prebend of Crantock (*ecc. S. Carantoci*) which Master Simon de Loges had voluntarily resigned. [Bishop's] Clyst, 3 September 1268.

698   Commendation, at the bishop's pleasure or until the commendation should be revoked, of Thomas de Hydon, rector of Hemyock (*Hemihec*), to Clyst Hydon (*Clist Hydon*). [Bishop's] Clyst, 3 September 1268.

699   Inst. of William de la Dene, subdeacon, to Diptford (*Depford*); patron, Sir Roger de Molys. London, 18 October 1268.

700   Collation of Master Edward de la Knolle, dean of Wells, to the prebend of Bosham which Henry de Bracton had held. Wallingford, 4 November 1268.

---

[45] The words concerning the presentation were written over an erasure.

701 Collation of Master J[ohn] de Esse to the prebend of Exeter which Sir Henry [de Bracton] had held. Wallingford, 4 November 1268.

702 Collation of Master William de Capella to the precentorship of Crediton, with letters of installation and induction. Wallingford, 4 November 1268.

703* 'Sir Philip Basset [a royal judge] and Sir Robert de Estall, archdeacon of Worcester, were summoned to Wallingford, having been chosen by the parties as arbiters, ordainers and friendly settlement-makers concerning secular property, with the assistance of the right reverend father, the lord R[oger Longespee], bishop of Coventry and Lichfield, Sir Henry [of Almain], eldest son of the illustrious king of the Romans, the lord abbot of Thame, Sir John de S. Walerico, Sir Geoffrey de Lewknor and Master Adam de Belsted, who likewise gave their consent and agreement. The lord bishop of Exeter, on behalf of himself and his church, and of the prior, convent and church of Bodmin, stated that many wrongs, losses and oppressions had been inflicted in Cornwall, contrary to God and justice and to its prejudice, on the said prior and convent by the bailiffs of the aforesaid lord king of the Romans. He delivered articles in writing concerning these and various other wrongs, losses and oppressions inflicted to the peril of their souls by the same bailiffs on him and on various ecclesiastical persons and others against common justice and against privileges granted under [pain of] anathema; likewise he exhibited before them, for their diligent examination with both discretion and zeal, articles recently delivered to him by the aforesaid lord king of the Romans which, if true, wronged the bishop and his people. After all the aforesaid articles had been diligently considered and precisely weighed, with the unanimous consent and agreement of all the aforesaid [arbiters], the same Sir Henry expressly approved and pronounced as just the complaint in the articles of the said bishop, including the selling off, waste, alienation, or occupation of the property of the aforesaid prior and convent, and he decreed that whatever had been attempted to the contrary had been done contrary to justice, and he gave judgment that a suitable fine should be imposed for this, and restored the said bishop and prior and their churches to their former status. Concerning the other articles exchanged, as was alleged, between the parties insofar as they related to various doings, he likewise determined that after a diligent inquiry had been carried out, before Christmas, into the truth of these doings by himself, or [fo.39] by other trustworthy and prudent men above suspicion, acting at his command, there should be a settlement and amends made, in accordance with justice, to be imposed and observed without delay, and made unshakeable. The contents of the submission of the king of the Romans was as follows:'[46] Wallingford, 6 November 1268.

704 Inst. of Peter de Totnes, priest, to the vicarage of Totnes parish church; patrons, the prior and convent of Totnes. [Bishop's] Clyst, 23 November 1268.

705* Identical institution of Peter de Totnes, but dated 25 November 1268.

---

[46] But no text of a submission was entered.

706 Collation of Sir Clement [de Langford], rector of Instow (*Innenestou*), to the treasurership of Crediton; he swore to be resident.[47] [Bishop's] Clyst, 25 November 1268.

707 Inst. of Roger, chaplain, to the vicarage of Fremington (*Fremeton*), presented by Sir Henry de Tracy with the consent of the abbot of Hartland. [Bishop's] Clyst, 25 November 1268.

708 Inst. of Walter Peverel to Ladock (*ecc. S. Ladoce*); patron, Sir William son of Ivo. [Bishop's] Clyst, 27 November 1268.

709 Inst. of Richard de . . ., priest, to Stockleigh English (*Stokeley Engles*); patron, Sir Hugh le English. Pawton, 20 December 1268.

710 Inst. of John de Burnham, priest, to the vicarage of Christow (*Cristenestou*); patrons, the prior and convent of Cowick. Pawton, 20 December 1268.

711 The bishop held an ordination. Launceston, 22 December 1268.

712 Inst. of Master Richard Vivian, subdeacon, to Lamorran; patron, Sir William de Halep. Lawhitton, 22 December 1268.

713 Inst. of Roger de Mills, subdeacon, to Doddiscombsleigh (*Legh'*); patron, by reason of her dowry, the lady Joan de Doddiscombe. Lawhitton, 22 December 1268.

714 Inst. of Robert de Week, subdeacon, to Boconnoc; patron, Sir Thomas de Kent. The bishop, in writing, ordered his official to induct Robert, saving any right the dean and chapter might have as regards the induction. Lawhitton, 22 December 1268.

715 The bishop gave to Master Roger de Leicester, papal chaplain, custody until the Ascension [2 May 1269], on the terms that follow, of the sequestrated church of Bideford (*Bydeford*), to which church he had been presented by the patron, Gilbert de Clare, earl of Gloucester. Master Roger was to show his dispensation in London to the bishop, or to one of his household having a proxy for that purpose, and the date must be notified in good time to Master Roger by Roger de Essex, grocer (*speciarium*) of London. Meanwhile the bishop did not recognize the rights of either patron or presentee, and no right was to be acquired by the presentee through this custody. St Germans, 26 December 1268.

[fo.39v] **716** Collation of Sir R[oger] de Dartford to the prebend of Exeter which Master William de Stanwey had held, and he was installed on the same day and assigned a seat in the chapter. 5 January 1269.

---

[47] *iuravit residentiam personalem pro rata temporis et beneficiorum que habet.*

717 Inst. of Richard de Teignmouth, priest, to the vicarage of South Brent (*Brentte*) with the duty of residence; patrons, the abbot and convent of Buckfast. [Bishop's] Clyst, 9 January 1269.

718 Inst. of Master John de Harberton to the vicarage of Harberton (*Hurberton*); patrons, the master and brothers of the Hospital of Bridgwater. [Bishop's] Clyst, 9 January 1269.

719 Collation of William de St Martin, priest, to the prebend of Crediton which Master William de Stanwey, formerly dean of Exeter, had held. [Bishop's] Clyst, 9 January 1269.

720 Inst. of John de Dorfington, priest, to Kilkhampton (*Kylcamton*), presented by the lord Gilbert de Clare, earl of Gloucester and Hertford, by reason of his guardianship of the heirs and lands of Richard de Grenville, the true patron. 19 January 1269.

721 The bishop gave to Master Henry de Bollegh the custody of the deanery of Probus (*ecc. S. Probi*) and its sequestered fruits. Crediton, 4 January 1269.

722 Collation of Master H[enry] de Bollegh to the deanery of Probus. [Bishop's] Clyst, 22 January 1269.

723 Collation of Matthew, called Bacon, to the prebend of Probus which Master Henry de Bollegh had held. [Bishop's] Clyst, 22 January 1269.

724[48] Collation of William de St Martin to the prebend of Exeter which Master John de Hanford had held. [Bishop's] Nympton, 1 February 1269.

725 Collation of Master Roger Barat to the prebend of Crediton which William de St Martin, priest, had held. [Bishop's] Clyst, 28 January 1269.

726 Inst. of Alured, priest, to Sutcombe (*Suthtecumb'*); patron, by reason of his wife's dowry, William Page. [Bishop's] Nympton, 4 February 1269.

727 The bishop granted by letters patent a pension of 20 shillings a year to Master William de Hancot, until he should be presented to a richer benefice in the diocese.[49] [Bishop's] Nympton, 4 February 1269.

728 Collation of Master Philip de Cancellis to the prebend of six marks [at Crediton] which William de Worplesdon had held. [Bishop's] Nympton, 5 February 1269.

---

[48] This and the next entry were written in in the wrong order, but reversed with marginal 'a' and 'b'.
[49] *quousque per se vel per aliquem de diocese suo sibi uberius in ecclesiastico beneficio sibi fuerit provisum.*

729 The bishop held a private ordination, and he ordained two subdeacons. Whitestone, 9 March 1269.

730 Inst. of Stephen de Renham, subdeacon, to Portlemouth (*Portlemue*); patron, Sir Alan son of Roald. Holsworthy, 9 March 1269.

731 The bishop dedicated churches in Devon and Cornwall throughout Lent. 1269.

732[50] The bishop issued statutes for the cathedral under his seal and under those of the dean of Wells [Edward de la Knolle] and the archdeacon of Exeter [probably Roger de Torridge still], and ordered them to be strictly observed; they begin: *Licet in operibus nature et humane conditionis institutione, etc.* Exeter, May 1269.

[fo.40] **733*** DEPOSITION OF JOHN CHUBBE, ABBOT OF TAVISTOCK.[51] 'In the name of the Lord, Amen. Just as it is fitting and right to cherish those fruitfully planted in God's church so that, when they are grown great, they may yield more abundantly the fruits of good works, so, by the same reasoning, it seems wholly expedient to uproot from the nursery of the Lord's house the dry and unfruitful ones whom no diligent cultivation will ever be able to induce to bear fruit, so that they may not uselessly take up the room of good trees, and to throw them out as far away as possible for burning, in grief and tribulation. Indeed, when we, Walter, by the grace of God bishop of Exeter, labouring in the Lord's vineyard as our pastoral duty requires, understood that John, called Chubbe, abbot of Tavistock, had been bound by our commissaries with the chain of greater excommunication because of his manifest offences and contumacies, the same abbot, coming to us in a spirit of devotion, as it appeared, recognizing his guilt and desiring, as he asserted, to mend his ways, after a corporal oath had been administered to him promised that he would make full satisfaction for the foregoing contumacies and offences, according to our will and ordinance without judicial clamour, voluntarily submitting himself totally to our ordinance; and he wished and granted that if at any time he should ever contravene any or all of the foregoing, he would be thrust back *ipso facto* into his former sentence of excommunication, and after these things had been done, we thought fit to grant him absolution at his instance.

Subsequently, however, the same abbot, hardening his heart, irreverently scorned the fulfilment of what he had sworn on oath to do; on this account we thrust him back into his former sentence of excommunication as justice demands. As time passed he returned, as he asserted, to a spirit of wiser counsel and desired to redeem the brand of disobedience and perjury through the merit of ecclesiastical discipline, and again sought urgently from us the benefit of absolution. And because, as he said, his means were at that time quite insufficient to make full satisfaction for the foregoing, concerning all the foregoing contumacies, offences and failures of obedience, for the second time he made a complete submission of himself and his position totally to our

[50] See Appendix II, from Dean and Chapter MSS.
[51] See Finberg, *Tavistock Abbey* p.23, cited in fn to **595**.

ordinance, grace and pleasure; after inspecting the holy gospels the same abbot took a second corporal oath, and he promised and voluntarily bound himself by virtue of the oath he had taken that concerning each and every item of the foregoing he would exactly undergo, observe and hold to our will or ordinance, nor would he ever at any time contravene it in any way; further, he wished and granted that if in any way he should ever contravene any or all of the foregoing he should *ipso facto* be deprived of his right and rule over the aforesaid abbey, as is all set out more fully in the letters of the abbot himself. Wherefore the same abbot under the aforesaid terms obtained the benefit of absolution.

The aforementioned abbot, however, unmindful of his own honour and salvation and not fearing the guilt of perjury, disobediently took no heed, despite frequent warnings, to fulfil what he had promised under oath to do. When subsequently, together with the foregoing matters, repeated reports had been made to us about this abbot which were not at all consonant with the honest observance of his Rule, we were roused by the repeated complaints of trustworthy men, and were urgently appealed to by monks of the same monastery; after associating with ourselves from the said monastery of Tavistock religious men of the same [Benedictine] order and of others, as the pastoral care of our office demands, we carried out an inquiry in legal form and had diligent inquiries made into the position of the said abbot, both in our own person and through our clerks, on diverse occasions, in the first place with the same abbot present and later when he was contumaciously absent. Wherefore, through the testimony of the monks of the same monastery and also through the testimony of other trustworthy clerks and sworn laymen, who have a better knowledge of the truth of what was done, it was found proven that the said abbot is an intolerable and manifest squanderer of the property of the said monastery by deserting the rule of monastic discipline to which he is bound by his vows of profession. On this account, by our authority, he was suspended from the administration of the temporal property of the same monastery.

Regardless of this suspension he put obstacles in the way of the keeper of the temporalities of the said monastery, appointed for this purpose by us with the consent of the monks in that same place, so as to prevent him administering the same for the benefit of the same monastery, squandering the same property as before, only more seriously and on a vaster scale. Spurning the discipline of the established regulations of the monastic rule, the same abbot, possessed by a spirit of madness, with the accomplices he had gathered to himself burst in upon one of his monks who was celebrating Mass, had him violently stripped of the sacred vestments in which he was clad, had him dragged out of the church and led captive to the abbot's own chamber, where he was detained for a further period. Not content with this, he set aside the fear of God and rashly laid violent hands on certain of the said monks and also on certain members of their household in their own cloister, [fo.40v] during the night. He made a terrible and outrageous assult on some of the monks who fled to the church for their own safety and were remaining there; breaking through the doors of the monastery with weapons of iron, he set fires in the aforesaid cloister; he smashed in the doors of the cellar, the church, and the treasury; he had violently carried off the chest – under the guardianship of two monks elected for this purpose by the convent – in which was kept the common seal, and also the charters and records of the said monastery included together with it, and also charters, books,

consecrated vessels, and many other various things, and he had those guardians
of the seal seized by violence in the church and brought captive to his chamber,
and he had them held prisoner there throughout the whole night, until he had
completely had his way with the said seal and the other things, and he
perpetrated other outrages to the peril of his soul, the prejudice of the
monastery, and the scandal of many. Further, the same abbot, although
bound by various sentences of excommunication, and not ignorant of these
sentences, irreverently took part in the sacraments.

We have considered all the foregoing with sighing of spirit and anguish of
heart, and have diligently pondered them, and understanding that according to
the rules of canon law it is more useful to have a few good ministers in the
church of God than many bad, and that a diseased limb should be thrown far
away from God's church, and having taken counsel from those learned in the
law we, by definitive sentence, depose, deprive and totally remove the
aforementioned John Chubbe, abbot, (whose absence — after his being lawfully
summoned and canonically awaited — has been supplied by the presence of
God) a man of ill desert who has brought loss on the aforesaid monastery on
account of the aforesaid and of other matters, from the administration of the
aforesaid abbey and from right and rule over the same. We give judgment that
the aforesaid monastery is vacant of the rule of an abbot *de facto* and *de iure*. And
because where the fault has been greater there the punishment must be the
more severe, we suspend the above-named John Chubbe from the celebration of
the sacraments for a period of three years, and by the same sentence we absolve
all the monks of the said monastery from their obedience to the same man, and
also the vassals, and any others whomsoever previously bound in any kind of
allegiance to him on account of the said monastery, from their fealty. But
because the same John seems to have incurred the brand of falling from the
Rule on many counts and for a variety of reasons, we reserve to ourselves and to
the see of Exeter the questions of his falling from the Rule so that they may be
more fully examined and debated in a judicial forum. Given and enacted in the
conventual chapter at Tavistock', 19 March 1269.[52]

[fo.41] **734** Inst. of Gilbert de St Crowan, priest, to the vicarage of Crowan (*ecc.
S. Crewene*) with the duty of residence; patrons, the abbot and convent of
Tewkesbury. To the vicarage was assigned all the altarage together with the
glebe and the five shillings that used to be paid for the glebe to the abbot and
convent; the vicar was to bear all the burdens due to the bishop and the
archdeacon, etc. Newlyn, 13 August 1269.

735 The bishop confirmed [cf **638**] the presentation by the prior and convent
of Bodmin of Master Odo Tureth to the vicarage of Padstow (*Allestowe*),
appointing to the vicarage an appropriate house and all the altarage, except
the tithes of fish and the mills and certain field tithes which were to remain in
perpetuity with the prior and convent. The vicar was to pay 40 shillings a year to
the prior and convent at the quarter days, and to bear all the due and customary
burdens. Newlyn, 13 August 1269.

[52] The rest of folio 40v — about a third of the page — was left blank.

736 The bishop confirmed the presentation by the prior and convent of Bodmin of Richard de St Endellion, priest, to the vicarage of Cubert (*vicaria S. Cuberti*), assigning to the vicarage all the altarage with the glebe, except the fish and mill tithes of Ellenglaze (*Helen*) and the field tithes of beans and peas which were to remain with the prior and convent. The vicar was to bear all the due burdens, etc. Newlyn, 13 August 1269.

737 The bishop taxed the vicarage of St Keverne. To the vicarage was assigned all the altarage, the vicarage buildings, and the bean and pea tithes of the old curtilage as presently understood, except the fish tithes and the tithes of beans and peas and vetch and all the other field crops which were to remain with the abbot and convent [of Beaulieu]; the vicar was to be responsible for all the customary burdens and also for the service books and vestments, as well as the chancel as long as it was sound (*necnon librorum et vestimentorum necnon cancelli dummodo ex toto non corruerit*). Newlyn, 13 August 1269.

738 Collation by lapse of Drogo de St Perran, priest, to the vicarage of Perranzabuloe (*ecc. S. Pyrani*). To the vicarage was assigned all the altarage of the mother church and chapel and all the offerings from the processions with the relics (*de turnis reliquiarium*); the vicar was to pay the dean and chapter of Exeter six marks a year, and to bear all the burdens, etc. Newlyn, 13 August 1269.

739 Collation by lapse of Eurinus de Helston, priest, to the vicarage of Gwennap (*ecc. S. Weneppe*). To the vicarage was assigned all the altarage of the parish church and the chapel of the Holy Trinity together with the glebe, except for three acres of glebeland on an appropriate site for building houses and barns; the vicar was to bear all the burdens, etc. Newlyn, 13 August 1269.

740 Collation by lapse of Amadasius, priest, to the vicarage of St Erth (*Lanuthno*). [fo.41v] To the vicarage was assigned all the altarage of the church together with the glebe, except for three acres for the rector to build houses and barns; the vicar is to pay to the warden of the cathedral fabric (*custodi operis ecclesie B. Petri Exon*) ten shillings a year, and to bear all the burdens, etc. Newlyn, 13 August 1269.

741 Collation by lapse of Robert de St Austell, priest, to the vicarage of St Anthony in Meneage (*ecc. S. Antonini in Manahet*). To the vicarage was assigned all the altarage together with the fish tithes and the tithes of garden beans and peas, together with an acre of glebeland suitable for building houses for the vicarage; the vicar is to bear all the burdens, etc. Newlyn, 13 August 1269.

742 Collation (*ad suam propriam custodiam spectantem*) of . . . de St Feock, priest, to the vicarage of Feock. To the vicarage was assigned all the altarage together with the glebe, except for the homage . . .; the vicar will bear all the burdens, etc. Newlyn, 13 August 1269.

743 Collation by lapse of William de Kaernemhec to the vicarage of Veryan (*Elerky*). To the vicarage was assigned all the altarage . . . Newlyn, 13 August 1269.

744[53]   The bishop issued letters patent. The state of the church of Crediton, formerly preeminent, and originally founded for eighteen canons, had now fallen to an establishment of twelve canons; the bishop has restored the original number with six canons and as many vicars. He ordained that the six vicars should be paid 20 shillings a year by the six canons even if that was not enough for their support (*licet exinde commode nequeant sustentari*). On account of the poverty of the collegiate church of the Holy Cross at Crediton, the bishop appropriated to it the parish church of Coldridge (*Colrigg'*) on the departure or decease of the current rector, with the consent of the patron, Sir John Wiger, knight, and also with the consent of the dean and chapter, reserving the assessment of an appropriate vicarage for that church, of which the patronage was to remain with the bishop. He laid down that the revenues of the former vicars, the annual 20 shillings a year to the new vicars, and the revenues of Coldridge were to be distributed equally among the eighteen vicars and their successors. The canons and vicars of the collegiate church and their successors were to celebrate in perpetuity the obits of the bishop and his predecessors and of Sir John Wiger and his ancestors. No vicar was to be admitted to the college without taking the oath to observe this ordinance, which the bishop had sealed. Crediton, 29 July 1269.

[fo.42] **745**   The bishop assessed all the vicarages in the rural deaneries of Trigg (*Trigesir'*) Major and Minor, and West and East Wyvel (*Wevelesir'*). The same day he first assessed the vicarage of St Minver (*ecc. S. Menwrede*), assigning to the vicarage all the altarage and all the glebe up to the value of ten shillings a year; the vicar is to bear all the due and customary burdens, but he is not to pay the five marks as was customary, until the bishop lays down otherwise.[54] St Breward, 17 August 1269.

746   To the vicarage of St Petrock, Bodmin, was assigned the livery of a canon for the vicar's daily wants, with forage for one horse, and four silver marks a year payable at the quarter days; the vicar is to bear none of the burdens. St Breward, 17 August 1269.

747   To the vicarage of St Teath was assigned all the altarage and the glebe to the value of two shillings a year; the vicar is to bear all the burdens, etc. St Breward, 17 August 1269.

748   Collation by lapse of Joel, chaplain, to the vicarage of Poughill (*Pohewill*), Cornwall, assigning to the vicarage all the altarage and four acres, English measure,[55] for a house. St Breward, 17 August 1269.

749   To the vicarage of St Gennys (*ecc. S. Gignasii*) was assigned all the altarage of the mother church and the chapel of St Julita, except for the hay tithe of the

---

[53] This entry seems to have been made subsequently on the blank bottom half of the folio.
[54] The last phrases were added in the margin; the payment was presumably due to the prior and convent of Bodmin, patrons of the vicarage.
[55] *Acras anglicanas*; the Cornish acre seems to have been much larger, perhaps equivalent to a virgate.

mother church and for half the mortuary payments of the chapel; furthermore, the vicar will have the glebe of the mother church and will bear all the burdens, etc. St Breward, 17 August 1269.

750 To the vicarage of North Petherwin (*Nordpydrewyn*) was assigned all the altarage together with the glebe assigned to the vicars from of old; the vicar is to bear all the burdens, etc. St Breward, 17 August 1269.

751 To the vicarage of Treneglos was assigned all the altarage of the mother church and chapel [of Warbstow] together with the garb tithes of Roose (*Ros*) and *Kenros*; the vicar is to bear all the burdens, etc. St Breward, 17 August 1269.

752 To the vicarage of Davidstow (*ecc. S. David*) was assigned all the altarage together with the glebe – for which the vicar no longer need pay two shillings a year – and all the hay tithes; the vicar is to bear all the burdens, etc, and must pay the prior of Launceston five shillings a year. St Breward, 17 August 1269.

753 To the vicarage of South Petherwin (*Suthpydrewyn*) was assigned all the altarage of the mother church and chapel; the vicar is to pay one mark a year to the prior of St Germans, and to bear all the burdens, etc. St Breward, 17 August 1269.

754 To the vicarage of Linkinhorne (*Lankynhorn*) was assigned all the altarage together with the glebe, on terms that the vicar pay two marks a year to the prior and convent of Launceston but be released from the other two marks which had been customarily paid, and he is to bear etc. St Breward, 17 August 1269.

755 To the vicarage of Lanreath (*Lanratton*) was assigned all the altarage of the mother church and the chapel of the Holy Trinity, and one mark's worth from the garb tithes because the vicar is enfeebled, on terms that on the departure or decease of Peter, that vicar, the said mark is to revert to the prior and convent of St Germans; the vicar is to bear etc. St Breward, 17 August 1269.

756 To the vicarage of Maker (*Macre*) was assigned all the altarage, together with the fish tithes, a house and eight measured acres of glebeland, and also a mark's worth of the garb tithes in an appropriate place; the vicar is to bear, etc. St Breward, 17 August 1269.

757 TAXATION OF THE VICARAGES OF THE ARCHDEACONRY OF EXETER. The bishop assessed all the vicarages east of the Exe. To the vicarage of Cullompton was assigned all the altarage, the whole hay tithe, and a house valued at half a mark; the prior and convent of St Nicholas, Exeter, are to take everything else, while the vicar is to bear all the burdens, etc. Sampford Peverell, 28 August 1269.

758   To the vicarage of Yarcombe (*Artecumb'*) was assigned all the altarage and the tithes of garden beans and peas; the prior [of Otterton] is to bear all the burdens, etc. Sampford Peverell, 28 August 1269.

[fo.42v] **759**   The bishop assessed the vicarage of Awliscombe, formerly assessed at ten marks, which he found actually worth seven marks, four shillings and a penny, due to the renovation of the farm buldings, and he restored it to ten marks. Sampford Peverell, 28 August 1269.

760   The bishop assessed the vicarage of Sheldon (*Shyeldon*) at five marks, made up from part of the altarage and of the garb tithes. Sampford Peverell, 28 August 1269.

761   The vicarage of Dunkeswell (*Donkewell*) was to have five and a half marks in hard cash (*in denariis siccis*); the abbot [of Dunkeswell] is to bear all the burdens, etc. Sampford Peverell, 28 August 1269.

762   To the vicarage of Seaton (*Sheton*) was assigned all the offerings of the church except for the garb tithes growing in the open fields, for the hay tithe and the main parsonage house (*et excepto capitali manso persone*). Sampford Peverell, 28 August 1269.

763   The bishop confirmed the assessment of Axmouth (*Axemuwe*) vicarage; the prior of Loders is to take two thirds of all the greater tithes and one third of the lesser, and the vicar all the rest, and the garb tithes were to be adjustable from year to year. Sampford Peverell, 28 August 1269.

764   To the vicarage of Aylesbeare was assigned four marks and sixteen shillings in fixed instalments and, further, all the tithes of *Poriford'* on the eastern side of the hill. Sampford Peverell, 28 August 1269.

765   To the vicarage of Sidmouth was assigned all the altarage and glebe valued at half a mark and valued in the annual census at two shillings, also eight marks, ten shillings and seven pence in fixed instalments, and a third of all the tithes from fish, ships and small boats. Sampford Peverell, 28 August 1269.

766   To the vicarage of Colaton Raleigh (*Coleton*) was assigned all the altarage and glebe, valued at six shillings, namely all the garb tithes of Bystock (*Boystok'*) and all the tithes from the old enclosures, whatever crop they carried (*et totam decimam veterum casetallagiorum vestatorum quodcumque genus grani plantetur vel seminetur in eisdem*). Sampford Peverell, 28 August 1269.

767   To the vicarage of Harpford (*Herpford*) was assigned five marks in fixed instalments, and four marks under penalty from the prior [of Otterton] at fixed dates, or the prior might assign them to him in fixed instalments; the vicar is to maintain a chaplain for Venn Ottery (*Fenotri*), and to bear all the burdens, etc. Sampford Peverell, 28 August 1269.

768 To the vicarage of Otterton was assigned all the altarage and hay tithes, but not the tithes from the mills and from the fodder for the prior [of Otterton]'s beasts. Sampford Peverell, 28 August 1269.

769[56] There is not yet a vicarage at Kenton, but the bishop assigned to a future vicar all the altarage with all its offerings, and a house and garden by the church for his residence. [Sampford Peverell, 28 August 1269.]

770[57] To the vicarage of Cowick was assigned five marks in fixed instalments. Sampford Peverell, 28 August 1269.

771 To the vicarage of Spreyton was assigned all the altarage and twelve acres of glebeland, and twenty shillings in fixed instalments from the garb tithes. Sampford Peverell, 28 August 1269.

772[58] To the vicarage of Brampford [Speke] (*Bramford*) was assigned all the altarage of the church and chapel, and twenty acres of land at Nether Exe valued at two shillings, or else two shillings from the prior [of St Nicholas, Exeter]; the vicar is to be exempt from the payment of the garb tithe on the glebe which he cultivates. The prior is to support a chaplain at Nether Exe. The bishop orders an inquiry into the portion of the chapel in order that the vicar may bear the burdens of the church and chapel and take from it a share to be assessed by the bishop. Sampford Peverell, 28 August 1269.

773[59] To the vicarage of Holcombe [Rogus] (*Holecumb'*) was assigned all the altarage, all the tithes of beans, peas and hay with the meadows of Burlescombe (*Botelescumb'*), worth 100 shillings in fixed instalments; if there should be a shortfall, it was to be supplemented from the glebe or the fixed rent. Sampford Peverell, 28 August 1269.

774 To the vicarage of Hockworthy (*Hokeworthy*) was assigned all the altarage and one mark's worth of the garb tithes; the vicar is to bear all the burdens, etc. Sampford Peverell, 28 August 1269.

775[60] To the vicarage of Halberton was assigned all the altarage and all the garden tithes of hay, linseed, beans and peas; the vicar is to bear all the due and customary burdens, and maintain a chaplain and a deacon. Sampford Peverell, 28 August 1269.

776 To the vicarage of Christow (*Cristenestow*) was assigned all the altarage with the mill tithes and 20 shillings from specified garb tithes. Sampford Peverell, 28 August 1269.

---

[56] See **809**, a year later.
[57] The entry is marked *pendet*.
[58] This entry is marked *pendet*; it was also scratched out with rough criss-cross lines. Cf **781**.
[59] This entry is marked *pendet*.
[60] Just beside this entry is written in very small letters *Gregorius*.

[fo.43] **777**   To the vicarage of Ottery St Mary (*ecc. Ottri S. Marie*) was assigned one tenth of the garb tithes of the parish and a tenth from the tithes of the 56 acres of ancient demesne formerly held in villeinage, all the the proceeds and offerings of the altarage of the said church, except for the tithes from the mills and the hay tithe from the lord's demesne, on terms that the vicar should pay annually to the dean and chapter of Rouen four marks, at the quarter days, and nevertheless is to bear all the due and customary burdens, and to maintain a chaplain, a deacon, and a clerk. Sampford Peverell, 28 August 1269.

778   To the vicarage of [East, as it later became] Budleigh was assigned all the altarage, all the garden tithes of beans, peas and vetch, all the hay tithe and a mark's worth from the garb tithes; the vicar will bear all the burdens, etc. Sampford Peverell, 28 August 1269.

779   To the vicarage of Pinhoe was assigned five marks in fixed instalments. Sampford Peverell, 28 August 1269.

780   To the vicarage of . . . . Sampford Peverell, 28 August 1269.

781[61]   To the vicarage of Brampford [Speke] was assigned all the altarage of that church and the glebe free from the payment of any tithes, the tithes of Cowley (*Couelegh*), and some 20 acres of land in Nether Exe together with the mortuary payments of all who died within the bounds of the chapel. Sampford Peverell, 28 August 1269.

782   The bishop assessed all the vicarages of the archdeaconry of Barnstaple. To the vicar of Brushford (*Brigford*) residing in the same place was assigned the whole [income from the] church of Brushford, with all its tithes and occasional offerings, except for the glebe; the vicar is to pay half a mark a year to the abbot and convent of Hartland on account of the parsonage. South Molton, 26 August 1269.

783   [The bishop] assessed the vicarage of Mariansleigh (*ecc. S. Marie Legh*), laying down that there should there be a perpetual vicar who . . . . South Molton, 26 August 1269.

784   To the vicarage of Mariansleigh (*Maringlegh*) was assigned all the altarage and three acres of glebeland in an appropriate place for building a house, and the four shillings rent from the land which Galfridus holds in Uppacott (*Oppecot*). South Molton, 26 August 1269.

785   To the vicarage of Fremington (*Fremiton*) was assigned all the altarage and glebe, except for two thirds of the patron's demesne. South Molton, 26 August 1269.

786   To the vicarage of Chittlehampton (*Chitelhamtone*) was assigned all the altarage and all the tithes of hay and pannage and also all the glebe — except for

---

[61] Cf **772**, which this entry replaced; Cowley is now in the parish of Upton Pyne.

twenty enclosed acres – to make up for the eight shillings lacking, or else as much of the garb tithes at true value as compensation for the rest of the glebe. South Molton, 26 August 1269.

787 To the vicarage of Braunton was assigned all the altarage. South Molton, 26 August 1269.

788 [The bishop] laid down that the vicar of [Peters] Marland (*Merland*) should have all the [income from the] church and its glebe; he was to pay an annual rent of ten marks on the quarter days to the prioress and convent of Cornworthy on pain of forfeiting the vicarage (*et si deficiat in solutione terminis statutis facienda cadat a vicaria*). South Molton, 26 August 1269.

789 To the vicarage of Monkleigh (*Monkelegh*) was assigned 60 shillings in fixed instalments, as assessed by Bishop Brewer, and an additional 20 shillings from the garb tithes unless the prior [of Montacute] can show proof that the earlier assessment was of legal force. South Molton, 26 August 1269.

790 To the vicarage of Buckland[62] (*Boclond*) [Brewer] was assigned all the altarage together with a house for the vicar, twelve acres [?of arable] and a half acre of meadow; the vicar is to have a chaplain, and he is to bear all the burdens, etc. South Molton, 26 August 1269.

791 To the vicarage of Abbotsham (*Albedesham*) was assigned all the glebe and altarage and two marks from the garb tithes. South Molton, 26 August 1269.

[fo.43v] **792** To the vicarage of Bishop's Nympton (*Nemeton Episcopi*) was assigned all the altarage and a plot next to the vicarage. South Molton, 26 August 1269.

793 To the vicarage of [Bishop's] Tawton was assigned ten marks in fixed instalments; the dean [of Exeter] is to support two chaplains and two clerks in the chapels. South Molton, 26 August 1269.

794 The bishop gave judgment that there should be a vicarage at Pilton (*Pelton*). South Molton, 26 August 1269.

795 [The bishop] gave judgment that there should be a vicarage at Ashford (*Esford*). South Molton, 26 August 1269.

796 To the vicarage of Dowland (*Duelond*) was assigned all the altarage. South Molton, 26 August 1269.

797 To the vicarage of Shebbear (*Sefbeer*) was assigned . . . . South Molton, 26 August 1269.

---

[62] Identified as such by Hingeston-Randolph; N. Orme points out that the other Bucklands did not have vicars.

798   To the vicarage of Winkleigh (*Wynkelegh*) was assigned all the altarage; the vicar was to pay three marks a year to the dean and chapter of Exeter. South Molton, 26 August 1269

799   The bishop gave judgment that there should be a vicarage at the parish church of Hartland. South Molton, 26 August 1269.

800   The bishop gave judgment that there should be a vicarage at the parish church of Frithelstock (*Frythelestok'*). South Molton, 26 August 1269.

801[63]*   Inst. of William Hurward, priest, to Yarnscombe; patron, John Hurward. Because William had been accused of fornication, he drew up letters patent for the bishop in these terms: 'Let all know that, since I was previously accused of fornication, I make a fresh promise to the venerable father, the lord Walter, by the grace of God bishop of Exeter, of the fruits of a better life henceforward, and I offer and grant to the same lord bishop gladly and of my pure and voluntary free will that if in the future it should happen that I be convicted of fornication of this sort − which God forbid − I am *ipso* [*facto*] to lose my right and possession in my church of Yarnscombe, to which he admitted me by special grace, reserving to myself thereafter no power of protesting, challenging, appealing, pursuing an appeal, or entreating the restoration of that church.' Paignton, 12 September 1269.

802   A proxy for the Roman curia was issued in letters patent appointing Master Nicholas de Honiton, clerk, the bishop's proctor at the papal court for bringing suit, challenging, and doing other things which fall within this remit, but the power of borrowing was specifically withheld from him. Nicholas also had power to swear in the bishop's name when there was need, and to substitute one or more proctors in the bishop's and his place when expedient; all earlier proxies were expressly revoked. Crediton, 5 February 1270.

[fo.44] **803**   The lord Robert was blessed as abbot of Tavistock. Newenham [Abbey], 6 April 1270.

804   Collation of Sir Alan de Nymet as archdeacon of Barnstaple. Chudleigh, 20 April 1270.

805   The lord Richard was blessed as abbot of Torre. London, 22 May 1270.

806   Master Reginald de Torrington ordained subdeacon and admitted to . . .; patrons, the abbot and convent of Buckfast. Titchfield, 7 June 1270.

807   Inst. of Richard de Chesterford, subdeacon, to Jacobstow (*Jacobostowe*) [Cornwall]; patron, Sir Henry de Champernowne. Faringdon, 9 June 1270.

---

[63] J.A. Brundage has pointed out that the mechanism here resembles, and may be modelled on, the practice of abjuration *sub pena nubendi*.

808 Admission of Sir Roger de Fontibus, monk, as prior of Tywardreath; patrons, the king of Germany and the abbot of St Serge, Angers. Horsley, 13 June 1270.

809 In letters patent the bishop assessed the vicarages of Kenton and West Alvington (*Alfinton*), with the consent of the dean and chapter of Salisbury to whom they were appropriated. The vicarage of Kenton was to consist of all the altarage except for the fish tithes, while the vicar was to have an appropriate house, the one the chaplain used to live in, together with the curtilage, to which was to be added an adjoining half-acre of glebe; the vicar was to bear all the ordinary burdens. The vicarage of West Alvington was to consist of all the altarage of the parish church and its chapels of South Milton (*Myddelton*), Malborough (*Marleberg'*) and South Huish (*Hywysh*), together with an acre in each place for building a house for the vicar or chaplain, but not the tithe of eels which was assigned to the said dean and his successors; the vicar was to maintain chaplains and suitable ministers to serve in these, to bear all the ordinary burdens, and to pay in perpetuity four marks a year at Michaelmas from the occasional offerings of the altarage for the maintenance of a chaplain saying his office for the bishop's soul and the souls of his successors and of all the faithful departed in the church of Exeter or the bishop's chapel [of St. Gabriel] there. The bishop also established that the vicarage of Yealmpton (*Ealminton*) should consist of all the altarage of the church and its chapel of Revelstoke (*Resulestok'*), with a suitable house; the vicar was to bear all the ordinary burdens. Winchester, 1 August 1270.

810 Robert [de Wickhampton],[64] dean of Salisbury, and the chapter, rendered obedience to the bishop for the prebend of Kingsteignton which they held in the cathedral of Exeter through the grant of the late bishop William [Brewer], with the assent of the Exeter chapter, and also of the former bishop of Salisbury, Robert [Bingham][65], and the chapter of Salisbury, and for their appropriated churches. Furthermore, they granted in perpetuity four marks a year at Michaelmas for the maintenance of a chaplain saying his office for the soul of the said bishop Walter, his successors and all the faithful departed, in the church of Exeter or his chapel there, as the bishop shall choose, to be paid at the hands of their vicar at West Alvington. Chidham, 5 June 1270.

[fo.44v] **811** Because the worship of God, and the safety of souls, was diminished on account of poverty, the bishop, in letters patent, annexed the chapel of Lower Creedy (*Crydie Wyg'*) with its appurtenances to the church of Upton Hellions (*Uppeton Hyliun*), with the consent of Sir John Wyger, patron of both, saving the right of the church of Crediton in the chapel; one rector was to serve both, having the cure of souls and acting through suitable ministers, and he is to bear all the burdens. Newenham, 6 August 1270.

812 Inst. of Reginald de Weare, priest, to the free chapel of Calverleigh (*Calwodelegh*); patron, Patrick de Calverleigh. Newenham, 6 August 1270.

---

[64] Dean 1262–74, and later bishop of Salisbury.
[65] Bishop of Salisbury 1229–46.

813   Collation of Alan de Helston, priest, to the vicarage of Sithney. To the vicarage was assigned all the altarage and, furthermore, all the hay tithes of Penventon (*Fentenvenham*) and St Elvan (*Seynthelven*), the tithes of garden beans and peas, the house where the priests customarily lived with the gardens beside it and with two fields between the field of Stultus, the priest, and the royal highway running from Helston to Hayle (*Heyl'*); the vicar is to bear all the burdens, and to pay 40 shillings a year to the canons of Glasney. [No place,] 21 August 1270.

814   To the vicarage of Kea (*Landege*) was assigned all the altarage of the mother church and of the chapels of Kenwyn (*Kenwen*) and Tregavethan (*Tregenfedon*), except for the tithes of field beans and peas, and all the houses pertaining to the said church and chapels, with the whole glebe; the vicar is to pay three pounds a year to the canons [of Glasney], and bear all the burdens. [No place,] 21 August 1270.

815   To the vicarage of Budock (*ecc. S. Budoci*) and the annexed church of Penryn (*Penren*) was assigned all the altarage of the said church and chapel, except for the tithes of fish, wool, lambs and field peas and beans, and the traditional parsonage house of Penryn with its gardens and the whole glebe of *Bethethlan*;[66] the vicar is to bear all the burdens. [No place,] 21 August 1270.

816   To the vicarage of Zennor (*ecc. S. Senare*) was assigned all the altarage, except for the tithes of fish, wool, and field beans and peas, and also the house where the rectors customarily lived, with all the glebe. [No place,] 21 August 1270.

817[67]   In view of the poverty of their resources, the canons of the church of Blessed Thomas, martyr, at Glasney obtained a letter from the bishop, confirmed by the dean and chapter of Exeter, granting them, for the daily distributions to the canons ministering there, the churches of Sithney, Zennor, Gorran (*ecc. de S. Gorono*), St Enoder and Kea with its chapels of Kenwyn and Tregavethan (*Tregefedon*), together with thirteen acres, English measure, in Glasney (*Glasneye*) measured in plots for houses and their outbuildings for the canons. The churches were to be held in perpetuity in free alms, immune from any secular service, and in each of them a perpetual vicar was to be established, to be instituted by the bishop of Exeter, with cure of souls and the duty of residence. Bishop's Clyst, 1 September 1270.

[fo.45] **818***   ORDINANCE. The bishop issued sealed letters patent. 'A matter of dispute seems to have arisen between our beloved sons the dean, R[oger de Torridge], and chapter of Exeter, and Master John, called Noble, archdeacon of Exeter, concerning the jurisdiction over certain chapels in the city and suburbs

---

[66] This is the site of the collegiate church of Glasney.
[67] Budock and Feock had already been appropriated to the collegiate church; see document C, Appendix 1, in vol.3. The college, known more widely as Penryn than Glasney, had been founded in 1264 or 1265 – on 26 March 1267 it was in the third year since its foundation.

of Exeter as also over those churches and manors within the boundaries of the aforesaid archdeaconry appropriated to the same dean and chapter; the said parties, totally abiding by our award and submitting themselves voluntarily to our ordinance, appeared before us in the chapter of Exeter on 3 September 1270, after lawful summons; after arbitration and determination we ordain, and ordaining we decree, with the express assent of the parties, in this manner: to wit, that the dean of Exeter for the time being is to have and exercise in perpetuity, inasmuch as it is annexed to and united with the deanery of Exeter by this our ordinance, saving in all matters the episcopal right and dignity, jurisdiction over all the canons, clerks, choir, both the vicars and others of similar status, the households of the canons, and also over the church of Heavitree (*Hevedtre*) and all the other churches appropriated to the said dean and chapter which are within the limits of our diocese and outside the city and aforesaid suburb, and also their manors – over such churches and manors as there is jurisdiction at present.

We ordain further that the archdeacon of Exeter for the time being is to have and exercise fully in perpetuity jurisdiction over the whole city of Exeter, namely over the clerks and laymen living or staying in the city and its suburbs, the parishioners of the chapels of St Sidwell (*ecc. S Sativol'*), St David, Holy Trinity, and the other churches and chapels of the city and its aforesaid suburbs, saving the jurisdiction of the aforesaid dean. On terms that the same archdeacon, from the proceeds of the same jurisdiction, provides one candle containing one pound's weight of wax, to be kept burning in perpetuity in the middle of the choir at Matins and before the high altar at High Mass. And if by chance it should happen that the archdeaconry of Exeter should be conferred at some future time on someone who is not a canon of Exeter cathedral, we desire and, with the express assent of the aforesaid dean and chapter, we ordain that the whole jurisdiction over the city and aforesaid suburb shall pertain to the dean of Exeter and attach to the deanery until the same archdeacon shall canonically acquire a canonry in the said cathedral or until the archdeaconry [is conferred] on another man who has been duly collated as a canon of the same cathedral, saving the episcopal rights in sequestrations and other matters when the aforesaid archdeaconry is vacant.' Sealed also by the dean and chapter and the archdeacon. Exeter, 4 October 1270.

819 The dean, R[oger de Torridge], and chapter, after lawful summons, had appeared before the bishop in the chapter of Exeter on 3 September 1270 and submitted the arrangements for their appropriated vicarages to his decision. The bishop laid down that the dean and chapter must, within a month of any vacancy, present a suitable parson for institution by the bishop; [fo.45v] anything pertaining meanwhile to the bishop by reason of a sequestration would accrue to the dean and chapter. To these letters patent were appended the seals of the bishop and of the dean and chapter. Exeter, 4 October 1270.

820 CONFIRMATION BY THE DEAN AND CHAPTER OF A PENSION OF TWO MARKS. In compensation for the loss to the bishop's rights from the late Bishop William [Brewer]'s ordinance, made with the consent of the Exeter chapter and also of Bishop Robert [Bingham] of Salisbury and of the chapter there, concerning the Kingsteignton prebend which the church of Salisbury holds in the diocese of

Exeter, Roger [de Torridge], dean of Exeter, and the chapter in letters patent (dated Winchester, 1 August 1270) granted in perpetuity two marks a year, payable at Michaelmas through the vicar of Harberton, a church appropriated to the cathedral by the aforesaid ordinance, for the support of a chaplain to pray for the souls of Bishop Walter [Bronescombe], of his successors and of all the faithful departed, in the cathedral or in his chapel [of St Gabriel] there, as the bishop shall choose. Exeter, 4 October 1270.

821   Master Henry de Hamtesfort resigned the church of Coldridge, for which the bishop established a vicarage; the vicars of the collegiate church of Crediton were to receive ten pounds a year in perpetuity, and the rest [of the income], together with the houses and glebe, was to be the portion of the vicar residing [at Coldridge]. Of his special grace the bishop laid down that Master Henry was to receive five pounds a year from the collegiate church until he should be better provided for. Exeter, 4 October 1270.

822   Inst. of Master Henry de Hamtesfort to Petrockstow (*Patrokestoh'*), vacant by the resignation of Sir William de S. Martin; patrons, the abbot and convent of Buckfast. Exeter, 4 October 1270.

823   Collation of Peter de Guildford, then the bishop's chaplain, to the portion of St Teath (*ecc. S. Etha*) vacant by the resignation of R[oger] Barat. Exeter, 4 October 1270.

824[68]   Gilbert de Tyting resigned the church of Cheriton Bishop (*Cheriton*), for which the bishop established that three chaplains should receive twenty silver marks a year in perpetuity . . .[69] of Thomas, canon, from the aforesaid church; the resident vicar is to take the rest [of the income], on terms that the said chaplains should celebrate in the cathedral of Exeter at the altar constructed by the same canon Thomas . . .

825   Inst. of Richard de Grangiis to Newton St Petrock (*Nyweton*), vacant by the death of Hugh Winter; patrons, the prior and convent of Bodmin. Exeter, 4 October 1270.

826[70]   AGREEMENT OF THE BISHOPS OF EXETER AND SALISBURY OVER THE PREBEND OF KINGSTEIGNTON. At Chidham on 5 June 1270 the bishop ratified the late Bishop William [Brewer]'s ordinance, made with the consent of the Exeter chapter and also of Bishop Robert [Bingham] of Salisbury and of the chapter there, concerning the Kingsteignton prebend which the church of Salisbury holds in the diocese of Exeter, and he confirmed the appropriation of Harberton to the dean and chapter of Exeter and the payment of the two marks, payable at Michaelmas through the vicar of Harberton, for the support

---

[68] This entry was cancelled by a *vacat*, and in the margin was written *quia aliter est ordinatum*. N. Orme points out that this seems to be the first attempt at setting up the chantry actually established from the revenues of Upottery; see **841**.

[69] Two illegible words erased.

[70] Cf **810** and **820**.

of a chaplain to pray for the bishop's soul, the souls of his predecessors and of all the faithful departed, in the cathedral or his chapel [of St Gabriel], as the bishop shall think fit to choose. Letters patent recording this were issued. Exeter, 4 October 1270.

827 Collation of Mark [de St Madron], chaplain, to the vicarage of Gorran (*ecc. de S. Gorrono*). Exeter, 4 October 1270.

[fo.46] **828** Collation of Master Roger de Okeston to the portion at St Teath (*S. Tthe*) vacant by the resignation of Roland de Pochifort. Exeter, 5 October 1270.

829 The dean of Exeter [Roger de Torridge] and Robert Everard appointed the bishop's commissaries in the matter of Walter son of Peter;[71] definitive sentence is reserved to the bishop. Exeter, 5 October 1270.

830 Collation of Mark de St Madron to the vicarage of Gorran (*ecc. S. Goroni*); to the vicarage was assigned all the altarage and all the lesser tithes, that is, of fish, apples and garden beans and peas, but not the corn or hay tithes. Exeter, 5 October 1270.

831 Collation of John de Paignton, priest, to the vicarage of Bishopsteignton. St Allen, 13 December 1270.

832 The bishop held an ordination in his chapel at Penryn; inst. of Master Adam Haym, subdeacon, to South Hill (*Suthhulle*); patron, Reginald de Ferrars. Penryn, 20 December 1270.

833 Inst. of William de Esse, subdeacon, presented by Sir Mauger de St Albans, to Martinhoe (*Matingho*), vacant by the resignation of . . . de Pyne, the former rector, who was instituted to Bow (Nymet Tracy); patron, Sir H[enry] de Tracy. Penryn, 20 December 1270.

834 Henry de Valle Torta ordained subdeacon and admitted to the portion in Marytavy (*ecc. S. Marie Tavi*) vacant by the resignation of Master Roger de Okeston from Petertavy (*ecc. Petri Tavy*) [sic]. Penryn, 20 December 1270.

835 Sir Thomas de Hertford, canon of Exeter, resigned his prebends at Crediton and Bosham. Paignton, 9 January 1271.

836 Collation of Sir Thomas de Hertford, canon of Exeter, to the archdeaconry of Totnes with all its rights and appurtenances. Chudleigh, 12 January 1271.

837 Collation of Master William de Ponchardon, priest, to the prebend at Bosham vacant by the resignation of Master Robert Everard. Chudleigh, 12 January 1271.

---

[71] Can this be the treasurer? See **489** and **552**.

838   Collation of Gilbert de Tyting, deacon, to the prebend at Crediton vacant by the resignation of Sir Thomas de Hertford. Chudleigh, 12 January 1271.

839   Collation of Sir Roger de Valle Torta to the prebend [at Bosham] vacant by the resignation of Sir T[homas] de Hertford. Chudleigh, 12 January 1271.

840   Inst. of John le Arcevesk to Sheviock (*Sevyhec*); patron, William de Alneto. Chudleigh, 12 January 1271.

841*   APPROPRIATION OF UPOTTERY (*Uppotri*). The bishop appropriated the church of Upottery (*Upottry*) to the dean and chapter of Exeter in sealed letters patent. 'Let all know that at the petition − or rather the pressing request − of our beloved son, Thomas de Hertford, archdeacon of Totnes and canon of our cathedral of Exeter, who is mindful of the benefices previously accepted by him as a grateful and deserving man should be, with the assent and express desire of our beloved sons Roger de Torridge, dean of Exeter, and the chapter of the same place, we, desiring to aid the salvation of souls, grant and by the tenor of these presents appropriate the church of Upottery (*Upottri*), of which we are the true patron, to the mentioned dean and chapter together with all its appurtenances, except for an adequate vicarage in the same, to be possessed in perpetuity for the support of three chaplains who are to minister at the altar dedicated to Saints John the Baptist, Blaise, and Piran in the nave of the said cathedral of Exeter, which is set aside for this purpose, on behalf of the souls of the venerable fathers William Brewer and Richard Blund, our predecessors as bishops of Exeter, our own, that of the said Sir Thomas and all the faithful departed. [The chaplains] are also to bear the other burdens written below: to wit, each of the aforesaid chaplains is to take by the hand of the stewards of the same cathedral of Exeter 60 shillings, but fourteen boys, for the time being and in future times appointed as choristers, shall be entitled jointly to take 28 shillings a year, proportionately, at the main quarter days, for hailing in perpetuity the glorious Virgin Mother of the Lord in sweet and sonorous voice every day after compline. After the said Sir Thomas [fo.46v] departs this life, the aforesaid dean and chapter are to celebrate his obit by distributing in the choir through their stewards twelve shillings every year, on the day of his obit, according to the ancient custom of the church of Exeter; and they are to find and adequately supply what is necessary − the bread, wine, candles, and all the other things − for the said chaplains, whom we wish hereafter to take part in all the sung hours in the said church, and whom we assign for the prayer to be poured out for us specifically and at all times in their Masses to Him who is Most High in life and in death at the aforesaid altar. The cure of souls of the aforesaid church of Upottery and the ordinary burdens in their entirety are to pertain to the vicar for the time being of the same.' [Bishop's] Clyst, 14 January 1271.

842   Collation of Master Thomas de Buckland to the prebend at Crediton which Master Alan le Gemel had held. [No place,] 17 November ?1270.

843   Collation of Richard de Colyton, priest, to the vicarage of Colyton (*Culiton*); to the vicarage was assigned all the altarage of Colyton and of the chapel of Shute (*Suthe*), and the hay tithe of Woodland (*Wodelond*), and the vicar is to bear all the due and customary burdens and a chaplain at Shute, and is to pay to the dean and chapter of Exeter 100 shillings a year on the quarter days. [No place,] 1269.[72]

844 Inst. of Michael [called] le Arcediakene to a pension of two marks from Offwell church, with a right of accrual by commendation; patron, Sir John de Courtenay by reason of his guardianship of Robert de Offwell and his lands. However, when Alured, now dead, had been vicar, the said Robert had *de facto* presented Osbert Giffard, priest, to the non-vacant church but the bishop had not thought fit to admit him; now he established him as vicar, laying down that Osbert should take the fruits and income of the church, and pay to Michael or his proctors 100 shillings from the property of the said church in equal portions on 30 November and 3 May, on terms that on the departure or decease of the said Michael the whole church should accrue to Osbert, if he had a claim *de iure* – all this in letters patent. [No place,] 1 September ?1270.

845* SETTLEMENT OF THE SUBMISSION MADE CONCERNING THE CONTESTED TITHES OF BOVEY TRACY (*bovi traci*). 'let all know who see or hear the present letters that sir henry de tracy and sir john de wolfrinton, perpetual vicar of the church of bovey tracy, have submitted totally to our judgment, arbitration, award and ordinance the decision of the question or dispute arisen between them over the tithes of the same sir henry's mills and of the meadow of broadmead (*brodemede*), which the said vicar has asserted to belong to his vicarage by the common law[73], while the said sir henry asserts to the contrary, alleging the same to have been assigned of old for the support of a perpetual chaplain to celebrate the mass of the blessed virgin in the same church, and that this chaplain has been established in peaceful possession of the receipt of the same for more than 40 years. we, walter by the grace of god bishop of exeter, after diligently examining, weighing and comprehending the nature of the aforesaid affair, question or dispute, assisted by the advice of learned lawyers, lay down, in our laying down decree, in our decreeing give definitive sentence and definitively give judgment that the vicar for the time being in charge of the said church shall receive in their entirety the said tithes of the aforesaid mills and meadow and hold them in perpetuity, and from that source he shall provide for a chaplain who is to celebrate continually in the said church masses in honour of the blessed virgin mary on behalf of the patrons, parishioners and other benefactors of the said church; [this chaplain is] to be presented hereafter to the archdeacon of the place [totnes] when there is need, on terms that the aforesaid parishioners shall pay the said vicar two marks sterling a year, in equal instalments at easter and michaelmas, for the support of the same chaplain, and if the aforesaid parishioners shall not pay, or refuse to pay, the aforementioned two marks, the vicars are to be released from responsibility for the said chaplain. if the vicar for the time being ministering in the said church should refuse to maintain a chaplain as aforesaid [fo.47] or

---

[72] Simply *Anno domini mcclxix* starts the entry.
[73] *de iure communi*; this seems rather more likely to mean the normal canon law than the Common Law of England.

should omit to present another within a month of the chaplain appointed for this duty being dead or removed, the parishioners are in his stead to present a suitable chaplain for the same duty to the said archdeacon, to be supported from the said tithes of the aforesaid mills and meadow and from the two marks to be paid by the parishioners at the prescribed dates.' bishop's clyst, 17 january 1271.

846[74]   Collation by lapse of Sir William de Esse, chaplain, to Ashwater (*Esse Valteri*), without prejudice to the rights of the patron, Sir Walter de Dunheved, or his heirs or assigns, nor to the rights of any other interested party. Paignton, 25 February 1271.

847   Inst. of Nicholas de Hylion to Powderham (*Poderham*) with a charter (*et habuit cartam in forma communi*); patron, Andrew de Powderham. Chudleigh, 22 February 1271.

848   Collation of Master Richard Paz, through his proctor Sir Roger de Dartford, to Whitestone [or Whitstone] (*Wytestan*), vacant by the resignation of Nicholas de Hylion. Chudleigh, 22 February 1271.

849   Collation of Roger Rufus to Lawhitton, vacant by the resignation through his proctor, R[oger de Dartford], of R[ichard] Paz. Chudleigh, 22 February 1271.

850   The abbot and convent of St Dogmell's (*S. Donmelis*)[75] and Master Thomas Ballard, vicar of Rattery (*Raktrue*), submitted their dispute to the bishop, who laid down that the vicar and his successors should have all the lesser tithes from the manor (*curia*) of the abbot and convent and all the other parishioners, together with the buildings and all the glebe, and forty shillings a year of rent; the beasts of the abbot and convent are not to be pastured on the glebe, nor the vicar's beasts on the abbey's land, but if a straying beast should cause damage they are, without argument, to pay compensation after legal arbitration. The bishop, the abbot and the vicar all appended their seals. Paignton, 26 February 1271.

851   The bishop took seisin at Totnes of the buildings and garden of Walter le Bon and his wife, with their consent, in the presence of a countless multitude; he ordered that a chapel should be built there, dedicated to the Holy Spirit and St Katherine. Totnes, 27 February 1271.

852   The bishop celebrated an ordination after a general citation made through the archdeaconry.[76] Totnes, 28 February 1271.

---

[74] The letters patent for this collation are given in full; cf **179**.
[75] Near Cardigan, in the diocese of St David's.
[76] Or by the archdeacon(s)? the MS merely has *per generalem citationem factam archidiacon'*.

[fo.47v] **853** Collation of Ralph de Butler, clerk, to a prebend of two marks at Probus. [No place,] 21 March 1271.

854 Collation of Master Robert de Totnes to a prebend of six marks at Crediton. [No place,] 27 March 1271.

855 Two proxies were issued for the Roman court. [In the first,] Master Alured son of Milo, the bishop's clerk (*clericum nostrum*), was made the bishop's proctor at the papal court, for requesting, challenging and accepting a judge, with special authority to substitute another proctor in his place for all or each of these, and the bishop would ratify and confirm whatever Master Alured or his substitute should think fit to do. All other proxies were expressly revoked, and the present appointment was to last until it should be revoked. Chidham, 13 April 1271.

856* The contents of the other proxy: To all, etc. 'You are to know that we give and grant free power to Master Alured son of Milo, clerk, the bearer of these presents, and we appoint the same Master our proctor for the purpose of contracting a loan at the Roman court with any merchants whomsoever up to the sum of 100 pounds sterling, to be spent at the same court on the affairs of ourselves and our church; and for the purpose of binding us, our property both moveable and landed, our church, and our successors, to the merchants with whom he shall contract the said loan for the payment of the said 100 pounds at a time and place which he shall assign to the same merchants, provided, however, that the said loan be undertaken with the advice of our venerable fathers the lords [John of Toledo], bishop of Porto and S. Rufine, and O[ttobuono], cardinal deacon of St Adrian, or either of them. We hold as right and approved whatever the said Master [Alured] shall think fit to do in our name in these matters.' Chidham, 13 April 1271.

857* LETTER OF INDEMNITY TO THE PRIOR OF TANDRIDGE FOR MASTER ROGER DE CAMPDEN. The bishop issued a sealed letter of indemnity: 'You are to know that the religious men the prior and convent of Tandridge at our request and petition have bound themselves to release us and our church from a pension of six marks a year to Master Roger de Campden, until the same Master Roger should be provided by the aforesaid prior and convent or someone other on their behalf to [a benefice of] ten marks without cure or twenty marks with cure of souls. We, wishing in full knowledge to prepare for this release for the aforesaid prior and convent in good time, promise in good faith to keep the said religious indemnified as far as the aforesaid obligation towards the aforesaid Master Roger and any others, binding ourselves by the tenor of these presents to the payment from our private purse of the aforesaid six marks a year, year by year during the week before the feast of St John the Baptist, to the same prior and convent until they should be completely freed from the aforesaid bond; and we ordain, for this part, by will or codicil, that if we should chance to die before the full deliverance or release of the aforesaid religious, the principal executors of our will are to make appropriate satisfaction from our estate to the aforesaid prior and convent before any other administration of our will.' London, 15 June 1271.

858* The bishop issued sealed letters patent of renunciation. 'Because we, on behalf of ourselves and the prudent men the dean and our chapter [of Exeter] and of Sir John Wyger, knight, Master Roger called Barat, and W. Gordet, clerk, and of any other party or parties who have or could have an interest, have from this time forward remitted all injury or action for injuries available now or in the future to us jointly or severally by reason of the sentences of excommunication, suspension and interdict promulgated *de facto* against us, as is alleged, by the precentor of Winchcombe on papal authority and by reason of the instigation of the same by Master R. de Campden, as is asserted; and we have renounced the lawsuit raised or to be raised against the same precentor and Master R. de Campden and the abbot and convent of the monastery of Winchcombe on account of the same sentences, [fo.48] and in good faith we record this by the tenor of these presents. We also undertake and promise, as far as in us lies, that no complaint will be raised in future against the aforesaid by anyone on account of the foregoing matters.' London, 14 June 1271.

859* Master Roger de Campden, clerk, issued a letter of renunciation to the bishop. 'In full knowledge, freely, voluntarily, absolutely and completely I resign into the hands of your holiness the canonry and prebend in the cathedral of Exeter, vacant by the death of the late Master Richard de St Gorran, to which I asserted I had been collated by the Holy See by the late Pope Clement, of pious memory, together with all the rights which I had or could have had in the same and their appurtenances, if indeed any right was appropriate or could be appropriate from a collation of this kind; and I renounce, in the form noted above, any letters of collation, confirmation and execution, or others touching on the said collation.' His seal and the abbot of Winchcombe's were attached. London, 15 June 1271.

860 Inst. of Stephen de Hardington, subdeacon, to Clayhanger (*Cleyangre*), vacant by the resignation of Geoffrey de Folam; patron, the Master of the New Temple, London. London, 15 June 1271.

861 Commendation of Peter Haym, clerk, to St Mabyn; patron, Sir Stephen Haym. [No place,] 9 August 1271.

862[77] Collation by lapse of Odo de Arundel to Buckland (*Bockelond*).[78] [No place,] 9 August 1271.

863 Collation of H[ugh] de Plympton, clerk, to the the prebend at St Buryan which Peter Haym had held. [No place,] 9 August 1271.

---

[77] This entry was inserted later.
[78] There were eight parochial Bucklands. Hingeston-Randolph identifies this as Buckland Monachorum; N. Orme suggests that the poverty of East (as also West) Buckland could explain why the patron was unable to fill the cure, so letting the patronage lapse to the bishop.

864 Collation of Master John de Winchester to a prebend of six marks at Crediton, vacant by the resignation of Master W[illiam] de Ponchardon. Bishop's Clyst, 8 September 1271.

865 In Crediton chapel the bishop ordained as subdeacon Master Peter Cornish – without title (*ad gratiam suam*) – and also Jordan de Prydias and Hamund de London; the aforesaid Odo [sic] de Prydias was admitted to Cardinham (*Cardinan*); patron, Sir Oliver de Dynham. Crediton, 19 September 1271.

866 Inst. of Hamund de London, subdeacon, to Newton St Petrock (*Nyweton Ilg'*); patrons, the prior and convent of Bodmin. Crediton, 19 September 1271.

867 Assessment of the vicarages of Gorran and St Enoder. To the vicarage of Gorran was assigned an acre, English measure, for building a house, and all the altarage, except for the tithes due from any boats over the number of twelve, for two thirds of the hay tithes, and for the rector's seine-nets and the field peas and beans; the vicar is to bear all the burdens. To the vicarage of St Enoder (*ecc. S. Enodri*) was assigned the house which Walter the reeve used to live in, thirteen acres, English measure, of the glebe and all the altarage except for the field beans and peas; the vicar is to bear all the burdens. [No place,] 22 September 1271.

868* The bishop granted the custody of Totnes hospital to Richard de Lyme, chaplain and priest. 'Because we have decided, God willing, to found a certain hospital in honour of the Holy Spirit on the ground which we recently acquired in Totnes next to the river by the charitable gift of our beloved Walter le Bon and his wife Agatha, to be applied to spiritual purposes, we commit to you the custody of the same land and the building to be erected there, ordering you to take special care of this and related matters, in the expectation that God will repay you as you deserve.' [No place,] 22 September 1271.

[fo.48v] **869** Before dinner on All Saints Day, on the way to table, while the bishop was standing,[79] Sir William Aguilon, knight, did homage to the bishop for all the land which he held from him by military service on Thorney Island, saving any other claim (*salvo iure cuiuscumque*), in the presence of Sir Alexander de Oxton and Sir Ralph de Arundel, knights, Roger de Dartford, Richard de Braundsworthy, Gilbert de Hemyock,[80] Robert de Candover, Hugh Splot, Richard de Grangiis, clerks, Philip de Cancellis, Alured son of Milo, William de Ponchardon, masters, Henry de Westbrook, Roger le Arcevek, Thomas de Merwe, Richard de Hydon, laymen, and many others. Chidham, 1 November 1271.

870 In the chapel of St Peter, Chichester, William Chauntemerle did homage to the bishop for a virgate of land which he held from him by military service on

[79] *ante prandium, in ingressu ad mensam, domino episcopo stante.*
[80] Titing is the only Gilbert regularly found with the bishop, but the MS reads something like *Hiyuuk*.

Thorney (*Torneye*) Island, in the presence of the above-named. And William swore fealty for the aforesaid virgate, and for another virgate on Thorney Island which he claimed to hold from the bishop in socage. Chichester, 6 November 1271.

871 The bishop received the fealty of the men (*de hominibus*) of Adam de Clochale, at his personal order, when he assigned them and their service to the bishop, in the presence of those named as hearing Sir William de Aguilon's homage. Thorney Island, 7 November 1271.

872 Adam de Clochale and Christiana, his wife, sold to the bishop the land which Adam held of him on Thorney (*Thornay'*) Island, without any reservation, and seised him of the same. Sir William Aguilon was holding the said land from Adam for a term of ten years, of which seven were still to run; these seven years he remitted and quitclaimed to the bishop in return for 35 marks, cash down. The bishop, however, granted that Sir William could freely and lawfully gather, and at harvest time dispose of as he wished, the next autumn's fruits from those acres which he had sown before the drawing up of the present letters. Thorney Island, 7 November 1271.

873 Collation of Payne de Liskeard, clerk, to a prebend at Glasney, vacant by the resignation the same day of Master John de Sackville. London, 9 December 1271.

874 Collation of Master J[ohn] de Sackville to a prebend of six marks at Crediton, vacant by the spontaneous resignation of Master William de Ponchardon. London, 9 December 1271.

875 Collation of Michael de Northampton, clerk, to a prebend at Crantock (*ecc. S. Canrantoni*), vacant by the spontaneous resignation of Odo de Arundel; and Michael resigned a prebend of less value at Crantock to which the bishop collated Ralph le Butler, clerk, who resigned his prebend at Probus. London, 9 December 1271.

876 Collation of Sir Clement [de Langford], rector of Instow (*Innestowe*), to a prebend at Exeter, vacant by the spontaneous resignation of Master William de la Cornere. Horsley, 4 December 1271.

877 Collation of Richard de St Gorran, clerk, to a prebend at Probus, vacant by the spontaneous resignation of Ralph le Butler. Chidham, 13 January 1272.

878 Collation of Master Richard de Bremhill, treasurer of Crediton, who resigned his prebend and the treasurership, to a prebend in the same college, vacant by the resignation of Sir Clement, rector of Instow. Crediton, 11 February 1272.

[fo.49] **879** Admission of Brother Theobald de . . ., monk of St Martin des Champs, Paris, as prior of St James', Exeter (*ad prioratum S. Jacobi extra portam australem Exon'*). Crediton, 11 February 1272.

880 Collation of Sir Thomas de Molland to the treasurership of Crediton, and he resigned his prebend at Crantock, in the presence of Masters William de Capella, William de Ponchardon, Richard Bremhill, Roger de Dartford, Peter de Guildford, chaplain, Hugh de Plympton, Richard de Grangiis, and others. Crediton, 12 February 1272.

881 Collation of Sir Stephen Haym to the prebend at Crantock which Sir Thomas de Molland had held, and he resigned the prebend he already had at that church. Reading, 7 April 1272.

882 Inst. of Sir . . . de Montacute, priest, to the vicarage of Ermington (*Herminton*); patrons, the prior and convent of Montacute. Great Milton, 15 April 1272.

883 Collation of Master Roger Barat to the prebend at Exeter which Master O[liver] de Tracy had held, who resigned his prebend at Crediton to which the bishop collated Sir Peter de Guildford, his chaplain. [No place,] 23 April 1272.

884 Inst. of Sir Thomas de Treverbin to Poundstock (*Pondestok'*), saving any other claim; patron, Sir Roger de Bodrigan. London, 13 May 1272.

885 Collation (*ad suam collationem spectantem*) of Master Nicholas de Honiton – who resigned Buckerell (*Bokerell'*) – to Payhembury (*Pahembery*), vacant by the spontaneous resignation of Sir Thomas de Wymondham, the former rector. And the bishop handed over to him all the documents and deeds concerning the litigation between Sir Thomas and the abbot and convent of Ford which had been raised before the *curia regis*. Fluxton, 5 June 1272.

886 Inst. of Master Peter de Crediton to East Ogwell (*Estwokewell*); patron, Robert de Malston. Fluxton, 5 June 1272.

887 Collation of John Pycot to Buckerell, vacant by the spontaneous resignation of Master Nicholas de Honiton, and he resigned St John's [by Antony] to which he had been admitted at the presentation of William de Alneto when still an esquire (*dum erat scutifer*). Chudleigh, 16 June 1272.

888 Inst. of Sir Henry de Montfort to Ilfracombe (*Hilfrincomb'*); patron, Sir Henry de Champernowne. Bishopsteignton, 17 June 1272.

889 The bishop blessed Simon, abbot of Buckfast (*Bufest'*). Paignton, 24 June 1272.

890 The bishop put his seal to a letter sent to the lord J[ohn of Toledo], cardinal [bishop] of Porto, on behalf of the prelates of England.[81] [No place,] 2 July 1272.

---

[81] *consignavit literam transmissam domino I. Portuen' cardinali, ex parte prelatorum Anglie.* This letter seems otherwise unknown.

891 Sir Henry de Tracy despatched a sealed letter containing a settlement (*forma pacis*) concerning the presentation made to Tawstock (*Taustok'*) church and the custody of the priory of St Mary Magdalene, Barnstaple; the letter remained with the bishop. Bishop's Nympton, 15 July 1272.

892 Sir Henry de Tracy, appearing before the bishop, confessed that he was excommunicated and sought absolution; and he was absolved, with many of his household, as appears more fully in the roll delivered to Sir Peter de Guildford. Tawstock, 16 July 1272.

893 In Barnstaple Priory the monks sought absolution from the bishop and, after swearing to obey the Church's commands and the bishop's ordinance, they were absolved, and Walter, vicar of St Peter's, Barnstaple, and rural dean, was appointed their custodian. Barnstaple, 16 July 1272.

[fo.49v] **894** The bishop reconsecrated Hartland parish church which had fallen under interdict on account of the shedding of the blood of the abbot [of Hartland] and his canons in the said church, and he reconciled Sir O[liver] de Dynham and the abbot, and had many of [Sir Oliver's] household absolved in legal form. Hartland, 23 July 1272.

895 The bishop wrote to the archdeacon of Barnstaple or his official concerning the will of the late Oliver de Tracy.[82] The archdeacon of Surrey had informed him that Master Oliver de Tracy owed him, the archdeacon, 206 marks; the executors were therefore to satisfy the archdeacon or his proctor however seemed best to them, or to collect all his monies and leave them in safe-keeping until they should receive further instructions from the bishop. Mean-while, nothing was to be distributed from his estate unless the executors should wish to satisfy the creditors and legatees; the archdeacon of Barnstaple was to report on the matter before 15 August. Lawhitton, 25 July 1272.

896 Inst. of . . ., chaplain, to Bradstone; patron, Robert de Cruwys. [No place,] 29 July 1272.

897 Collation (*ad suam collationem spectantem*) of Master Hamund [Parleben] to Colan (*ecc. de S. Choulano*), vacant by the spontaneous resignation of John Julius. Pawton, 6 August 1272.

898 Collation (*ad suam collationem spectantem*) of John Julius, chaplain, to St Breward (*ecc. de S. Bruereto*), vacant by the voluntary resignation of Thomas de Treverbin. Pawton, 7 August 1272.

899 Inst. of Nicholas Blundell, chaplain, to Clannaborough (*Chouenebur'*); patrons, the prior and convent of Taunton. Cargoll, 9 August 1272.

900 Dispensation was granted to two chaplains, John de Pillaton and Reginald de Morthoe, for having been ordained to all sacred orders by foreign

---

[82] Himself a former archdeacon of Surrey – **349**.

(*transmontanis*) bishops, as had appeared from inquiry made of John and through the testimonials of the cardinal bishop of Albano;[83] he had letters that he could celebrate *nos autem spiritus et requiem*,[84] but that he should not be admitted to the cure of souls without special episcopal licence. Penryn, 15 August 1272.

901 Richard Kalynnal appeared and confessed himself excommunicated for sharing in the crime of Simon de Gorney, prior of Barnstaple, who had been excommunicated by the bishop, as was his desert; Richard sought absolution and, the following day, in the morning (*mane*), received the benefit of absolution in legal form. [No place,] 20–21 August 1272.

902 Richard Blund, clerk, proctor for Sir Robert Burnell, who had been presented to Tawstock by Richard Kalynnal when still excommunicate, appealed for his principal's rights. [No place,] 21 August 1272.

903 Induction of William, chaplain, then vicar of Dawlish, to Atherington (*Hadrinton*), without cure of souls or òath of obedience (*cui non erat commissa cura nec iuravit obedientiam*). Pawton, 22 August 1272.

904 Inst. of Roger de Leicester to Silverton (*Silferton*); patron, Sir Thomas Corbet. Pawton, 22 August 1272.

905 Induction of . . . de Lew, chaplain, to the vicarage of North Lew (*Lyw*), without cure of souls or oath of obedience; patron, Master Richard de Bolevile, the rector. Pawton, 22 August 1272.

906 Induction of Roger de Cargoll, chaplain, to the vicarage of St Enoder. Pawton, 19 August 1272.

907 Henry de Christow in letters patent resigned his prebend at Crediton. Lawhitton, 29 August 1272.

908 Collation of Sir Henry de Christow to the portion at St Teath (*S. Hetha*) vacant by the spontaneous resignation of Peter de Guildford, the bishop's chaplain. Lawhitton, 29 August 1272.

909 Master William de Capella received a letter of institution concerning the precentorship of Crediton,[85] and a letter of commendation in special form to St Allen; they had been sealed at Horsley on 25 June. Newenham, 30 August 1272.

---

[83] *Albi cardinalis*: Rudolf de Chevrières? or Berard?
[84] Mr Michael Kennedy of the University of Glasgow suggests to me that these could be incipits; *nos autem* is the introit on Maundy Thursday and at feasts of the Holy Cross, *Spiritus* [*Domini*] at Pentecost, and *requiem* at masses of the dead. However, there also appears to be a *salvis* before *nos autem*.
[85] **702** of 4 November 1268 records his collation, with letters of installation and induction.

[fo.50] **910** The bishop gave permission to Sir Henry de Champernowne for his wife lawfully to remain in Polsloe Priory.[86] [No place,] 31 August 1272.

911 Collation of Master H. de Sackville to the prebend at Crediton which Henry de Christow had held. [Bishop's] Clyst, 31 August 1272.

912 Inst. of Adam de Clyst St Mary, chaplain, to the vicarage of Harpford (*Herpeford*); then patron (*tunc*), the prior of Otterton. Bryanston, 5 September 1272.

913 The bishop held an ordination; John called Forbur, clerk, was ordained subdeacon and inducted to Lydford with cure of souls, after taking the oath of obedience and fidelity; patron, Sir Edmund [the new earl of Cornwall]. Waverley, 24 September 1272.

914 Induction of Robert de Bickleigh, ordained subdeacon, to Jacobstow (*ecc. S. Iacobi de Penalym*); patron, Sir Henry de Champernowne, knight. Waverley, 24 September, 1272.

915 Master Robert de Penhard ordained subdeacon, without title (*ad gratiam*). Waverley, 24 September 1272.

916 The bishop issued sealed letters patent. Sir Stephen Haym was canonically presented to Georgeham (*Hamme*), patron, Sir Mauger de St Aubyn, but for various reasons the bishop deferred admitting him, while wishing by virtue of his office to make ampler provision for him; yet, in view of what Stephen's merits demanded, he was given custody of the said church at the bishop's pleasure. Horsley, 29 September 1272.

917 Inst. of John Haym to the prebend at St Buryan vacant by the death of Master Robert de Aveton, at the presentation of Sir Stephen Haym; and he had letters of induction addressed to Sir Stephen's chaplain, Robert Chancellor, saving the rights of the archdeacon. Horsley, 29 September 1272.

918 Inst. of Master Robert de Penhard to St John's by Antony (*ecc. S. Iohannis de Antone*), vacant by the resignation of John de Exeter;[87] patron, Sir William de Alneto. Horsley, 1 October 1272.

919 The bishop in letters patent gave the custody of his houses at Salisbury to Master Philip de Exeter for a year, unless he should meanwhile make some other arrangement for them. Philip had letters close for obtaining enfeoffment of the houses from Master Robert de la Strode, canon of Salisbury. Horsley, 6 October 1272.

---

[86] *concessit domino Henrico de Campo Hernulfi quod uxor eiusdem Henrici potuit licite perhendinare in prioratu de Polslo.*
[87] In **887** John is called Pycot; under this name he became dean of Exeter in 1281.

920 Collation of Peter Haym to the prebend at Glasney vacant by the death of his brother, Durandus Haym. London, 14 October 1272.

921 Collation of Ralph le Butler to the prebend at Crediton vacant by the death of Master John de Winchester. London, 16 October 1272.

922 Collation of Richard de Candover to the prebend at Crediton vacant by the resignation of Master Henry de Sackville. London, 16 October 1272.

923 Collation of John de St Aubyn to the prebend at Crantock vacant by the resignation of Ralph le Butler. London, 17 October 1272.

[fo.50v] **924*** The bishop wrote to the bishop of Winchester, N[icholas of Ely]: 'On the advice of our brothers, our fellow-bishops of the province of Canterbury, we entrust to your fatherhood the bringing an end, in both temporal and spiritual aspects, to the matter of dispute between the noble lord Edmund, son of the late illustrious king of Germany, on the one part, and us and our household on the other, concerning the throwing down of our park at Cargoll and the violence inflicted on our clerks in the same place. We shall ratify whatever you see fit to lay down in the foregoing.' London, 17 October 1272.

925* OBIT OF THE CANONS OF GLASNEY. The bishop issued sealed letters patent. 'Although [all] the husbandmen labouring in the vineyard of the Lord are in truth worthy of reward, yet we believe that those whose more fruitful labour and longer hire have caused them to excel others take prior place in the degree of recompense. Since, therefore, our beloved sons, Masters Henry de Bollegh, the provost, Stephen Haym, Roger de St Constantine, Nicholas de Tregoreth, Roland de Podiford, Richard Vivian, William de St Just, Robert son of Robert, Walter Peverel, Walter Fermesham, Durandus Haym, Payne de Liskerret, and Walter de Tremur, first canons of the church of St Thomas the Martyr at Glasney and participators in the original foundation of the same place, constructed buildings, dwelling houses, orchards and greens on the rough site assigned to the individual prebends and canons on a scale lavish in relation to their means, we wish to reward their temporal industry and the fruitfulness of their labour with spiritual recompense. Therefore, by the tenor of these presents, ordaining we decree and decreeing we ordain, with the lawful assent of our dean and chapter of Exeter, that each of the successors of the aforesaid canons in future times to come, being inhabitants of such buildings, dwelling houses and greens, shall pay eight shillings a year on the anniversary of the death of each of the canons expressly listed by name above annually in the chapter of the aforementioned place for the obit to be celebrated in perpetuity; we wish each canon to receive annually two pence, each vicar in priest's orders a penny, the other vicars in lower orders and the clerks present at the obit Mass one halfpenny each, on condition that whatever shall remain from the aforesaid monetary sum of eight shillings is to be distributed in bread, to be shared out for the use of the poor as seems good to the provost or the steward of the same place, on behalf of the soul of the deceased canon whose obit is celebrated on that day.' Horsley, 22 October 1272.

926[88]*   The bishop issued sealed letters patent. 'Having been numbered – not by our own meritorious action but by the disposing clemency of the eternal King – among the successors of the apostles, we are advised and led to follow in their footsteps to the extent of our inspiration and to make good, as far as we are able, the divisions and the rights – which have too long been weakened – of the church which He planted with His blood, considering it the duty of our office that divine worship be increased in our days and that the people serving God be enlarged in merit and number. Indeed, the church of Crediton, formerly most celebrated in its rank, marked out by pontifical dignity[89], and adorned from olden times by the famous relics of diverse saints and by miracles, and also splendidly endowed with papal indulgences and other benefactions of the holy fathers, but now by the passage of succeeding time having lost its dowry, been reduced in divine worship, and robbed of its former dignity, giving forth the sigh of the dove instead of the song, bewails its banished glory in tearful lamentation as it awaits the remedy of support. Therefore, moved by piety to take pity on its lamentations and sighings, and desiring to soften its wrinkles [fo.51v[90]] with the healing ointment of salvation by mercifully impregnating its barren womb with the due number of sons, we have already decreed the addition of – and decreeing we have added in accordance with the status of ancient times – six canonries and prebends to the twelve formerly existing in the same place, and we have appropriated to the same church of Crediton, according to the canons, the church of Egloshayle (*Eglosheyl*), of which the advowson is recognized as belonging to the bishop's table, laying down that every year each of the six canons whom we have created anew should receive six marks each year, and each of their vicars twenty shillings, to be granted to them along with the other twelve vicars, on account of the prebend or vicarage.

Because the revenues and income from the aforesaid church of Egloshayle are inadequate for the burdens of the said six prebends, we recall the same church to its former status, and so that the increased number of canons may receive their portions from an adequate and assured income, in place of the said church of Egloshayle, for the salvation of our soul and for the souls of our ancestors, by the attestation of the present charter we join by perpetual appropriation the church of Lelant (*Lannant*) to the aforementioned church of Crediton and the canons of the same place, and by annexing it with canonical joinder we irrevocably appropriate it to their own use to be possessed completely in perpetuity, with the lawful consent of our beloved sons the dean and chapter of Exeter. We have canonically acquired the advowson of Lelant, with its appendages, to wit an annual pension of 30 shillings, by the gift and grant of our beloved sons, the prior and convent of Tywardreath, which [now] belongs to our collation with all that relates to it, exempt and quit of the payment of the aforesaid pension; an adequate vicarage was assigned, consisting in accordance with our ordinance of all the altarage, except, that is to say, the tithes of fish, of lambs, and of wool, and it is to be conferred according to the canons by us and our successors on suitable persons who shall bear in perpetuity all the ordinary,

[88] Cf **352** and **744**.
[89] Bishop Leofric moved the see from Crediton to Exeter in 1050.
[90] The continuation of the entry on fo.51 was spoiled and cancelled, with a note made that the continuation was on the lower half of the verso.

due and customary burdens. Furthermore, one [fo.52] acre of land, English measure, in the vill of Penbeagle (*Penbegel*), which is commonly known as *Tremarruc*, which we recently acquired by the gift and grant of the said prior and convent, as we have said before, together with the aforementioned advowson, and we reserve that and the right of patronage for us and our successors in token of our title, protection, warranty and defence.

In addition we also decree and in decreeing ordain that the portions of the aforesaid six prebendal canons and of the vicars of the same are to be distributed annually to the aforesaid canons and vicars on the principal quarter-days by the hand of the precentor of Crediton for the time being, as long as he is in personal residence, and otherwise by the hand of some resident canon appointed for this purpose by the community of brothers with the acquiescence of us and our successors; but the remainder of the income of the said church of Lelant we assign in perpetuity to be spent in future times on daily distributions for the resident canons. If any person, ecclesiastical or lay, should presume with rash daring to breach this deed of our appropriation or grant, or to disturb or diminish the rights of the aforementioned church of Crediton, if he does not repent after a second or third warning, let him know that he has incurred the curse of Almighty God, of the glorious Virgin Mary, of all the saints, and our own, and he is to be forbidden the most holy Body and Blood of the Lord; but on all observing the rights of the same place let there be the peace of our Lord Jesus Christ so that in this life they may receive the fruit of their good actions and before the inescapable judge they may find the rewards of eternal peace.' Horsley, in October 1272.

[fo.51[91]] **927** A copy of the letter about Crediton was issued, but without the clause concerning the consent of the dean and chapter. Horsley, in October 1272.

928 Collation of the rector of East Horsley to the prebend at Probus vacant by the spontaneous resignation of Master Hamund Parleben. Horsley, 23 October 1272.

929*[92] 'Let it be recorded that William de Hasebexsh, who had been presented to the church of Tawstock, appeared before the lord bishop of Exeter, humbly seeking the benefit of absolution from the sentence of excommunication imposed on him which he was alleged to have incurred in that Nicholas de N., priest, his proctor, at his order and command, had intruded in the name of Sir William in the aforementioned church, without having requested the diocesan's consent, and taken over and partially consumed the property of Master O[liver] de Tracy which he found in the aforesaid church and its glebe, and in that he attempted other outrages against the lord bishop and the archdeacon of Barnstaple. After he had taken a corporal oath, touching the holy sacrament, to make satisfaction to the said lord bishop at his

[91] See previous note.
[92] Cf 891–92 and 1089; see also *Select Canterbury Cases*, Selden Society vol. 95 (1978–9), pp.232ff. J.A. Brundage points out that the burden of proving his absolution rested upon the excommunicate; hence the value of this sort of memorandum.

pleasure, or at the decision of good men to whom the same bishop should delegate his pleasure, in the doorway of the lord bishop's chapel he obtained the benefit of absolution from him.' Witnesses: Sir A[lan de Nymet], archdeacon of Barnstaple, J[ohn] Wyger, knight, H[enry de Bollegh], provost of Glasney, R[oger] de Dartford, canon of Exeter, Master W[illiam de Capella], precentor of Crediton, Master W[illiam] de Ponchardon, and others. London, 19 September 1272.

930* 'Let it be recorded that William de Oxton, John de Fenton, Alured de Porta,[93] Richard de Carswell and Thomas Donectan, burgesses of Exeter, appeared before the lord bishop, in his chamber, humbly seeking on behalf of themselves and in the name of the community of fellow-burgesses that the anger which he had conceived against the aforesaid citizens for the diverse crimes and robberies committed against himself, the dean and all his canons of Exeter at various times should be abated, and that he should deign to recall the canons whom he had ordered to absent themselves from the cathedral of Exeter. Accordingly, after they had sworn that in future they would not commit such acts nor, having been condemned, permit them to be committed in future – and if perchance such were committed, they would pursue such malefactors in accordance with the law of the land and the rigour of justice – and that for the future they would be friends to the lord bishop, the dean and canons of Exeter cathedral, and the other clerks and their households, and also that they would faithfully ensure that the mayor and their fellow-burgesses would take an identical oath in the presence of the dean and canons of Exeter, the same bishop remitted his aforementioned anger and restored them to his grace[94] . . .'

[fo.51v] **931** The bishop, at the request of Sir Henry de Chekehill, knight, issued letters patent, granting that he might have a suitable chaplain, to be supported by him and presented by the canons of Bosham, to celebrate the divine office in his oratory or chapel of *Trusehara* as long as he lived and held that land, saving an indemnity in all things to the mother church. Horsley, 24 October 1272.

932 The bishop gave Simon de Bodmin, chaplain, custody of St Minver (*ecc. S. Menurede*); patrons, the prior and convent of Bodmin. Horsley, 18 November 1272.

933 The bishop gave William de Tragev, deacon, custody of the mediety of St Endellion (*ecc. S. Endeliane*), vacant by the death of Master John de Winchester; patrons of the mediety, the prior and convent of Bodmin. Horsley, 18 November 1272.

934 Inst. of Master Richard de Carswell to Doddiscombsleigh; patron, the lady Joan [de Doddiscombe]. Horsley, 23 November 1272.

---

[93] Later mayor of Exeter.
[94] The bottom of the folio is badly worn and nothing is to be read; the last few words are uncertain.

935 The bishop gave Adam de Bremelle, chaplain, custody of the church of Lydford. Horsley, 27 November 1272.

936 Inst. of Nicholas de Stratford-on-Avon to the vicarage of Halberton (*Alberton*); patrons, the abbot and convent of St Augustine's, Bristol. Horsley, 7 December 1272.[95]

[fo.52] **937** Collation of Master John de Sackville to the prebend at Crantock which Sir Stephen Haym had resigned on the receipt of another. London, 16 December 1272.

938 Inst. of Master Godfrey de Pecham to Woodleigh (*Wodele*); patron, Sir Roger Prawle. Horsley, 26 December 1272.

939 Inst. of John Haym to Morwenstow (*Morwennestohe*); patron, Sir Herbert de Pyn. London, 20 January 1273.

940 Admission of Henry de Beaupré to the prebend at St Buryan, vacant by the spontaneous resignation that day of John Haym; patron, Sir Stephen Haym. London, 20 January 1273.

941 Inst. of John son of Gilbert, chaplain, to the vicarage of [East] Budleigh (*Boddele*); patrons, the prioress and convent of Polsloe. Mitcham? (*Meygham*), 21 January 1273.

942 Collation of Master Richard called Paz to the prebend at Crediton vacant by the spontaneous resignation of Master John de Sackville, and he was inducted on the order of the bishop (*et ad mandatum episcopi in eandem est inductus*). Horsley, 22 January 1273.

[fo.52v] **943** Collation by lapse of Sir Robert Burnel to Tawstock. London, 19 February 1273.

944 The bishop gave John de Furbur custody of Lifton. [No place,] 7 March 1273.

945 Inst. of the chaplain of Sir Alan [de Nymet], archdeacon of Barnstaple, to Hollacombe (*Holacumb'*).[96] Crediton, 10 April 1273.

946 Inst. of Alan de Baucombe to St Mary de Gradibus [Exeter]; patron, Richard son of Richard. Exeter, 22 April 1273.

947 Inst. of Robert, chaplain, to the vicarage of Dawlish; patrons, the dean and chapter of Exeter. [No place,] 23 April 1273.

---

[95] Here follows the second part of **926**.
[96] Hingeston-Randolph's identification.

948   Collation of Master Robert de Totnes to the prebend at Crediton vacant by the death of Thomas Achym. Bishop's Clyst, 27 March 1273.

949   Inst. of William Wancy, clerk, to Broadwoodwidger (*Brawode Vypund*); patron, Sir John Wyger. His letters of induction had the clause 'the bishop reserves the power of increasing or decreasing the portion of the same Elias [sic]'. Cerne Abbas, 25 April 1273.

950   Institution of Peter de S. Antonino as prior of Plympton. Paignton, 2 April 1273.

951   Collation by lapse of Richard de Mabe to the vicarage of St Clement (*Moresc*). London, 2 May 1273.

952   Inst. of William de Malborough, chaplain, to the vicarage of Broad Clyst (*Cliston*); patrons, the prior and convent of Totnes. London, 4 May 1273.

953   Collation of Master Walter de Laking to the prebend at Probus which had been held by Sir Peter, the vicar. Tonge, 8 May 1273.

954*   PROXY. The bishop wrote to the dean of Exeter [Roger de Torridge]: 'So that the benefices which shall fall vacant while we are travelling overseas[97] may not be deprived of pastoral care, we give special power to you, whom we have previously chosen for a variety of reasons to have a share in our cares, to receive presentations to such benefices made by their true patrons, to grant letters of inquiry, and to do whatever else shall be lawful with the advice of the chancellor of Exeter[98] [John de Esse] and of R[oger] de Dartford, canon, our steward, when he shall happen to be present, in the terms which the same Roger will tell you. And we shall henceforward hold ratified what you shall do in the foregoing matters.'[99] Canterbury, 9 May 1273.

[fo.53] **955**   The previous letter was repeated but dated 10 May (*vi Idus Maii*), and itself dated Canterbury, 7 May (*in crastino S. Iohannis ante Portam Latinam*) 1273.

956   Collation of Master William de Ponchardon, chaplain, to the prebend at Exeter vacant by the voluntary resignation of Master Robert Everard. [No place,] 11 May 1273.

957   Collation of Payne [de Exeter], chaplain, to the portion at Gerrans vacant by the death of Master Roland [de Podiford?]. [No place,] 10 August 1273.

---

[97] The bishop was going to Gascony to meet Edward I on his return from Crusade.
[98] John de Esse may have been diocesan chancellor – **971**; of the chancellors of the cathedral, Oliver de Tracy had been dead for a year – **895** – and Richard de Bremele was collated in September 1274 – **997**.
[99] Cf **971**. J.A. Brundage remarks that Durandus' *Speculum iudiciale* 1.3 tit. *de procuratore* §4.1 suggests that such an undertaking to ratify might not be binding.

958 In letters patent the bishop appointed Master William de Capella, precentor of Crediton, as his proctor, with power to appoint or substitute one or more other proctors as seemed most beneficial for the bishop and his church, and with power to cancel and replace such proctors, in all actions raised or defended by the bishop of whatever kind and before whatever judge, ordinary or delegate, anywhere in the province of Canterbury. The bishop would ratify whatever was done under this proxy. He also gave William, or any substitute, power to raise, defend, counter-petition, enter exceptions and replications, supplicate, appeal, pursue an appeal, swear on the bishop's behalf, seek restoration to original status, and do all the other things that the bishop might have done, had he been present, saving what was restricted to his order,[100] but he witheld the power to come to a settlement or compromise without his being consulted; he also ratified the furnishing of security by anyone acting as his advocate before whatsoever judge. Bayonne, 18 October 1273.

959 Collation of John de Hanok, clerk, to Stockleigh Pomeroy. [No place,] 23 September 1273.

960[101] In letters patent the bishop admitted Master Gervase de Crediton by title of commendation to West Down (*Westdon'*), patron, Ralph Beaupel, together with the church of Calstock (*Kalestok'*). Paris, 24 September 1273.

[fo.53v] **961** Collation of Master William de Capella, precentor of Crediton, to the prebend at Bosham which Master William de Ponchardon had held. Bayonne, 11 October 1273.

962 Collation of Sir John de Pyleton, chaplain, to the vicarage of Coldridge, which was to be assessed. Bayonne, 12 October 1273.

963 Master William de Capella received a letter from the bishop of Winchester acknowledging a debt of 100 pounds to the bishop of Exeter, and a letter of credit from the citizens and merchants of Florence based in Paris for 40 shillings, at need. Bayonne, 21 October 1273.

964 The bishop wrote to the partners Nicholas Bonivicini and James Bonacursi, citizens and merchants of Florence based in Paris, appointing Peter de Montagu his proctor for borrowing from them 115 marks sterling. Bayonne, 12 November 1273.

965 The bishop wrote to Nicholas Bonivicini and James Bonacursi in similar terms, appointing Robert de la Hallelond, clerk, his proctor for borrowing from them 50 pounds sterling. Bayonne 12 November 1273.

---

[100] *agendum, defendendum, reconveniendum, excipiendum, replicandum, supplicandum, appellandum, appellationem prosequendum, in animam nostram iurandum, in integrum restitutionem petendum, et omnia alia faciendum que, si presentes essemus, salva ordinis seu conditionis nostre disciplina, facere possemus seu debemus* . . .; cf **976**.
[101] The letter was given in full.

966* LETTER TO THE CURIA. The bishop wrote to Pope G[regory X]. 'There came into my presence Walter and Alan de Lostwithiel, clerks of the diocese of Exeter, bearing letters from you concerning their defect of birth and their receiving the orders of subdeacon and deacon from an Italian bishop without my letters dimissory and contrary to the decree of C[lement IV] of happy memory, your predecessor, in which you gave me a command that I should with your authority mercifully dispense these clerks concerning the aforesaid defect of birth and receipt of orders, attaching the limit and conditions which are more fully contained in your aforesaid letter. I, however, while wishing diligently to give effect to your command, have found them to be begotten of a deacon and different unmarried women, and to be insufficiently lettered, and incapable of proving that their orders were conferred on them according to proper usage. Furthermore, it stirs and stings my conscience that scarcely any men in these days receive orders so that they may devoutly serve God in the same, but rather that they may prolong in this world their unhappy lives with evil living, whence they become a source of scandal for the people; again, in addition to those things, they shrink from entry into religion, and there are also other circumstances which have been fretting my conscience as to their future example.Wherefore, dreading to burden my protesting conscience by dispensing the aforesaid [clerks] while they remain in their worldly life, lest conscience should later accuse me and the truth of reason provide no excuse, I have thought fit to send back these clerks to the apostolic see, so that where grace and the plenitude of power abound their defects may be made good.' Bayonne, 7 December 1273.

[fo.54] **967** Collation of John Ferre to the prebend at Crediton vacant by the death of William Poynz. [No place,] 9 December 1273.

968 Appointment of Master Richard de Carswell, clerk, as the bishop's proctor at the papal court for requesting, challenging and accepting a judge, giving him power to substitute another proctor in his stead for all the above, and the bishop ratified whatever would thus be done. All other proxies at the papal court were expressly revoked; the present one was to be valid until 1 May. Bordeaux, 27 December 1273.

969 Appointment of Master Richard de Carswell, clerk, as the bishop's proctor at the papal court for claiming and receiving from the executors of Master Alured son of Milo, formerly the bishop's proctor, any debts, obligations, contracts with merchants, also letters of payment and receipt and other liabilities of the deceased to the bishop. The bishop ratified what Master Richard should think fit to do whether by way of action or of settlement. Bordeaux, 27 December 1273.

970 Appointment of a proctor [Master Richard again?] with power to claim and receive from Philip Rodulphi and his partners, citizens and merchants of Florence, up to the sum of twenty marks from the money which had been paid to them by Master Alured son of Milo, formerly the bishop's proctor at the papal court. Paris, 20 February 1274.

971* The bishop wrote to John de Esse, his official and chancellor of Exeter. 'We recall that when we went away we gave a special power to our dean of Exeter [Roger de Torridge] to grant in our absence letters of inquiry to those lawfully presented to ecclesiastical benefice, and in our stead to entrust to the same suitable persons custody [of their benefices][102]. However, because we are unable, on account of the orders of our superiors over our wishes, to return as we were hoping to our own concerns, meanwhile, on account of the risk to souls and so that the church should not lack her due service, by the tenor of these presents we give you special power to institute the aforesaid men who have been admitted to the custody [of their benefices] if you should find them suitable – the rule of law and the Council [of 1268][103] of the previous legate [Ottobuono] being everywhere observed – and we order that this same should be done in each and every case, provided only that there is no canonical obstacle in the foregoing to their presentations or to themselves.' Vitry, 6 March 1274.

972 Collation of Master Robert de la More to the prebend at Glasney vacant by the death of Master Richard Vivian. Vitry, 5 March 1274.

[fo.54v] 973 Appointment of Master Richard de Carswell and Master Philip de Exeter, clerks, jointly or severally, as the bishop's proctors to receive on the bishop's behalf and for his business at the papal court 30 marks sterling – reckoned at 13s. 4d. a mark – from Johannis Gerardini and Philip Spina of Pistoia, merchants and partners of Jacobus, Bartholomew and Baudouin, the sons of the lord Amanati, and of Jacobus lord of Agolens, and of Laus, lord of Anio, their fellow citizens; the bishop promised to ratify whatever these proctors should see fit to do. He also promised to repay the money to Jacobus of Agolens and Laus, or one of them, in London before Pentecost [20 May], binding himself and his successors and all their property, and renouncing any defence of fraud, present action, invalid forum or being on crusade, and any privilege allegedly granted to the prelates and clergy of England that they should not be justiciable overseas.[104] Vitry, 18 March 1274.

974 In letters patent the bishop admitted Sir A[maury] de Montfort, papal chaplain, by title of commendation to Helston, of which he had previously had custody through his proctor, after having been presented in his absence by the patron, Richard of blessed memory, king of the Romans and earl of Cornwall.[105] Vitry, 5 April 1274.

975 The bishop acknowledged a debt of 790 marks – reckoned at 13s. 4d. a mark – received from Renaldus Guelf, Galterus Scoldi, Franco Plebanelli, and Jacobus Renero, partners and citizens and merchants of Florence, paid on behalf of themselves and of Ubertus Renaldi, Jacobus Rembertini, Nicholas

---

[102] Cf **954**.
[103] c.30; see *Councils and Synods* II 2, 777–9.
[104] Cf Lateran IV, c.37.
[105] The letter is given in full, presumably because of the high status of the parties involved. (A piquancy is added in that Guy de Montfort had murdered Richard's son, Henry of Almain, at Viterbo in 1271.)

Bonevicino and Jacobus Bonacursi and all their other partners. The said merchants and their partners had received this sum from the bishop and his proctors in London between 2 February 1273 and 12 March 1274 and were bound to repay it. The bishop released them from this debt, renouncing the defence of the money not having been counted out and paid; he promised, on behalf of himself, his successors and his see, to make no further claim, and desired that any instruments which might turn up concerning this debt should be void. He promised all this on penalty of forfeiting double the sum, renouncing the defences of things done, privilege of clergy, of Crusade, of the canon on two diets of the Council,[106] and all other defences. Paris, 7 April 1274.

[fo.55] **976*** PROXY AT THE PAPAL COURT. In sealed letters patent the bishop issued a proxy. 'In the case which is pending or is expected to be pending at the papal court between us and Thomas de Carvenal, clerk of our diocese, we make, ordain and appoint our beloved sons in Christ, Masters Nicholas [de Honiton], rector of the church of Payhembury (*Hambyri Coffin*), and Philip de Exeter, clerks, our proctors, jointly or severally, on terms that there is to be no better status for the one in occupation, ratifying and confirming whatever shall be done or arranged by them or either of them in our name in the foregoing matters. Furthermore, we give to the same men, jointly or severally, full and free power to raise an action, defend one, lodge a complaint, enter an exception or a replication, swear in our name, put forward *positiones* or reply to them, substitute one or more proctors as shall seem expedient to them, revoke such substitute or substitutes, depute one or more proctors in their place, appeal, pursue an appeal, claim expenses and costs, and do all the other things which true and lawful proctors can and should do; however, the power is withheld from them to compromise or settle without consulting us. And we signify this same to the opposing party and to all whom it concerns.' Lyon, 11 May 1274.

977 Collation of Anthony Bek, the king's chancellor, to the prebend at Bosham vacant by the death of Master Roger de Torridge, dean of Exeter. Lyon, 18 May 1274.

978 Collation of Master John de Pontoise to the prebend at Exeter vacant by the death of Master Roger de Torridge. Lyon, 18 May 1274.

979 Acting on a mandate from the papal penitentiary, the bishop in letters patent announced that he had heard the confession of the prior of Bodmin, had accepted his contrition, and had imposed as penance on him that he should not have any knowing dealings with those under excommunication, and that, on the days on which the shire court was held in the borough of Bodmin and at other formal assemblies of laymen suspected of being excommunicate, the prior was not to permit the daily Mass to be celebrated in the conventual church with singing but to be said in hushed voices, with the gates of the choir closed and known excommunicates excluded. Moreover, the prior was himself to refrain from the solemn celebration of Mass until the said excommunicates had been

---

[106] Lateran IV, c.37.

absolved, but he could celebrate on St Petrock's Day (4 June) and thereafter in the form prescribed above. Lyon, 24 May 1274.

980 Collation, at the prompting of charity, of Master John de Esse, the official, to Egloshayle (*Eglosheil*) by title of commendation, since the bishop believed his discretion and industry could restore the decayed rights and possessions of the church.[107] Vitry [sur Seine], near Paris, 2 April 1274.

[fo.55v] **981** Collation of Hugh de Plympton, deacon, to the prebend at Crediton which Sir Adam [de Ilchester] had held. Lyon, 10 June 1274.

982 Appointment of Edmund de Warfield, clerk, as the bishop's proctor at the papal court with power to request both ordinary and special letters (*tam simplices literas quam legendas*), challenge and accept a judge, and to substitute another proctor in his place. The bishop expressly revoked all other proxies of this sort. Lyon, 16 July 1274.

983* The bishop wrote to the cathedral chapter:[108] 'Wishing – as we are bound – to assent to your petitions, which have been confidently put to us by our beloved sons J[ohn] de Exeter and W[illiam] de Worplesdon, your brothers and fellow-canons, both in your letters and by their authoritative utterance, we grant to you and them free power to elect a dean, insofar as it ought apparently to pertain to you, and saving our rights and those of anyone else over the advowsons of the churches of Braunton, Bishop's Tawton, Landkey (*Landeke*) and Swimbridge (*Swynbrigge*), and reserving our power to provide a dean to the same church of Exeter in case of lapse or any other canonical ground.' La Charité sur Loire, 22 July 1274.

984 Master John de Pontoise granted letters dimissory, valid for a year, to receive holy orders from any Catholic bishop. Paris, 29 July 1274.

985 The bishop wrote to the clergy and people of the archdeaconry of Cornwall, informing them of the collation of Master John de [fo.56] Esse, the official, to the archdeaconry. Horsley, 23 August 1274.

986 Master John de Esse, the official, was ordered to cite all beneficed clergy in the archdeaconries of Exeter, Totnes and Barnstaple who were not in priest's orders to an ordination at Tiverton on 22 September; the same notice was to be given to all abbots and priors. Horsley, 23 August 1274.

987* The bishop wrote to the cathedral chapter:[109] 'Just as, in showing justice to all, the tie of nature makes us careful debtors to the common law, so much the more submissively in the preserving of our rights do we believe that a similar repayment should be made to us by our subjects whereby, in a meritorious exchange, we specifically restore it in the bowels of charity. Indeed, although

---

[107] Cf **926**; the letter is given in full.
[108] Cf **987**.
[109] Cf **983**.

overcome by the prayers and diligent – we shall not say importunate – entreaty of our beloved sons, John of Exeter and William de Somerford,[110] your fellow-canons and proctors, knowing that our rights endure everywhere, we gave you licence in writing to elect a future dean, a saving clause on our rights was inserted into the same document. Being mindful of the power devolved on us by lapse of time of providing a future dean to the aforesaid church, in virtue of the obedience and duty by which you are held to us and the aforementioned church, we inhibit you by the tenor of these presents, under canonical sanction, from proceeding to the election of the said dean *de facto* (since for the aforesaid reason and for others which we forbear to enter here you cannot proceed *de iure*) to the prejudice of our rights, as you shall hope to avoid canonical vengeance.' Horsley, 23 August 1274.

988   Master John de Esse, archdeacon of Cornwall, resigned his prebend at Crantock. Fluxton, 5 September 1274.

989   Collation of John de Esse, archdeacon of Cornwall, to the prebend at Penryn which Master Jordan Aiguel, formerly archdeacon of Cornwall, had held. Fluxton, 5 September 1274.

990*   The bishop wrote a sealed letter to [John de Esse] the archdeacon of Cornwall or his official, Master John de Withiel, and the dean of Powder. 'Borne by common report which seems to amount to notoriety, relating it in sorrow, we have recently learned that Sir Richard de Seaton, knight, steward of the noble lord, the earl of Cornwall, has not shrunk from having our beloved sons Roger, rec[fo.56v]tor of Little Petherick (*Nasfonteyn*), Roger, vicar of St Petrock's, Bodmin, and Andrew Gydion, all priests, unjustly arrested and had them committed to an abominable prison, after falsely weaving a fabric of untrue charges against them, to the peril of his own soul, the prejudice of the Church's privilege, and the scandal of many. Wherefore we command you, etc., that on receipt of these presents, after associating some ecclesiastical persons with you, you should warn the aforementioned steward, and effectually bring him to release the aforementioned clerks thus imprisoned within three days of your warning, and to let them go in peace once released. Otherwise, you are peremptorily to cite him to appear on the next juridical day after Michaelmas, in the cathedral church of Exeter, before us or someone acting in our stead, to make his response concerning the arrest and detention of the said clerks, and to receive what justice will urge. The same steward also, as has struck our ears from the repeated outcry of our subjects, does not fear with rash daring to attack, mutilate, diminish, infringe and overthrow ecclesiastical rights and privileges, to the ruin of the status of Church and clergy: to wit, he drags clerics and ecclesiastical persons unwillingly to court in personal actions before himself in the secular forum, against the decrees of the sacred canons; he extorts from the same fines and monetary penalties on an enormous scale by searching rigour and calculated malice; he gives judgment *de facto* concerning wills and the property of deceased persons, marriages, tithes and the right to tithes, and the receiving of the sacraments and sacramentals; and he disposes at his pleasure of

[110] Presumably the same man as William de Worplesdon.

the same and of other matters which without doubt pertain to ecclesiastical jurisdiction; he also wrongfully arrests other clerks and ecclesiastical persons, imprisons them and extorts a heavy ransom from some of them; he commits sacrileges also and other outrages – which we do not wish to, and must not, pass over uncorrected with conniving eyes – against God and the sanctions of the canons.' Therefore they were commanded, all or any of them, to cite Sir Richard to appear to answer these and other possible charges as well, and to inform the bishop of what they had done in letters patent. [Bishop's] Clyst, 10 September 1274.

991 Inst. of Brother Luke, canon of St Pierre de Fougères, as prior of Ipplepen (*Ypelepenn'*), vacant by the resignation of Brother Thomas; patrons, the abbot and convent of St Pierre, Fougères (*S Petri de Filger'*).[111] Paignton, 14 September 1274.

992 Inst. of Philip de Harraton to Bigbury (*Bykebyr'*); patron, Sir William de Bigbury. Exeter, 12 September 1274.

993 Inst. of Bartholomew, priest, to the vicarage of Broad Clyst (*Clystone*) vacant by the death of William de Malborough; patrons, the prior and convent of Totnes. Exeter, 12 September 1274.

994 Inst. of Hugh Splot [de Plympton], deacon, to Exminster (*Exemenistr'*), vacant by the death of William de Bisimano; patrons, the prior and convent of Plympton. Bishop's Clyst, 9 September 1274.

995 Commendation of Hugh [Splot de Plympton] to Ugborough (*Uggebyr'*), presented by the prior of Plympton. Bishop's Clyst, 9 September 1274.

[fo.57] **996** Collation by lapse of Master John Noble, archdeacon of Exeter, to the deanery of Exeter cathedral, and he was installed by the bishop's official. Exeter, 20 September 1274.

997 Collation of Master Richard de Bremhill, who resigned his prebend at Crediton, to the prebend at Exeter which Sir Walter de Merton had held,[112] and to the chancellorship of Exeter, and he was installed by the dean. Exeter, 20 September 1274.

998 The bishop gave William de Worplesdon, canon of Exeter, custody of the hospital of St John, Exeter, with discretion in the administration of its property. [Bishop's] Clyst, 20 September 1274.

999 Master Thomas de Buckland given charge, until the bishop should otherwise provide, of the archdeaconry [of Exeter], with powers to issue sentence

---

[111] Knowles and Hadcock explain (p.161) that Ipplepen was a cell of St Pierre de Rillé, to which the community of Notre Dame de Fougères moved c. 1143 after adopting the Augustinian rule.
[112] Elected as bishop of Rochester.

of suspension, excommunication and interdict. [Bishop's] Clyst, 20 September 1274.

1000 Letter to the archdeacon of Totnes [Thomas de Hertford] to induct Robert[113] de Elwell, priest, collated by lapse to Ashbury (*Aissebyri*). Crediton, 22 September 1274.

1001 Inst. of Joel de Valle Torta, subdeacon, to North Tawton (*Northtauton*), vacant by the death of Osmund de Valle Torta; patron, John de Valle Torta. Crediton, 23 September 1274.

1002 Inst. of Master Conan de Trumputt to Cheriton Fitzpaine (*Churiton Santon'*), vacant by the death of William son of Richard; patron, Roger fitzPayne. Crediton, 23 September 1274.

1003 Collation of Master Nicholas de Paignton, subdeacon, to Hollacombe (*Holecumb'*).[114] Crediton, 23 September 1274.

1004 Collation of Master Gervase de Crediton to the prebend at Crediton vacant by the resignation of Master Richard de Bremhill, and he was installed. Crediton, 23 September 1274.

1005 Collation of Master Richard Paz to the prebend at Crediton which Master Gervase de Crediton had held, and he was installed by the precentor [William de Capella]. Crediton, 23 September 1274.

[fo.57v] **1006** Collation of Sir Robert Giffard to the prebend at Crediton vacant by the resignation of Hugh Splot [de Plympton]. Crediton, 23 September 1274.

1007 Collation of Sir Nicholas de Raleigh to the prebend at Exeter which Martin de Littlebury had held. Crediton, 23 September 1274.

1008 Inst. of Gilbert de Tyting to Bridestowe (*Briztestowe*); patrons, the prior and convent of Plympton. Crediton, 24 September 1274.

1009 Collation – pertaining to the bishop – of Sir Peter de Guildford, the bishop's chaplain, to Cheriton Bishop, vacant by the resignation of Gilbert de Tyting. Crediton, 24 September 1274.

1010 Collation of Matthew Bacon, priest, to St Michael Penkevil (*Pencavel*), because the patron, Sir John de Treiagu, had been unable to make a valid presentation since he was excommunicate (*inhabilis fuit propter conspirationem*

---

[113] Also called John in this entry.
[114] Hingeston-Randolph identifies this as Holcombe Burnell, but that was annexed to a prebend of Wells, which one would expect to be mentioned; similarly, Holcombe Rogus was in the patronage of the prior and convent of Montacute. Hollacombe therefore seems more likely.

contra episcopum et clerum factam); at the bishop's order, Matthew was inducted by the archdeacon of Cornwall. [Bishop's] Clyst, 25 September 1274.

1011   Collation of Sir Walter called Gascon, chaplain, to the vicarage of Lelant. [Bishop's] Clyst, 25 September 1274.

1012*[115]   The bishop issued a sealed letter to [John Noble] the dean of Exeter, [Ralph de Hengham?[116]] the precentor of Exeter, and [John de Esse] the archdeacon of Cornwall. 'We make you our commissaries, jointly and severally (to all, to two or to one, whoever shall happen to be present), in all matters concerning Sir Richard de Seaton, steward of Cornwall, and any of his accomplices in this affair, for any right of action or objecting to the office of a judge, and lodging complaints of whatsoever kind against the same and prosecuting them in our stead.' [Bishop's] Clyst, 26 September 1274.

1013*   The bishop issued a letter to [John Noble] the dean of Exeter, [Ralph de Hengham] the precentor, and [Richard de Bremhill] the chancellor. 'In the legal and other business touching us and our church of Exeter, on the one part, and Sir Richard de Seaton, knight, steward of the noble earl of Cornwall, and certain others, on the other, we make you our commissaries, jointly and severally (on terms that two of you or one, when the other or others is not expected to be present, may competently proceed in the foregoing), and we ratify and confirm whatever you all – or the one or two of you who happen to be present – should think fit to do.' Fluxton, 27 September 1274.

[fo.58] **1014**   Collation of Master Robert de Trillawe to the prebend at Crediton which Sir Robert Giffard had held. London, 10 October 1274.

1015   Collation of Master W[illiam] de Middleton to the prebend at Bosham which Roger de Valle Torta had held. London, 10 October 1274.

1016   Collation of Master Ralph de Merlawe to the prebend at Probus which Matthew Bacon had held. Horsley, 1 November 1274.

1017   Appointment under seal of Master Richard Paz as the bishop's proctor at need (*ad opus*) at the Court of Arches; the transcript remained etc. Horsley, 1 November 1274.

1018   Dispensation, by papal authority, of Thomas de Withiel, born of a subdeacon and a spinster, from his defect of birth. Horsley, 21 November 1274.

1019   Collation of Master Richard Griffin to the prebend at Crediton which Master Richard Paz had held. Salisbury, 2 December 1274.

---

[115] On this and the following entry, see **990**, and **1024–5**, **1044** & **1058**; J.A. Brundage has pointed out that the bishop is clearly desperate that someone should do something, whatever the risks.
[116] With **1012** & **1013**, see also **1429**. On the identity of the precentor, see O.F. Robinson, 'The wages of virtue' *JLH* 15 (1994), 73–6.

1020   Inst. of Sir John de Leicester, chaplain, to the prebend of Kingsteignton in Salisbury cathedral vacant by the resignation of Master William de la Cornere; patron, the bishop of Salisbury. [Bishop's] Clyst, 10 December 1274.

1021   Obedience of Master Walter Scammel, dean of Salisbury, for the churches in the diocese of Exeter appropriated to the dean and chapter of Salisbury. Salisbury, 9 December 1274.

1022   Inst. of Sir . . ., priest, to Trusham; patrons, the abbot and convent of Buckfast. Chudleigh, [December] 1274.

1023   Inst. of Sir William, rector of St Martin's, Exeter, to the vicarage of Colyton (*Coliton*); patrons, the dean and chapter of Exeter. Chudleigh, 21 December 1274.

1024*   The bishop isued a letter to Master H[enry] de Bollegh, provost of Glasney, and the official of the archdeacon of Cornwall [Master John de Withiel]. 'By the authority of the lord archbishop of Canterbury, deputed as judge delegate by the holy see, we command you, firmly enjoining you by your duty of obedience, that you should have all those who laid sacrilegous hands on Master Jordan [Aiguel], then archdeacon of Cornwall, and other ecclesiastical men in the church and parish of St Allen, and dishonoured them in other ways, and those who gave authority, counsel, aid and reckless companionship in crime for such sacrileges, publicly and solemnly denounced in every parish church in the archdeaconry of Cornwall, on Sundays and feastdays, during the celebration of Mass. The same for all those who arrested, imprisoned and long held captive that prudent man, Master John de Esse, our chancellor and official, while he was carrying out the office entrusted to him, and who maliciously accused him of felony, [fo.58v] and those by whose authority, command or order the foregoing were done. The same for all those who entered into a conspiracy or plot, confirmed by oath or writing, against the church of Exeter, us and our clerks. The same for all those who unlawfully brought wrongs, losses and troubles upon us, our men and our clerks, contrary to the privileges of the Church and the laws and customs of the realm. All these are to appear in person before the doors of the cathedral church of St Peter, Exeter, on 22 December, each in his own degree, to make fitting compensation and satisfaction concerning the foregoing matters to the persons they have injured and oppressed. You are also to give notice to the aforesaid injured and oppressed persons that they are to appear at the said day and place, either in person or through suitable proctors, to receive satisfaction and compensation according to the canons. But in no way do we wish or command this denunciation to be extended to the person of the noble earl of Cornwall. If, however, it is not possible for both of you to take part in carrying out these matters, either one of you may nonetheless put them into effect without waiting for − or receiving an excuse for − the presence of the other.' They were to inform the bishop by the said date of what they had done. Chudleigh, 15 December 1274.

1025*   The bishop wrote to the official of Cornwall [Master John de Withiel]. 'As we have heard from trustworthy men, so great an error − with risk of damnation – has flourished in Cornwall that certain men, who have been excommunicated by name and publicly denounced, as their deserts merit, by the archbishop of Canterbury, believe themselves able, without having yet obtained the benefit of absolution, to associate everywhere and anywhere with Christ's faithful on the pretext that they have taken a corporal oath to observe the commands of the Church, or that they allege they were provisionally absolved in the court of Canterbury. So that there may in the future be no more illicit communion through this sort of error between such excommunicates and Christ's faithful (by which the Lord's flock is blemished), we command you to give notice publicly to each and every person that they should not presume to consort in any instance not permitted by law with the aforementioned excommunicates until these have deserved to obtain the benefit of absolution; if they do – which God forbid – let them be deprived of participation in the sacraments.' Chudleigh, 18 December 1274.

1026 The bishop confirmed under seal the charter drawn up between Sir Nicholas son of Martin and Master Henry de Sackville, rector of Dartington, concerning certain lands and other things of the said church granted by Sir Nicholas. Paignton, 21 December 1274.

1027 Collation of Richard de Candover, subdeacon, to the prebend at Crantock vacant by the resignation of Master John de Esse; the archdeacon was to induct him. Crediton, 27 December 1274.

1028 Collation of the rector of Morchard Bishop[117] (*Morcerd*) to the prebend at Crediton which Richard de Candover had held; he was installed by order of the bishop. Morchard Bishop, 31 December 1274.

1029 Inst. of Reginald de Molendinis, priest, to the vicarage of Hockworthy (*Hockeworth'*); patrons, the prior and convent of Canonsleigh. Crediton, 27 December 1274.

1030 Collation by lapse of Thomas de Brellelawe, clerk, to Northam (*Norham*). Exeter, 24 December 1274.

1031 Inst. of Master William Bloyo, subdeacon, to Lew Trenchard (*Liw Trenchard*); patron, Michael Trenchard. Exeter, 24 December 1274.

1032 Sir Roger de Donesland, priest, given custody of Widworthy (*Wyde-worth'*). Exeter, 24 December 1274.

1033 Collation of Master J[ohn] de Pontoise to the archdeaconry of Exeter. Paignton, 22 December 1274.

[fo.59] **1034** Collation of Master William de Hococ, subdeacon, to Stockleigh Pomeroy, vacant by the resignation of John de Hanok. [Bishop's] Clyst, 2 January 1275.

---

[117] The last named rector was Nicholas, in May 1258 – 35.

1035 Dispensation, by papal authority, of Matthew de St Wenn, born of a deacon and a spinster, from his defect of birth. [Bishop's] Clyst, 2 January 1275.

1036 Dispensation, by papal authority, of Henry de Tredinsolse, born of a priest and a spinster, from his defect of birth. [Bishop's] Clyst, 2 January 1275.

1037 Collation of Sir Richard de Otterham, priest, to the vicarage of [South] Petherwin. [Bishop's] Clyst, 2 January 1275.

1038* The bishop wrote to his official [John de Esse]. 'We grant you by the tenor of these presents full power validly to present for ordination to the venerable father, the lord [Thomas], bishop of Leighlin, in our stead, religious and beneficed clerks of our diocese [for promotion] to holy orders and inferior clerics to acolyte's orders, and also those presented to vacant benefices (as long as they furnish you with special letters from ourselves concerning this), and to call upon the same lord bishop to carry out during our absence the other things which cannot be put into effect without the office of a bishop's orders; the present letters are to last until Easter.' [Bishop's] Clyst, 6 January 1275.

1039 Inst. of Robert de Cotton, subdeacon, to Clyst Hydon; patron, William de Hydon. [Bishop's] Clyst, 8 January 1275.

1040 Inst. of Stephen de Uffculme, priest, to Blackborough (*Blakebergh*); patron, the lady Philippa de Bollegh. [Bishop's] Clyst, 8 January 1275.

1041 Inst. of Simon de Hydon, subdeacon, to Hemyock (*Hemyok*); patron, Sir John de Hydon. [Bishop's] Clyst, 8 January 1275.

1042 Collation by lapse of Master Thomas de Buckland to the portion without cure of souls at St Endellion which Master John de Winchester had held. [Bishop's] Clyst, 8 January 1275.

1043 Collation, because the prior and convent of Bath had presented an unsuitable candidate (*eo quod . . . personam minus ydoneam sibi presentaverant*), of Henry de Lenna, subdeacon, to Bampton. [Bishop's] Clyst, 8 January 1275.

1044* The bishop wrote to Master Thomas de Buckland, canon of Crediton. 'We have made that man of venerable prudence, our beloved son the dean of Exeter [John Noble], our commissary to receive compensation according to the canons from those of Cornwall who, violating the Church's privilege, conceived a certain conspiracy against the church of Exeter, us and our successors, and, moved by a spirit of evil intent, put the same into practice as far as in them lay; and also to grant the benefit of absolution on fixed terms to such violators of ecclesiastical privilege as have been bound by an automatic sentence of greater excommunication but are displaying signs of contrition for their crimes by seeking that the fruits of penitence be bestowed on them. Bearing in mind, however, that one man, even of such great abilities, without a yokefellow for this task and distracted by the press of other business can be overburdened in many ways, we command you to give assistance in the same aforementioned business to the same dean of Exeter [fo.59v] and, in accordance with God and justice and for the honour of the Church, to bring about by your prudence that such transgressors are recalled to the bosom of Mother Church, conducting yourself in such a way in dealing with this sort of business that your diligence, which is deservedly commendable by us, may gain in reputation therefrom.' [Bishop's] Clyst, 8 January 1275.

1045   The bishop wrote to the dean [John Noble] in almost the same terms as in the preceding entry to inform him of the appointment of Master Thomas de Buckland, canon of Crediton, as his assistant. [Bishop's] Clyst, 8 January 1275.

1046   Collation of Master Robert de Trillawe, subdeacon, to the prebend at Exeter vacant by the death of Sir William de Bisimano. London, 3 February 1275.

1047*   The bishop wrote to the warden of the Franciscans at Oxford. 'In order that the last will of Master William de Ponchardon, recently a clerk of our household, who died a praiseworthy death after duly drawing up his testament, may have its due effect, we have thought fit earnestly to entreat you to have account fully made to Simon de Ponchardon, rector of the church of West Buckland, and the co-executors or any one of them or to their proctor, who shows you these our letters patent, for the books and other property deposited in good faith by the same [William] in your house for safe-keeping, charitably speeding on the aforesaid will, as far as you may, and in no way holding it back.' London, 3 February 1275.

1048   Collation of Richard de Candover, subdeacon, to a pension of 20 marks from St Merryn, vacant by the death of Roger de Valle Torta. London, 4 February 1275.

1049   Sir Payne de Exeter, chaplain, resigned Gerrans. Horsley, 6 February 1275.

1050   Inst. of Payne de Exeter, chaplain, to Broadhembury (*Brodehembyri*), vacant by the death of Sir Martin de Littlebury; patron, the king, as guardian of certain lands of Joan de Ferlingeston (*ratione quarundam terrarum Iohanne de Ferlingeston' in manu sua existentium*). Horsley, 6 February 1275.

1051   Collation of John de Hanok, subdeacon, to Gerrans, vacant by the resignation of Sir Payne de Exeter, chaplain. Horsley, 6 February 1275.

1052   Collation of Master W. de Farnham to the prebend at Crediton which Master Robert de Trillawe had held. Windsor, 17 February 1275.

[fo.60] **1053***   The bishop wrote to John de Pontoise, archdeacon of Exeter. 'Although the responsibility for all the churches of our city and diocese is ours, we have undertaken the care of the priory of St Mary Magdalen in Barnstaple, vacant for so long that for the moment it deserves our pity, and this the more willingly because the prior and convent of St Martin des Champs in Paris, to which the same priory is alleged to be immediately subject, are separated from it by so great a distance. And since the said priory has been weakened in so many ways for lack of a good ruler in both temporal and spiritual matters, we command you, firmly enjoining etc, to take with you one or more creditworthy inhabitants of Paris, and to warn the aforementioned prior and convent of St Martin on our behalf that they should not delay to present to us, before 1 May, a suitable person for the rule of the aforesaid priory. Otherwise, we shall be unable thereafter to disregard the risk to ourselves any longer, and we shall take steps to provide for the safety of the said church, as God shall inspire us, and to ward off the risks that threaten.' He was to inform the bishop of what he had done, in letters patent sealed by himself and those who had accompanied him, within a month of the receipt of the present letters. London, 25 February 1275.

1054 J[ohn] de Pontoise, archdeacon of Exeter, granted letters dimissory to receive the priesthood from any Catholic bishop. London, 25 February 1275.

1055 Letter patent confirming that the bishop had ordained Master John de Pontoise as deacon at Paignton on 15 December 1274, and had collated him to the archdeaconry of Exeter. London, 25 February 1275.

1056 Inst. of Ralph de Hydon, clerk, to Clayhidon (*Hydon*); patron, Sir John de Hydon. Horsley, 27 February 1275.

1057 Inst. of Robert de Kermerdyn, subdeacon, to Slapton; patron, Sir Guy de Brian. Horsley, 27 February 1275.

1058* The bishop wrote to the provost of Glasney [Henry de Bollegh] and the official of the archdeacon of Cornwall [John de Withiel]. 'When a patient ignores the warnings [of his doctor] it readily brings him to a speedy death. Certain of our subjects in the archdeaconry of Cornwall whose names are as yet unknown, in addition to those who have been convicted by name, believe themselves allowed to do illicit things, in a greater reckless companionship in crime than those sacrilegious persons who with rash violence laid hands on Master Jordan, formerly archdeacon of Cornwall, and other ecclesiastical persons at St Allen and in the park of Cargoll, dishonoured the clerical garb which they wore, castrated some of their horses and killed others, and committed other outrages there; further, those who gave consent, counsel, aid and encouragement for the arrest of our official and for the charge of felony trumped up against him, and also for the conspiracy conceived against us and our church; further, they imposed intolerable losses and burdens on our manors and privileges, to the peril of their souls and to the prejudice and oppression of ecclesiastical privilege, on account of which they have fallen *ipso facto* under sentence of excommunication, and after being denounced by papal authority and that of the lord archbishop of Canterbury, they remain thus bound generally. We, therefore, being zealous – as we are bound to be – for the salvation of the souls of our same subjects, command you, firmly enjoining you by virtue of your obedience, that immediately on the receipt of these letters [fo.60v], postponing all other business, you convoke special meetings of the chapters in each deanery on this matter, and make diligent inquiry as to what persons are culpable under the foregoing articles or any of them, so that being thus advised we may be able to remedy the health of their souls. Let them inquire, moreover, into who has associated with those excommunicated by name after canonical notification had been made.' They were to inform the bishop of what they had done, in sealed letters patent, before the middle of Lent. Horsley, 1 March 1275.

1059 Collation of Sir Richard de Brendesworthy, deacon, to the prebend at Exeter vacant by the death of Sir Adam de Belstead. Horsley, 27 February 1275.

1060 Collation of Sir Ralph de Ingham to the prebend at Crantock which Richard de Candover had held. Horsley, 28 February 1275.

1061[118] Collation by lapse of Sir Reginald de St Crantock, priest, to the portion at St Endellion (*ecc. S. Endelyente*) which Master John de Winchester had held. [Bishop's] Clyst, 28 March 1275.

1062 Inst. of Hamelin de Heanton, priest, to Kentisbury (*Kentesbyr'*); patron, William Lou. Exeter, 13 April 1275.

1063 Inst. of Sir Thomas, chaplain, to Morthoe (*Mortaho*); patron, Philip de Beston. Exeter, 13 April 1275.

1064 Inst. of John de Aqua, subdeacon, to Luffincott (*Luffingecote*); patron, Jordan de Luffincott. Exeter, 13 April 1275.

1065 Inst. of John called le Cornu, subdeacon, to Thornbury (*Thornbir'*); patron, William called le Cornu. Exeter, 13 April 1275.

1066 Collation of . . . to the vicarage of . . . . [No place,] 15 April 1275.

[fo.61] **1067*** A settlement was made between the bishop and Edmund, earl of Cornwall, who had submitted their disputes to the judgment of the archbishop of Canterbury [Robert de Kilwardby]. 'It has finally pleased the aforementioned parties and been agreed between them, after the intervention of common friends and following various discussions, that the said contention be laid to rest by way of a settlement for the sake of peace in the form set out below:
To wit, that the said earl of Cornwall desires and grants that the Church and its ministers should have peace in Cornwall and in the other lands and demesnes of the said earl in the city and diocese of Exeter, just as they had in the time of the lord king of Germany, his father [and previous earl], and in his time, until the time when the contention between the said lord bishop and himself had arisen. The said earl of Cornwall also desires and grants that on behalf of the manors of Pawton and Penryn four free and law-worthy men only from each manor should have suit of court each year at two shire courts and two sheriff's tourns, as was customarily done in the time of the aforesaid king of Germany and of the said earl, until the time the said contention arose; and that on behalf

---

[118] Cf **1042**.

of the manors of Tregear (*Treigaer*) and Lawhitton one free and law-worthy man only from each manor should have suit of court each year at two shire courts and two sheriff's tourns, as was customarily done in the time of the said king of Germany and of the said earl, until the time the said contention arose. Further, the said earl desires and grants that the said bishop should hold the assize of bread and ale in his manors of Pawton, Penryn, Tregear, Lawhitton and St Germans, as he had customarily held in the time of the said said king of Germany and of the said earl, until the time the said contention arose; and that the pillory and tumbrel[119] of the free borough of Penryn which had been thrown down should be re-erected, and the privilege of the said borough entirely restored. Further, that the [bishop's] park at Cargoll should be made good within a fixed and suitable time, and that the privileges of the manor of Cargoll should be fully observed, as was more fully contained in the charter of the aforesaid king of Germany which had been drawn up over this. And also that all the other privileges in the aforesaid episcopal manors and in others which had been injured or violated should be restored and returned to their former state, as they had been in the time of the king of Germany and of the said earl, until the time the said contention arose.

Because various losses and wrongs had been many times inflicted on the said lord bishop of Exeter and his church by various malefactors (not within the knowledge of the earl, as is believed, and which the same earl completely disavows), the same earl promises in good faith that he will protect nobody against the said lord bishop recovering his losses, but help him in pursuing his rights. Further, that the lands and holdings, the rents and services, which were unlawfully usurped (from the time when the aforesaid disturbance arose) by the servants of the said earl for his benefit and to the harm and loss of the said bishop and of his church of Exeter should be restored and returned to their former state. Further, the said earl grants that if Sir Richard de Seaton, John Goshelm, and others who are not of the diocese of Exeter, had extorted or unlawfully seized anything from the bishop's men, his clergy, or from the property of the said bishop, which had been acquired by the aforesaid earl, he would restore it in good faith. And if the same earl has not received what was thus extorted, he will in good faith help the lord bishop to obtain full satisfaction concerning it from the said malefactors. Further, the said earl desires and grants that the said lord bishop should have full restitution, seisin and possession of all the privileges and other aforesaid things which the same bishop and his predecessors were used to have, and that he should enjoy the same well and peacefully, as said above, saving the rights of the same earl if he should wish to speak out for them, on terms that the aforesaid shall remain inviolably and without hindrance with the said bishop until it should happen that the aforesaid earl should prove any right he should have in [fo.61v] the foregoing through due process of law.'

The archbishop of Canterbury approved and confirmed this settlement, entered into for the sake of peace, with the advice and consent of John [Chishull], bishop of London, Walter [Merton], bishop of Rochester, Anian, bishop of St Asaph, and Robert [Burnell], bishop-elect of Bath and Wells. The

---

[119] Or cucking-stool; it seems to have been a variant of the ducking-stool, or something similar.

bishop and the earl sealed the settlement as a cyrograph, along with the seals of the said prelates, and faithfully promised to observe it. Lambeth, 5 March 1275.

1068 The bishop inspected and confirmed under seal the charter of Bishop William [Brewer] to the burgesses of Penryn, given at Penryn, 29 August 1230. They were to hold from the bishop in free burgage, free from all services in return for 12 pence a year, paid in two instalments on 1 November and 1 May, for each whole acre; reliefs on transfer or death were to be paid at 12 pence an acre; larger or smaller holdings were to pay rent and relief proportionately. Sixpence was due for any amercement following a reasonable decision in the bishop's court, unless – which God forbid – for laying violent hands on the bishop or his bailiffs. Beyond that, the burgesses were to enjoy their privileges and free customs in perpetuity. Exeter, 13 April 1275.

[fo.62A[120]] **1069*** The bishop issued a letter to [Henry de Bollegh], the provost of Glasney, [John de Withiel], the official of the archdeacon of Cornwall, and Master Thomas de Buckland, canon of Crediton. 'The duty of our office requires us to watch over the health of the souls of the members of our flock, and if holy scripture teaches that great and small must be judged alike – for to distinguish between one leper and another is reserved to the papal office – yet, as equity urges, help must be given to weak, old, and wretched persons and those to whom we are father and lord. Certain persons, already named, of the county of Cornwall were present at the dishonouring of the clerks which occurred previously at St Allen and in our park at Cargoll (*Gargaul*), and were companions to those who dishonoured them, although short of laying hands on them – but we have accepted that they were under orders or even forced – and consented to the conspiracy of these identical persons against us, our church and clergy; some, indeed, communicated with the excommunicates, although not in the crime yet *de facto*, on which account there is no doubt that they fell under sentence of excommunication. We, burning the more zealously for the salvation of the souls of the members of our flock, as for all weak, old and wretched persons or those to whom we are father and lord in the said county, have considered the condition of each of those who were ordered or forced against their will to be present at the aforementioned dishonouring, and further, all those who consented unwillingly and not freely to the aforesaid conspiracy, and also all those who associated with the excommunicates but not in their crime, and have received from them appropriate satisfaction so that they be not excessively afflicted. We therefore grant you full power, by the authority of the metropolitan and ourselves, to absolve them in legal form, provided that they take a corporal oath reverently to receive and perform the salutary penance to be imposed on them by us. If, however, you should find by inquisition or otherwise any who are at fault according to the canons in the aforesaid articles or any of them, you are to warn them and effectively induce them to return to the bosom of the Church, and to make satisfaction appropriately for their misdeeds. Otherwise, you are to have them publicly and solemnly denounced by name as excommunicate through all Cornwall, until they make adequate

---

[120] See Introduction, Bronescombe's Register, vol.1, p.x.

satisfaction. But if you cannot all take part in the execution of these matters, my sons and the official, the foregoing is to be effected by any of you.' Crediton, 16 April 1275.

1070   Inst. of Walter, priest, to the vicarage of Egg Buckland (*Heckebokelond*); patrons, the prior and convent of Plympton. Exeter, 17 April 1275.

[fo.62Av] **1071**   Collation of Ralph le Butler, subdeacon, to the prebend at Crediton vacant by the resignation of Sir Robert Giffard. London, 6 May 1275.

1072   Collation of Sir H. de Montfort to the prebend at Crediton vacant by the resignation of Ralph le Butler. London, 6 May 1275.

1073   Collation of Sir Ralph de Hengham to the prebend at Exeter which Sir Walter son of Peter had held. London, 6 May 1275.

1074   Collation of Sir Henry de Godalming, priest, to the prebend at Bosham vacant by the resignation of Sir Andrew [Pruz]. London, 6 May 1275.

1075   Inst. of Sir William de Somerford, priest, to Uffculme (*Ufculm'*) with a charter (*et habet literas etc. et cartam*); patrons, the prior and convent of Bath. London, 7 May 1275.

1076   Master Roger le Rus resigned Lawhitton into the bishop's hands. London, 7 May 1275.

1077   Inst. of Master Roger le Rus to North Hill (*Northulle*), after judgment (*per sententiam diffinitivam adiudicatam*);[121] patron, Sir John de Mules. London, 7 May 1275.

1078   Inst. of Sir William de Chardstock, priest, to Marhamchurch (*Marwenecherche*); patron, Sir Hugh le English. Horsley, 15 May 1275.

1079*   'To all inspecting the present [sealed] letters, William de Alneto, knight, greeting in the Lord. Let all know that I, led by wise counsel, humbly recognize myself guilty of the conspiracy which I undertook with certain others of the county of Cornwall against the venerable father, the lord bishop of Exeter, his church and his men, and that I have associated with certain men excommunicated by authority of the lord archbishop of Canterbury, and I urgently and sincerely seek the benefit of absolution. And, offering fitting satisfaction, having touched the holy gospels, I swear that before 30 November I shall make adequate satisfaction for my guilt of conspiracy and association with the aforesaid to God and the Church and the aforementioned bishop. And if — which God forbid — I should not do this, I desire and from this moment grant that, without previous warning, I shall at once be thrust back into my

---

[121] There is nothing to say whether this was a case in the church or the secular courts.

former sentence of excommunication, or *ipso facto* be thrust back and bound.'
London, 9 October 1274.[122]

[fo.62B] **1080**   The archdeacon of Totnes [Thomas de Hertford] was ordered
in a letter to induct Master William de la Wyle (whom the bishop had already
admitted) to the church of Kingsteignton, a prebend in Salisbury cathedral,
saving the rights of the Exeter see; patron, the bishop of Salisbury. Compton,
30 May 1275.

1081   Inst. of Sir Gilbert de Molton, priest, to the vicarage of North Molton
(*Northmolton*); patron, Sir Richard Hureward, the rector, with the consent of Sir
Nicholas son of Martin, patron of the church; the vicarage was to be taxed if it
had not already been (*vicariam taxandam si rite non fuerit taxata*). Fluxton, 5 June
1275.

1082[123]   Thomas de Kent, knight, issued a sealed letter seeking absolution. He
had been present at the outrages at Cargoll, and had been an accomplice in
them, and moreover, he had consented to the conspiracy against the bishop; on
this account he had fallen *ipso facto* under sentence of the greater excommunication. At last, through those intervening for his salvation, he came to himself; he
promised under oath to pay 50 marks to the bishop, on days the bishop should
appoint, as amends and satisfaction for these crimes, and he also swore never
thereafter to commit such violent wrongs against the Church or ecclesiastical
persons, on pain of 40 marks to be paid within a month of conviction for such
offences. He swore to do all this on pain of automatically falling back into
excommunication; he also renounced any remedy of law by which such falling
back might be prevented or delayed. Witnessed by Sir Ralph de Arundel,
knight, Sir Hugh de Plympton, John le Chamberlayn, Richard de Dartford,
clerk, Thomas de Tremilla, clerk, Thomas, rector of Boconnoc, Roger de
Guynes, and others. Titing, 18 May 1275.

1083   The bishop issued sealed letters patent, acknowledging receipt from
Thomas de Kent, knight, of 50 marks in good and legal money (*bone et legalis
monete*), for which he was liable on account of the losses and trespasses inflicted
on the bishop and his clerks when the park at Cargoll (*Gargaol*) was laid waste,
and of the conspiracy wickedly set on foot against the bishop and his church,
and of the other wrongs and troubles inflicted on the bishop and his men by the
same Thomas. The bishop promised to take the 50 marks in full satisfaction.
Titing, 18 May 1275.

[fo.62Bv] **1084**   In letters patent the bishop acknowledged full satisfaction of
John de Beaupré's payment of 100 marks on account of the offences and wrongs
inflicted on the bishop [at Cargoll and elsewhere]; his bond of good behaviour
for a further 40 marks was nevertheless to remain in force. Lawhitton, 21 June
1275.

---

[122] *Anno regni regis Edwardi secundo* – the date is given by a layman.
[123] The language of this submission, although much shorter, is frequently identical to
that in **1085**.

1085* 'Let all know who see or hear the present letters that I, John de Beaupré, knight, former steward of Cornwall, was present at the violence and dishonouring wrongfully and violently inflicted on the priests and clerks at the dismantling of the park at Cargoll (*Kaergaol*), in the diocese of Exeter, on 30 August 1272, and wickedly furnished brazen help and fellowship to others doing worse wrong, and ordered the [enclosures of the] said park to be levelled, and, not content with all this, I organised a conspiracy formed against the venerable father Walter, by the grace of God bishop of Exeter, his church and clergy, and secured its approval by others, some freely and others unwillingly, and authorised the illegal arrest of Master John de Esse, official of Exeter, by ordering him to be led to prison and detained there too long, and besides, I inflicted, without right, other intolerable losses and injuries on the said lord bishop and his men, both free and villein, as regards their rights, liberties, manors, cultivated lands, and demesne lands, by illegal arrests and detentions of their draught animals and various other extortions and injuries, to the prejudice of the said lord bishop and the manifest harm of ecclesiastical privilege. On account of this I fell *ipso facto* under sentence of the greater excommunication.

In this state I persisted for upwards of two years, rejecting the oft-repeated admonition made against me publicly and solemnly by authority of the archbishop of Canterbury, with hardened heart scoffing irreverently at the said sentence. At last I came to myself, humbly and devoutly recognizing my offence, by the intervention of sons of peace who urged the salvation of my soul. Having taken a corporal oath to make satisfaction and to obey the commands of the Church, in virtue of the same oath I promise to give, render and pay the same lord bishop 400 marks sterling at the dates and on the conditions set out below, by way of compensation and satisfaction for the aforesaid losses and injuries thus inflicted by me on the said lord bishop and his church of Exeter, in his own person and in those of his villeins.

To wit: I shall give, render and pay to the same lord bishop, or to his appointed messenger showing letters patent, in the cathedral church of St Peter, Exeter, 100 marks at the next coming Michaelmas, in the month of September, and 100 marks at the next mid-Lent Sunday, with no further delay or any kind of subterfuge, on condition that the 200 marks then remaining, and their payment under the terms written below, will be respited and in no wise demanded of me, as long, indeed, as I behave devoutly and faithfully towards the aforementioned lord bishop and his successors in the lawsuits and affairs of the Church, and do not in future harm persons such as those I harmed before, nor acquiesce in their harm (unless repelling force by force, and [then] with care to show fitting moderation[124]). I desire that if I should act otherwise and be convicted, or confess, on these heads, or any of them, or should my wrongdoing appear manifestly notorious, I be absolutely bound to the full payment of the said 200 marks remaining, and be immediately brought by the said lord bishop and his successors under sentences of suspension, excommunication and interdict, without summons to court or hearing of the issue.

For the faithful performance and completion of all these things, I bind myself and all my goods, moveable and immoveable, to whomsoever [fo.63] they

---

[124] *et cum moderamine inculpate tutele*; J.A. Brundage sees it as the equivalent of pulling his punches.

should belong and wheresoever they should be found, to the same lord bishop, his church, and his successors, until the payment and completion of each and every item of the aforesaid; each and all of the aforesaid goods I recognize as being pledged and hypothecated to the said lord bishop, his church and his aforesaid successors, to the extent that, on my decease, there is to be no execution whatever of my will or disposal or distribution of my said estate until full satisfaction has been given to the same for the aforesaid 400 marks in the aforesaid form. I expressly renounce, as regards each and all of the aforesaid, all defence, cavil, appeal, dilatory defence, evasion, privilege of forum, indult for those who have taken or are about to take the Cross, custom, statute, royal writ of prohibition, and all remedy of canon, civil or customary law, either requested or able to be requested, which could bar this instrument or deed or by which the effect of this present bond could be denied, invalidated or deferred.

Because, indeed, various losses and wrongs have on numerous occasions been inflicted on the said lord bishop and his church by various malefactors – whose acts I totally disavow and whom I do not consider included under this agreement – I promise in good faith, in virtue of the same oath offered, that I shall not protect anyone or procure in any way the protection of anyone against the said lord bishop in the recovery of his losses, but that I shall faithfully aid him in the pursuit of his rights, and that I shall have the lands, holdings, rents, custodies, possessions and services, in any way damaged or usurped by me or through me to the harm, loss or prejudice of the said lord bishop and his church of Exeter, brought back to their former state, and I shall effectively bring about their complete restoration as far as I am able.

Furthermore, I have given to the same lord bishop and his church as guarantors for the observation of the foregoing the distinguished men written down below, namely Sirs William de Botterell, Roger de Pridias, Ralph de Arundel, and Hugh Peverel, knights, who have jointly pledged themselves as principal debtors in the following terms: "We, the aforenamed, having heard the present bond read and recited before us in the vulgar tongue, and having fully understood its contents, will guarantee on behalf of Sir John de Beaupré, knight, before the venerable father, the lord bishop of Exeter, the aforesaid monetary sum of 200 marks to be paid only and completely [*tantum et absolute*] on the prearranged dates, and in full understanding make ourselves jointly principal debtors in the aforesaid manner and form; we renounce completely and expressly on behalf of ourselves and our heirs all those remedies of law and of fact which the aforesaid John de Beaupré renounced on his own behalf above. In testimony whereof I, John de Beaupré, have sealed the present document, and we, the aforesaid William, Roger, Ralph, and Hugh, in testimony of our obligation, have in due order attached our seals." Launceston, 22 June 1275.

1086* 'To all inspecting these [sealed] letters, John de Treiagou, Ralph de Dynton, and William de Cerisy, knights, greeting in the Lord. Let all know that we, appearing in person before the venerable [John Noble], dean of Exeter, and the archdeacon of Taunton, the commissaries of the lord archbishop of Canterbury, have recognized and freely confessed that we have taken part in the unlawful conspiracy recently and wickedly set on foot in Cornwall against the venerable father, the lord bishop of Exeter, and his successors; for which reason we, the aforesaid John and Ralph, coming to our right minds, offer and pledge

20 marks, in equal portions, and I, William, 100 shillings sterling, to the same lord bishop as reparation; we promise by lawful stipulation to pay the assessed sum of money to the aforementioned bishop within a fortnight of his demanding it or having it demanded. Having touched the sacraments, we also swear that never again will we conspire or consent to a conspiracy or its making against ecclesiastical persons in the future.' This was done in the presence of [John de Pontoise] the archdeacon of Exeter, Henry [de Bollegh], provost of Glasney, William [de Capella], precentor of Crediton, Masters Gervase de Crediton, Philip de Exeter, William de Hancock, Richard de Carswell, Peter de Guildford, chaplain, and others. 3 January 1275.[125]

[fo.63v] **1087** Brother Theobald de Curtipalatio, monk, given custody of Barnstaple Priory; patrons, the prior and convent of St Martin des Champs, Paris. He gave his obedience there in the presence of Sirs William de Worplesdon and Clement [de Longford], canons of Exeter, Master Gervase de Crediton, Master Roger le Rus, Sir Peter de Guildford, Sir Hugh de Plympton, Richard de Grangiis, Richard de Dartford, and others. [Bishop's] Clyst, 29 June 1275.

1088 Dispensation of William de Tryl, acolyte, born of a priest and a spinster, from his defect of birth. [Bishop's] Clyst, 29 June 1275.

1089*[126] LETTER OF THE ABBOT OF FORD. 'Let it be recorded that Brother William, abbot of Ford of the Cistercian Order in the diocese of Exeter, was reproved before the venerable father, the lord Walter, bishop of Exeter, because it was alleged that the same abbot, contrary to the virtue of obedience and respect for episcopal dignity, issued and promulgated certain sentences of excommunication against the same venerable father in certain executory letters arising from the sentence recently definitively given by the authority of certain apostolic letters on behalf of Master William de Ditton, clerk, concerning the church of Tawstock of this diocese, or in some way implied or proclaimed that the same bishop had fallen under such sentences, or also involved the same lord bishop in such sentences or assumed him to be involved. The same abbot appeared in person with his sworn council on 9 July 1275 in the hall of the same lord bishop in Exeter, in the presence of the dignitaries of the city of Exeter and the greater part of the clergy of Devon, gathered solemnly there over a tax for the Holy Land, and of his free will, in good faith and with a clear conscience denied each and every one of the aforementioned complaints against him, in the terms which follow: "I, William, abbot of Ford, publicly make profession that it neither was nor is my intention to promulgate any sentence of excommunication against the lord bishop of Exeter, nor to involve him in any such sentence, whatever may be contained in my letters executing the sentence given on behalf of Master William de Ditton concerning the church of Tawstock. And if anything besides was enacted in the same letters, or the occasion giving rise to them, I withdraw it as a nullity." Also [John Noble] the dean of Exeter, being present there as principal judge, who had not appointed commissaries, in the

---

[125] MS has 1274, but this seems unlikely.
[126] See **929**, and its footnote.

presence of the aforesaid gathering went on to make an identical and solemn revocation. As supporting witnesses the aforementioned dean [of Exeter], [Edward de la Knolle] the dean of Wells, the archdeacon of Wells, the abbot of Hartland, the treasurer of Exeter, the priors of Barlinch and Frithelstock, [William de Capella] the precentor of Crediton, Master Thomas de Buckland, Gilbert de Tyting, and Peter de Guildford, canons of Crediton, all sealed the record, in the presence of the following invited witnesses, namely, Master William Wancy, Robert de Cotton, Richard de Grangiis, Master John de Wolfrinton, Richard de Gundewyne, Richard de Dartford, and others.' Exeter, 9 July 1275.

[fo.64] **1090** In sealed letters patent, John de Leicester, canon of Salisbury, former holder of the [Salisbury] prebend of Kingsteignton in the diocese of Exeter, submitted himself completely to the bishop as regards the fruits of that church with all its appurtenances.He invited [Edward de la Knolle] the dean of Wells, the treasurer of Exeter, and Masters William de la Wyle, canon of Salisbury, Clement [de Langford], canon of Exeter, Thomas de Buckland and Peter de Guildford, canons of Crediton, to act as witnesses, and they added their seals. Bishop's Clyst, 11 July 1275.

1091* A letter was issued. 'Walter, by the grace of God bishop of Exeter and deputed by the holy see as administrator for the Crusade in the city and diocese of Exeter, to his beloved son, Master Thomas de Buckland, canon of Crediton, greeting, grace and benediction. Since the holy see has granted the indulgence of many privileges to those undertaking the Cross, we commit to you, in our stead, the protection of the privileges of those going on crusade from our diocese and jurisdiction over cases concerning them, and bringing them to a due conclusion. If you should in due form pass sentences of suspension, excommunication or interdict against rebellious persons, we shall have them inviolably observed until, God willing, fitting satisfaction shall be made. The commission is to last until we have thought fit to revoke it.'[127] [Bishop's] Clyst, 13 July 1275.

1092* CITATION.[128] The bishop to Master J[ohn de Esse], his official: 'It is our duty, if we wish to avoid the stigma of reprehensibility and disobedience, to be attentive to the performance of the law as regards the statutes of the holy fathers, although they may contain no express threat of penalty. It was recently laid down at the Council of Lyons that beneficed clergy, particularly those to whose benefices the cure of souls was attached, should, within set periods of time, have themselves ordained priest[129], and numerous previous statutes of holy canons have been issued concerning such ordination of beneficed clergy, whose publication has as yet borne scanty fruit in many parsons in our diocese. Accordingly, so that we should not fear a penalty for culpable negligence, where reward for diligent execution of the law might deservedly be expected, we command that you should peremptorily cite and have cited, publicly and solemnly, all the rectors and vicars of parish churches in our diocese who are

---

[127] This sentence was added later.
[128] Cf **23** and **986** for notices of citations.
[129] Canon 13 of Lyons II, 1274. The bishop attended this General Council.

not already in priest's orders, omitting nobody, and including those holding prebendal benefices in collegiate churches, to present themselves in our sight in the parish church of Torrington[130] on the Ember Days next before Christmas [ie 18, 20, 21 December], to receive holy orders as the status of each requires, under the penalty contained in the canons of the aforesaid Council and others. But because there are some who, defrauding the Church of her property by squandering the fruits of their churches, are accustomed to waste a whole year's subsistence in a short space of time, and having thus willingly made themselves so to speak destitute, are too poor easily to be able to be coerced to such [ordinations] and other similar ones, ordinary or extraordinary, we command you by strict order that, if you find any in our diocese to be suspect on that account, you should first of all – as justice demands – suspend them from the admi[fo.64v]nistration of ecclesiastical property which they hold in our diocese, then you should sequestrate the fruits of their benefices in whoever's possession they are, making them liable under farmed sequestration until they give effective obedience to the law in this respect. You are to see to it that you inform us, at the said day and place, through your letters patent including the content of this [letter], of how you have executed our command.' [Bishop's] Clyst, 20 July 1275.

1093   The bishop ordered the issue on 9 August of a sealed letter recording his collation of Sir Roger de Gorcheny, priest, to the vicarage of St Enoder. To the vicarage was assigned thirteen acres, English measure, of glebeland together with the house which Walter the reeve (*prepositus*) used to live in, and all the altarage except for the tithes of field beans and peas; further, the vicar was to bear all the due and customary burdens. Exeter, 30 September 1275.

1094   Inst. of Master Robert de Stokes, subdeacon, to Creed; patron, the earl of Cornwall. Chudleigh, 20 July 1275.

1095   Admission of Brother Vincent de Fulchis, monk, as prior of Modbury (*Mouber*); patrons, the abbot and convent of St Mary at St Pierre sur Dives [Calvados]. Chudleigh, 21 July 1275.

1096   Dispensation of William de Haltona, clerk, born of an acolyte and a spinster, from his defect of birth. 13 August 1275.

1097   Dispensation of Richard called Haym of Bodmin, clerk, born of a subdeacon and a spinster, from his defect of birth. 16 August 1275.

[fo.65] **1098*** CHARTER. 'To all the sons of holy mother Church who see or hear this present document, Walter, by divine compassion bishop of Exeter, eternal greeting in the Lord. Let all know that we, in consideration of the lack of ministers in the church of Blessed Thomas the Martyr, Glasney, at the prompting of divine charity have granted and conferred on the same church of St Thomas for the perpetual maintenance of two chaplains who are to say one

[130] Presumably Great Torrington; the MS originally read 'the chapel of St James at Teignmouth (*Teyngmue*)'.

mass a day for St Mary and another for our soul and the souls of Master Henry de Bollegh and Sir Walter de Fermesham and the souls of all the faithful departed in the aforesaid church, and who thereafter are to be present in that place for singing the psalms at the canonical hours, the church of Manaccan (*Menstr'*) of which we are patron, together with all its rights, offerings, and all its other appurtenances, to be possessed for their own use in perpetuity by the aforesaid chaplains, saving an appropriate vicarage in the same church of Manaccan to be taxed by ourselves or our successors and to be filled whenever it shall fall vacant. We also desire and ordain that the provost and sacristan[131] of Glasney for the time being, if they are present in the diocese — failing which, whichever one of them happens to be present — shall present to us and our successors, for the celebration of the aforesaid offices, chaplains as aforesaid on the departure or decease of their predecessors; we assign to the same chaplains, for them to live in, at the wish and consent of the aforesaid Henry and Walter, the houses and buildings with all their appurtenances which the same Henry and Walter have built near Glasney Bridge, on terms that the aforesaid chaplains have and hold these houses and buildings in perpetuity, freely, with immunity, and released from all oppressive imposition and secular service. In testimony whereof we have had our seal affixed to the present document. Witnessed by Master John le Noble, then dean of Exeter Cathedral, Master John de Pontoise, then archdeacon of Exeter, Master John de Esse, then archdeacon of Cornwall, Sir Richard de Braundsworthy, canon of Exeter, Sir Hugh de Plympton, canon of St Buryan, Sirs Alexander de Oxton, Ralph de Arundel, and John de Treiagu, knights, and others.' The Park of Cargoll, 17 August 1275.

1099 The bishop issued a letter of quittance to Master Thomas de Buckland, canon of Crediton and one of the bishop's clerks, for all that he had received through his administration of the archdeaconries of Exeter, Barnstaple and Totnes.[132] Paignton, 9 September 1275.

[fo.65v] **1100*** The bishop wrote to Robert Kilwardby, archbishop of Canterbury. 'We are unable to be present at the consecration of the venerable father, the lord Thomas [Cantilupe], bishop-elect of Hereford, to be celebrated in Christchurch, Canterbury, on the coming feast of the Nativity of the BVM (8 September) — at which we would gladly have been present by reason of his uprightness[133] and because his own merits and those of his ancestors demand it — since we are hindered by various and difficult affairs. These include: the offences and oppressions inflicted recently on the church and clergy in Cornwall, which we hope to be set right by the arrival of the earl of Cornwall around the time of the said feast, and that an end be made to the disputes arising therefrom; the solemn celebration of orders which had been advertised throughout our diocese long before we received your command;[134] also, the

---

[131] Was this Walter de Fermesham?
[132] Cf **999**, which only mentions the Exeter archdeaconry.
[133] He was later canonized.
[134] The ordination set for the December Ember Days (**1092**) had originally been scheduled for the Ember Days before St Matthew, ie 18, 20 & 21 September.

commemoration of St Gabriel to be celebrated, God willing, on 2 September in our cathedral church;[135] and there are various other matters occupying us which, saving our honour, cannot be in any way passed over. We entreat you, as our father, with regard to the foregoing, that you should be pleased to hold us excused. As to the aforesaid consecration, as far as in us lies, we joyfully give our consent and approval.' [Bishop's] Clyst, 31 August 1275.

1101* The bishop wrote to the archdeacon of Exeter. 'We understand from what certain persons have told us that some minions of Satan, desirous of breaking the sinews of ecclesiastical discipline and striving to extend their power to things which are unlawful, have purposed to dispossess by superior force and with an armed band William de St Gorran, deacon, rector of Ottery St Mary in our diocese, (to which same he has been canonically instituted) from the same church, its fruits, and the rights pertaining to it, contrary to the liberties of the Church and the peace of the lord king and his realm. Wherefore we command you that to foil so iniquitous a plan, when you see signs that such a crime is being committed, you should summon together all the priests of the rural deanery of Aylesbeare, and others in the neighbourhood as you shall see fit, and send them to that place [Ottery St Mary presumably], dressed in their priestly vestments and walking in procession to the aforesaid church, to warn such doers of violence that they should desist absolutely from so nefarious a purpose, under penalty of incurring *ipso facto* the greater excommunication. Otherwise, if they persist in their evildoing, [the priests] are to proclaim publicly and solemnly, with lighted candles and ringing of bells, that such evildoers have fallen under the law through the published sentence, and they are diligently to seek out the names of the evildoers. You are to inform us through your letters patent, including the content of this [letter], as speedily as you can, of how you have executed our command.' Paignton, 8 September 1275.

1102 Collation of Sir Solomon de Rochester to the prebend at Crantock (*ecc. S. Karentoci*) which Sir Henry de Montfort had held. Exeter, 2 September 1275.

1103 Collation of Master Robert de Penhal to Lawhitton (*Lawinton*). [Bishop's] Clyst, 17 September 1275.

[fo.66] **1104** Collation by lapse of Master Nicholas de Paignton, subdeacon, to Buckland (*Bocland*).[136] [Bishop's] Clyst, 17 September 1275.

1105 Collation of Nicholas Strange, subdeacon, to Knowstone (*Kontston*). [Bishop's] Clyst, 17 September 1275.

1106 The bishop in letters patent (dated 14 September) appointed Sir Clement [de Langford], canon of Exeter, his attorney to receive at Michaelmas 100 marks from Sir John de Beaupré,[137] and other debts due from many of the

---

[135] Gabriel was the bishop's patron, and it is in St Gabriel's chapel that he is buried; cf **1297**.
[136] See note to **862**; here too Hingeston-Randolph suggests Buckland Monachorum.
[137] See **1085**.

bishop's knights and free tenants, with power to grant letters of quittance. [Bishop's] Clyst, 17 September 1275

1107 Admission[138] of Brother Adam de Buris, monk, to Cowick Priory; patron, the abbot of St Mary, Bec. [Bishop's] Clyst, 16 August 1275.

1108 Collation by lapse of John de Eledon, subdeacon, to Roborough (*Roheberg'*). Wells, 22 September 1275.

1109 Dispensation, by authority of the lord Ottobuono, the former papal legate in England, of Roger la Zusche, born of a bachelor and a spinster, from his defect of birth. Wells, 22 September 1275.

[fo.66v] **1110*** The bishop wrote to the prior of St Nicholas', Exeter, and Master W[illiam] de Capella, precentor of Crediton: 'In the course of leading back our church of Exeter from its crooked ways to its due and ancient state, we published certain healthgiving statutes [see **732**] which our dean and chapter accepted and approved, and were pleased to confirm by oath and in writing, which statutes, so far, they have taken so little care to observe that we forbear to mention their shame. We purpose shortly, if God wills, to visit our city and diocese, and to begin with its head. We therefore command you, firmly enjoining you by your duty of obedience, in our stead and with our authority diligently to warn the aforesaid dean and chapter, and effectively persuade them to have the aforesaid statutes read and recited every week on Saturdays, at least once, in chapter at the hour of Prime, after the martyrology, in their presence and that of the cathedral clerks, and to see that what has been recited is effectually observed, as they wish to avoid the shame of disobedience and the stigma of perjury. Thus it will not happen that in the execution of our duty of visitation, when it occurs, we have the duty of convicting them – which God forbid – of lack of obedience, contempt and perjury.' The prior and William were to report back before 1 November, in letters patent, what they had done. Wells, 23 September 1275.

1111 Collation by lapse of John de Eledon, subdeacon, to Roborough (*Rogheberhe*). Wells, 23 September 1275.[139]

1112 Inst. of Master John de Pontoise, archdeacon of Exeter, to Tawstock; patrons, the prior and convent of St Mary Magdalen, Barnstaple. London, 19 October 1275.

1113 A proxy was issued for the court of Canterbury to Richard de Kingston and Ralph de la Pole as alternates in all actions raised by or against the bishop, at any time or place, with power to take an oath in the bishop's name, seek restoration to original status, object to crimes and defects,[140] claim expenses, and do all the other things required of proctors in the bishop's name. The bishop

---

[138] MS says *installatio* in margin.
[139] This seems a mistaken repetition of the previous day's entry – **1108**.
[140] *crimina et defectus obiciendi*; such as irregular ordinations, J.A. Brundage suggests.

would ratify whatever they did and promised to pay out on their behalf. [fo.67] London, 19 October 1275.

1114[141]* John of Pontoise, archdeacon of Exeter, issued a sealed letter. 'Let all know that when the lord Walter, by God's grace bishop of Exeter, admitted me after I had been canonically presented by the true patron to the church of Tawstock, and inducted me into corporal possession of the same church, saving any other claim, not wishing the said lord bishop to be troubled on the pretext of my induction or anything else, I promise firmly, by the tenor of these presents, that I shall manfully[142] protect my possession in the same church against whomsoever, and I shall keep the said lord bishop immune from loss under a penalty of 100 marks, to the payment of which I desire, if I default in the foregoing, the said lord bishop to be able to compel me wherever I may be within a month of giving notice; I renounce all general and special defences of forum, privilege or of any other legal device as an aid which could be competent to me against the aforementioned lord bishop.' [No place,] 22 October 1275.

1115 The bishop issued a sealed letter granting John de Lardario 40 shillings a year from his private purse, payable at All Saints and Pentecost, until he should receive, from the bishop or on the the bishop's behalf (*per alium contemplatione nostri*), a more adequate benefice. London, 22 October 1275. This letter was cancelled in London on 6 May 1276, when John received a prebend at Probus.[143]

1116 Collation of Master Ralph de Merlane to the prebend at Crantock vacant by the voluntary resignation of Sir Michael de Northampton. London, 19 October 1275.[144]

1117 Collation of Sir Robert de Scarborough to the prebend at Crediton vacant by the voluntary resignation of Master Ralph de Merlane. London, 19 October 1275.

1118 Collation of Sir Ralph de Hengham to the chancellorship of Exeter, vacant by the death of Master Richard de Bremble. London, 19 October 1275.

1119 Sir Ralph de Hengham, presented by the earl of Cornwall, given custody of Lanteglos until 1 April 1276.[145] London, 19 October 1275.

1120 Collation by lapse of Master Nicholas de Musele to the pension which Master Robert Everard had held in the church of Pelynt, on the same terms. London, 19 October 1275.

---

[141] This entry was added at the bottoms of ff.66v & 67.
[142] Reading *viriliter*, at J.A. Brundage's suggestion, although the MS clearly gives *viliter*, which would mean the opposite.
[143] This sentence was clearly added later.
[144] But the entry ends: *Datum de Poltone*.
[145] He was admitted on 6 May – **1168**.

1121 Sir John de Kirkby, presented by the earl of Cornwall, given custody of St Buryan until 1 April 1276. London, 21 October 1275.

1122* LETTER CONCERNING IRELAND. A letter was issued in this form: '[Walter], bishop of Exeter, and [Nicholas of Ely], bishop of Winchester, appointed judges-delegate by the lord pope in the business of the election of a dean for St Patrick's cathedral, Dublin, to their venerable brethren, the bishops of Ferns [fo.67v] and of Ossory,[146] and to the prudent abbot of St Thomas near Dublin, greeting in the Author of salvation. We have received the command of the lord pope [Gregory X] in these words: "Gregory, bishop, servant of the servants of God, to his venerable brothers the bishops of Exeter and Winchester, greeting and apostolic blessings. Our beloved sons, the chapter of the cathedral of St Patrick, Dublin, have indicated that lately, since the deanery of the aforesaid church was vacant, and since the election of a dean in that church pertains to the same chapter, they canonically and unanimously elected our beloved son, Master John de Sanford,[147] canon of that cathedral, to the deanery of the same church. But, since the see of Dublin is alleged at present to lack a pastor – to whom the confirmation of such an election pertains – a humble supplication was made to us on behalf of the said chapter that we should, of our apostolic good will, command that election to be confirmed. We therefore, condescending to their supplications, command you, our brothers, in these papal letters, that, having inquired with much diligence for the truth into the manner of the aforesaid election, the intentions of the electors and the merits of the one elected, if you should find that the aforesaid election was of a suitable person and canonically conducted, you should, by our authority, confirm it. Otherwise, having formally quashed it, you should see to the provision through a canonical election of a suitable person to the aforesaid deanery, constraining any who challenge you with ecclesiastical censure, setting aside any appeal. It will be no bar if an apostolic indult has been granted to any persons that they cannot be put under interdict, suspension or excommunication, unless their apostolic letters make full and express mention of an indult of this kind. We do not wish, however, that, through this kind of commission given you by the authority of the presents, any prejudice should be engendered against the chapter of the church of Holy Trinity, Dublin, as regards their claim that their church is a cathedral. Lyons, 7 January 1275." Because we are hampered by various matters of business in the realm of England, we are unable to put the said matter on foot and to bring it to full completion; we have therefore, by the authority entrusted to us and according to its tenor, thought fit to summon you to the expedition, conduct and completion of the said business of the election. But if not all of you are able to take part in the conduct and completion, two of you may nevertheless deal with the foregoing.' London, 23 October 1275.

1123 The bishop, principal papal judge-delegate in the lawsuit between Robert, son of William de Bingham, the appellant, and Sybilla, called Oliver, a woman, the respondent, wrote to Masters Ralph de Merlane, canon of Crantock, and Richard Paz, canon of Crediton, appointing both or either of

---

[146] Hugh de Lamport, 1258–82, and Geoffrey St Leger, 1260–87.
[147] Later archbishop of Dublin, 1286–94, so presumably this election was confirmed.

them his commissaries, with canonical power of coercion; [fo.68] he reserved
definitive sentence to himself. London, 24 October 1275.

1124* The bishop sent a sealed letter to Robert Kilwardby, archbishop of
Canterbury. 'When our beloved son, Richard de Grenville, presented to us the
prudent Sir Bogo de Clare,[148] canon of Exeter, for the vacant church of
Kilkhampton in our diocese, the same Bogo pursued such presentation through
a proctor, showing before us the contents of his dispensations, and the proctor
requested that his principal be admitted to the aforesaid church. We, wishing for
good reason to deliberate over the foregoing, appointed for the same proctor a
peremptory date a fortnight after Michaelmas for doing what justice must
recommend. Since the same proctor was not satisfied with our appointment and
appealed the aforesaid case to your court, we, out of reverence for the see of
Canterbury, have given way to his appeal, and have thought fit to send on the
aforementioned proctor with the whole dossier for the affair and his aforesaid
deeds for your examination.' [Bishop's] Clyst, 17 September 1275.

1125 The bishop wrote to the official of Canterbury, acknowledging his letter
dated Lambeth, 23 October 1275. Bogo de Clare, dean of Stafford, had claimed
that Bronescombe's refusal to admit him after lawful presentation was unrea-
sonable (*ad eandem ecclesiam minus iuste admittere recusastis*). The official inhibited
the bishop from doing anything which would prejudice Bogo's case while his
appeal was pending. The bishop was cited to appear before the Court of the
Arches on the fourth legal day after Martinmas; he was to inform [fo.68v] the
official of any action he took after the receipt of the letter of inhibition. The
bishop repeated what he had told Kilwardby.[149] London, 26 October 1275.

1126*[150] The bishop acknowledged the letter of the official of Canterbury,
dated London, 22 October 1275. It ran: ' "A complaint has been made to us by
Agnes de Crues, a woman of your diocese, that although she had not been
legally warned, or cited, or convicted, nor had she confessed, or been
contumaciously absent, you incorrectly promulgated, or ordered the promulga-
tion, without reasonable cause of a sentence of excommunication against her,
contrary to the canons of the general council,[151] to her considerable prejudice
and the scandal of many. On account of this, the same Agnes approached the
court of Canterbury, humbly beseeching us for a healthful remedy. Wherefore
we command you, reverend father, if the facts are thus, that you should in legal
form relax the said sentence of excommunication within eight days from your
receipt of the present letter; otherwise, we cite you peremptorily to appear before
us or our commissary in the church of St Mary of the Arches in London, in

---

[148] Son of Richard, earl of Gloucester, and the most notorious pluralist in England.
[149] The case suggests that Bronescombe thought Bogo's pluralism and non-residence
beyond reason; cf **966**. The result seems to have been a compromise, since *The Rolls and
Register of Bishop Oliver Sutton*, ed. R.M.T. Hill (Lincoln Record Society, 1950), vol. II,
p.3, shows him receiving a pension of 10 marks from the parish.
[150] The source of the trouble – a dispute over land in Ottery St Mary – is to be found in
C.C.R., Edward I, 1272–9, p.253; see also footnote to **1177**.
[151] See c.6 of Lateran III, c.47 of Lateran IV, and c.7 of Lyons I.

person or through a suitable and adequately instructed proctor, on the third legal day after Martinmas, to answer to the said Agnes concerning the foregoing matters and to admit what due process of law demands. You are to certify to us or our commissary, at the said day and place, by means of your letters patent, including the content of this letter, what you have done from the day you received this present letter." We hereby indicate to you that, since we have not excommunicated this Agnes – as the court of Canterbury alleges – we cannot bestow on her the benefit of absolution. Yet out of reverence for the aforesaid court, we have made an offer to the same Agnes that, when we return to our diocese, if we find her to have been bound by the chains of excommunication by our official or commissaries, we shall have bestowed on the same the benefit of absolution in legal form.' London, 27 October 1275.

[fo.69] **1127** Collation of Richard de Grangiis, subdeacon, to the prebend of Probus vacant by the voluntary resignation of Master Ralph de Merlane. Horsley, 30 October 1275.

1128 The bishop wrote to the dean and chapter of Exeter giving notice that he would make a visitation on 14 November, and ordering all of them to be present in the cathedral. Horsley, 1 November 1275.

1129 The bishop wrote to [John de Pontoise] the archdeacon of Exeter, ordering him peremptorily to cite the abbot of Ford to answer, in Exeter cathedral on 12 November before the bishop or his commissary, for the breaking of the bishop's sequestration of the fruits from Ottery St Mary,[152] and various other transgressions. Horsley, 1 November 1275.

1130 The bishop issued letters patent acknowledging that Sir John de Beaupré had fully paid the instalment [100 marks – **1085**] of his fine due at Michaelmas. Exeter, 16 November 1275.

1131 Inst. of Odo de Luders, deacon, to East Allington (*Alinton*); patron, Sir Hugh de Treverbyn, knight. [Bishop's] Clyst, 18 November 1275.

1132 Inst. of Sir Henry, called Potel, chaplain, to Lympstone (*Laveneston*); patron, William de Albemarle. Crediton, 20 November 1275.

[fo.69v] **1133** Inst. of Sir Robert de Sidbury, priest, to the vicarage of Salcombe (*Saltcumbe*); patrons, the dean and chapter of Exeter. Paignton, 9 December 1275.

1134 The bishop held an ordination; the names of the ordinands were held by Master J[ohn] de Esse, official of Exeter. Torrington, 21 December 1275.

1135 Collation of Reginald le Arceveske, subdeacon, to the prebend at Exeter which Sir Thomas [de Hertford], archdeacon of Totnes, had held. Sampford Peverell, 21 December 1275.

---

[152] Was there a connection with the events of **1101**? See **1175**, etc.

1136   Collation of Master Henry de Bollegh to the archdeaconry of Totnes, with letters for clergy and people (*et habet literas clero et populo in forma communi*). Paignton, 25 December 1275.

1137   Collation by lapse of Robert Tone, deacon, to Ashton (*Asshereston*). Bishopsteignton, 28 December 1275.

1138   Dispensation by papal authority of John de Helston, acolyte, born of an acolyte and a spinster, from his defect of birth. Bishopsteignton, 29 December 1275.

1139   Inst. of Master Adam Heym, subdeacon, to Menheniot (*Meyniet*); patron, ...[153] Paignton, 26 December 1275.

1140   Collation of William de Tracy to Bow (Nymet Tracy); patron, Sir Geoffrey de Canvile. [Bishop's] Clyst, 11 January 1276.

1141   Sir Robert Giffard resigned the church of Farringdon (*Farndon*) into the bishop's hands, and Sir Peter de Guildford, the bishop's chaplain, was given custody until the bishop thought fit to recall it. [Bishop's] Clyst, 12 January 1276.

1142   Collation of Sir Reginald le Arceveske, subdeacon, to St Breward (*ecc. S.Brueredi*). [Bishop's] Clyst, 12 January 1276.

1143   Inst. of Sir Thomas de Willand, priest, to Warkleigh (*Warkel'*); patron, Sir Walter de Raleigh. [Bishop's] Clyst, 12 January 1276.

1144   Inst. of Sir John Pycot, deacon, to Merton; patron, Sir John de Wyger. [Bishop's] Clyst, 15 January 1276.

1145   Inst. of Sir Adam de Campbell, subdeacon, to Horwood (*Horwode*); patron, William Lamprey. [Bishop's] Nympton, 20 January 1276.

1146   Inst. of William de Stoke, priest, to Kelly; patron, John de Kelly. [Bishop's] Nympton, 22 January 1276.

1147   Master Thomas de Swansea given custody of Bratton Fleming (*Bratton*) until the Ascension; Master David, son of Sir Nicholas son of Martin, had been presented to the same church by the true patron.[154] [Bishop's] Tawton, 26 January 1276.

[fo.70] **1148**   The bishop confirmed the election of Johel as prior of Frithelstock (*Frithelestok'*); patron, Sir John de Beauchamp. [Bishop's] Tawton, 27 January 1276.

---

[153] It was William de Tregrille in 1260 – **251**.
[154] See **1163**.

1149 A proxy was issued to Nicholas de Musele, clerk of the Temple at London, to act for the bishop in his dispute – and any related matters – with the abbot and convent of Ford, of the Cistercian Order, with powers to take oaths on the bishop's behalf and to make substitutes. Previous proxies were to remain in force. [Bishop's] Clyst, 12 February 1276.

1150 A letter was issued to Master Henry de Bollegh, archdeacon of Totnes and canon of Glasney, who had resigned as provost of Glasney. The bishop was postponing any installation to the provostship until suitable provision had been made for its maintenance; meanwhile, Henry was entrusted with the discipline of the canons and other clerks and all other matters pertaining to the provost's jurisdiction, including its delegation, until the bishop should provide otherwise. Glasney, 8 March 1276.

1151 Dispensation of Robert de St Wenn, acolyte, in common form, with the additional clause that if in future he should fall back into the same offence[155] and be duly convicted, the dispensation would be invalidated. Glasney, 8 March 1276.

[fo.70v] **1152** Dispensation of Robert de St Lalluo, acolyte, in common form, with the same additional clause. 20 March 1276.

1153 Inst. of Sir Michael de Leigh, priest, to Ashprington (*Assprinton*); patrons, the prior and convent of Totnes. Paignton, 26 March 1276.

1154* The bishop issued a sealed inspeximus[156] to the dean, John [Noble], and chapter of Exeter, who, at Exeter, on 2 April 1276, had written: 'Let all know that we, having weighed and examined the utility and honour of our church of Exeter, and with the lawful consent of our venerable father, the lord Walter, bishop of Exeter, and of the prudent Master John,[157] precentor of Exeter, have granted to Elias de Cirencester, at that time vicar[-choral] of Master Thomas de la Knolle, [the headmastership of] the house of the choir scholars together with the succentorship of the cathedral church of Exeter, which he is to hold in perpetuity, receiving all the emoluments and bearing all the burdens thereof on these terms: to wit, that on account of this our communal grant, the said Elias causes to be built at his own expense an appropriate, adequate and decent house for the use of the succentor and the boys of our choir to be possessed for the aforesaid choir school in the place previously arranged. We further desire that the said house with all its appurtenances, and with the succentorship, should remain with the said Elias in perpetuity; after the death of the said Elias it shall remain immune and free with all his successors who shall be for the time being succentors and vicars of the said precentor and his successors, and with the the boys of our choir, to be maintained at their own expense by the said Elias and the succentors who will succeed him in future

---

[155] Presumably fornication.
[156] However, this seems confirmation of a new office rather than a true inspeximus.
[157] The precentor was actually Ralph de Hengham – see 'The wages of virtue', cited for **1012**; 'John' seems to echo the name of the dean.

times. With this modification, that the said precentor and his successors after him shall make provision for a suitable and decent man for the succentorship and the rule of the same scholars, and shall present the same to us for the said office.' The bishop confirmed the grant for himself and his successors. Exeter, 3 April 1276.

1155 Collation of Richard de Grangiis, subdeacon and the bishop's chamberlain, to St Teath, vacant by the death of Master Roger de Oxton. Exeter, [?3 April] 1276.

[fo.71] **1156*** SIR HENRY DE LA POMERAY'S BOND. 'To all Christ's faithful who see or hear the present letters, Henry de la Pomeray, knight, eternal greeting in the Lord. Let all know that, on account of various and manifest offences and wrongs wickedly inflicted by me and my household on the venerable father, the lord bishop of Exeter, and other ecclesiastical persons of the diocese of Exeter, I had been bound by a sentence of the greater excommunication, and, coming to myself and desiring to make satisfaction for the said crimes, had promised faithfully in fixed form to make satisfaction, and had undertaken thereafter to be faithful to the church of Exeter and its bishop, taking a corporal oath, as is more fully set out in my written bond drawn up on this matter. But then, the chain of the same promise and undertaking constrained my heart less strongly than was fitting and, contrary to the terms of the fidelity owed, I unlawfully climbed over the dikes of the park of Paignton with my followers and many others of my household of Berry [Pomeroy] who were accompanying me, and in the said park of the lord bishop of Exeter, without seeking out him or his bailiffs, I caught and killed, or had caught and killed, in person and by my men, certain wild animals, to the prejudice of that bishop and the harm of ecclesiastical liberty. Coming to myself under a renewal of divine influence, I saw that these acts could in no wise be passed over uncorrected and in silence without peril to our souls. Therefore, making a personal approach to the aforesaid father and liege lord of mine, the lord bishop of Exeter, and having taken a corporal oath, I promise in good faith and under the duty of the oath I have taken that I shall in future, without backsliding, be faithful to the same lord bishop, his church, and his liberties and rights, and I shall not disobey by deed or word, or procure or permit such disobedience where I am able to oppose or resist it. And if – which God forbid – I should contravene the foregoing or any one of them, I desire and grant of my free will that *ipso facto* I should be thrust back under the earlier sentence of excommunication, and from then continually be denounced as excommunicate until I should make full and effective satisfaction both for the crimes set out above included in the earlier bond and for the contents and penalty of the present bond. And I shall restore the aforesaid park with suitable wild animals before next All Saints' Day at the dictate of Durandus, bailiff of the said lord bishop, save for three beasts which Sir John son of John caused to be caught in the same park. I promise to observe this formula of peace in good faith without any disobedience, under penalty of 100 marks to be paid to the same lord bishop if I should be duly convicted on this head, and I desire that this should apply to my person alone, reserving offences against the lord king, if – which God forbid – it should happen that I disobey in something. I renounce in this regard appeals, defences

– general as well as particular – royal writs of prohibition, and all [similar procedural devices] whether requested or able to be requested. In testimony whereof I have had my seal affixed to the present document. And at my request Sir Henry de Montfort and Solomon de Rochester, justiciars of the lord king, and the dean of Exeter [John Noble] affixed their seals. Witnessed by: Sirs J[ohn] Wyger, William de Fishacre, and Alexander de Oxton, knights'. Exeter, 22 July 1265 [sic].

1157 Collation by lapse of Brother Richard called Jordan, monk of Mont St Michel, as prior of Otterton (*Oterynton*). Fluxton, 11 April 1276.

1158 Collation by lapse of Brother Richard Perer, monk of Mont St Michel, as prior of St Michael's Mount. Fluxton, 11 April 1276.

[fo.71v] **1159** The bishop issued a sealed charter,[158] granting to Michael de Exton, smith, a perch of land to the east of the bridge at Bishop's Clyst (*Clyst Episcopi*), alongside and to the north of the king's highway where it runs east,[159] and to Richard Grendel, clerk, half an acre of land there, and a perch of land each there to Richard Proutz, John Clement, and Roger Clotere; the said Michael, Richard,[160] Richard, John and Roger, and their heirs and assigns, were to hold all the aforesaid lands, together with their appurtenances, in return for homage and service, from the bishop and his successors, in free tenure. They were to pay 12 pence annually, at the quarter days, for each perch of land as quittance for all secular service, although the bishop reserved the right to demand suit of court twice a year at his court of Clyst – by a reasonable summons (*per rationabilem summonitionem*); the relief payable on death or departure of a freeholder was six pence. Witnessed by Sirs Henry Champernowne, John son of Geoffrey, Roger called le Arceveske, Matthew de Egloshayle, knights, Michael de Bridewell, Serlo de Grendel, and Henry de Holbrook. [Bishop's] Clyst, 12 April 1276.

1160 In the hall of the bishop's London house, the abbot of Hailes swore obedience to the bishop, in the presence of Master John [de Pontoise], archdeacon of Exeter, Master Gervase [de Crediton], canon of Crediton, Sir Peter [de Guildford], chaplain, Richard de Grangiis, Sirs John Wyger, Roger le Arceveske, Roger de Priddy, Matthew de Egloshayle, and John Beaupré, knights. London, 27 April 1276.

1161 Inst. of Sir Adam de Stratton, subdeacon, to Milton [Damerel] (*Middelton*); patron, Amice, countess of Devon and lady of the Island (*domine Insule* [of Wight]). London, 29 April 1276.

---

[158] Mr N.W. Alcock suggests that this charter marks the foundation of the modern Bishop's Clyst, and that the village had formerly been at the north end of the manor, beside the bishop's court.
[159] This may well be the old Roman road between Lyme Regis and Exeter via Colyford.
[160] An otiose John has crept into the MS between the two Richards.

1162[161] The bishop, in a sealed letter, gave his consent to the case between John de Pontoise, rector of Tawstock, and William de Ditton, concerning the church of Tawstock, falling under the jurisdiction of the official of Canterbury. London, 26 April 1276.

1163[162] The bishop wrote to [Richard Carew], bishop of St David's, commissioning him to inquire further into the personal suitability of David, son of the noble Sir Nicholas son of Martin, as coming from his diocese. David had been canonically presented to the church of [fo.72] Bratton [Fleming], but the bishop was not sufficiently satisfied concerning the morals, orders, age, etc. of David to be able to institute him. The bishop of St Davids was to report his course of action to Bronescombe. London, 3 May 1276.

1164 Inst. of Odo de Arundel, subdeacon, to Lanivet; patron, Sir Laurence son of Richard, knight. London, 3 May 1276.

1165 Collation of Ralph de Arundel, clerk, to the prebend at Crantock which Stephen Haym had held. London, 3 May 1276.

1166 Inst. of Hugh de Cave, subdeacon, to Torbryan (*Thorrebrian*); patron, Guy de Brian. London, 4 May 1276.

1167 Collation of Master William de Wymondham, subdeacon, to the portion at St Teath which H[enry] de Christow had held. London, 5 May 1276.

1168 Inst. of Ralph de Hengham to Lanteglos; patron, the earl of Cornwall. London, 6 May 1276.

1169 Collation of John de Lardario to the prebend of Probus which Richard de Grangiis had held; John gave back the letter granting him a pension of 40 shillings,[163] which was cancelled. London 6 May 1276.

1170 Master Walter de Laking resigned his prebend at Probus. London, 6 May 1276.

1171 Inst. of David, son of Sir Nicholas son of Martin, subdeacon, to Bratton Fleming; patron, Richard de Fleming. Horsley, 10 May 1276.

1172 Inst. of Sir Payne de Liskeard, deacon, to St Stephen's, Cornwall;[164] patron, the earl of Cornwall. London, 6 May 1276.

1173 Master Hamund Parleben resigned Colan (*ecc. S. Culani*) in Cornwall, in the presence of Sir R[oger] de Dartford, Hugh Splot, Richard de Grangiis, and others. London, 6 May 1276.

[161] See note to **1177**.
[162] See **1147** and **1171**.
[163] See **1115**.
[164] St Stephen's in Brannel? Or by Saltash? Both lay in manors of the earl of Cornwall. Hingeston-Randolph preferred Saltash.

1174   Collation of Master William de Middleton, archdeacon of Canterbury, to the prebend [*ultra Exam*, in Exeter Castle] vacant by the voluntary resignation of Master Thomas de Wymondham. Faringdon, 17 May 1276.

[fo.72v] **1175***   The bishop wrote to [John de Esse], his official: 'The more the harmful appetite of offenders seeks to creep into what is forbidden, and the more damnably it drags them, fallen back into lawlessness, down to the doom of Gehenna with their accomplices, so much the more straitly must their audacity be punished. Brother William de Crook, abbot of Ford of the Cistercian Order in our diocese, on account of his manifest offences and repeated contumacies has been bound by the chains of the greater excommunication, as justice demands, both by us and by others, relying both on papal authority and that of the ordinary, and has been bound by a similar sentence by authority of the canons and proclaimed as thus involved, but he persists in his malice, drinking up curses like water, and has with hardened heart for too long endured such excommunication. Lest then the flock of the Lord which has been entrusted to our care may be infected dangerously by association with the said abbot, we command you, firmly enjoining you by your duty of obedience, that, in our cathedral church of Exeter and in every conventual, collegiate and parish church of our city and diocese, you should, both in person and through others whom you know to be trustworthy, on every Sunday and feast day, with ringing of bells and throwing of lighted candles to the ground, publicly and solemnly proclaim and have proclaimed that the said abbot is thus excommunicate, warning and having warned, according to the canons, all Christ's faithful who are subject to us to abstain from associating or trading with, serving or obeying the said abbot, and in any other kind of social (*civili modo*) way from adherence or support to him for whom no excuse may be made, until such time as he returns to the unity of the Church and deserves to obtain the benefit of absolution. If indeed you shall find, after due investigation, that any persons are associating with the same abbot after your canonical warnings, you are to chastise them, punishing them with canonical sanctions. And you shall write back to us in latters patent, including the content of these letters, within a month of their receipt, as to how you have performed our command.' Horsley, 23 May 1276.

1176   The bishop wrote to R[obert Burnell], bishop of Bath and Wells, repeating much of his previous denunciation of William de Crook, abbot of Ford, and asking that, since Abbot William was frequently in the diocese of Bath and Wells, its bishop too should solemnly excommunicate him throughout the diocese with bell and candle [fo.73], until the abbot submitted and was absolved. London, 25 May 1276.

1177[165]   In a letter of signification the bishop notified the king that William de Crook, abbot of Ford, William de Ditton, clerk, and Agnes de Cruwys, all of his

---

[165] See O.F. Robinson, 'Canon law in theory and in practice: insights from a thirteenth century diocese' *Index* 22 (1994), 473–80. For letters of signification generally, see F.D. Logan, *Excommunication and the Secular Arm in Medieval England* (Toronto: Pontifical Institute of Mediaeval Studies, 1968).

diocese, were obdurate in their excommunication for more than 40 days; he therefore prayed the aid of the secular arm against them. London, 24 May 1276.

1178   Inst. of Sir Philip de Stoke Gabriel, priest, to the vicarage of the parish church of St Petrock, Bodmin; patrons, the prior and convent of Bodmin. Bishopsteignton, 28 July 1276.

1179   Inst. of Arnulph de Prawle, priest, to Woodleigh; patron, Sir Roger de Prawle. Bishopsteignton, 28 July 1276.

1180   Inst. of Nicholas de Totnes, priest, to St Olave's, Exeter; patrons, the prior and convent of St Nicholas', Exeter. Fluxton, 4 August 1276.

1181   A proxy for the court of Canterbury was issued to Master Richard Paz, canon of Crediton, to act on the bishop's behalf in the proceedings due on 17 August before the archbishop of Canterbury, with power to give security under pledge of the bishop's property. [Bishop's] Clyst, 6 August 1276.

1182   Collation of Sir Michael called the Archdeacon, subdeacon, to the prebend at Glasney vacant by the voluntary resignation of Master Robert de la More. Cargoll Park, 30 August 1276.

[fo.73v] **1183**   Dispensation by papal authority of Richard de St Mawgan, clerk, born of a subdeacon and a spinster, from his defect of birth in common form, with the additional clause that if in future he should fall into the same sin of incontinence and be duly convicted, the dispensation would be invalidated. Penryn, 7 September 1276.

1184   Dispensation of Michael de St Martin, clerk, born of a priest and a spinster, in identical form. Penryn, 7 September 1276.

1185* CHARTER. APPROPRIATION. A charter was issued in this form: 'To all who inspect the present letters Walter, by divine compassion bishop of Exeter, eternal greeting in the Lord. The purer the zeal and the greater the solemnity with which the Highest Majesty, by whose nod all things are disposed, is honoured from the fruit of our transitory possessions, the greater the wholesomeness whereby our human condition lawfully acquires such possessions. Wherefore, desiring that the famous memory of the highest herald of the heavenly court and the messenger of man's reparation, St Gabriel the Archangel, should be celebrated annually and forever with devout and solemn service on the second ferial day at the beginning of September in the collegiate church of St Thomas the Martyr at Glasney, we appropriate and by canonical appropriation annex and we bestow – with our beloved sons, our dean and chapter of Exeter, assenting to this with lawful consent – the church of Colan (*ecc. S.Coelani*) (of which the right of patronage and collation belongs to us by lawful acquisition, along with the fruits of the same) to be possessed in perpetuity to sustain perpetually the burdens of that service, on the aforementioned church of the aforesaid martyr and on the canons serving God and the Blessed Virgin there, for the salvation of the souls of us, our successors and our benefactors. We reserve an adequate vicarage, consisting of all the altarage, the glebeland and the greater tithes in fixed places to the value of 40 shillings a year, to be conferred by us and our successors in future times. We lay down that the sacristan of the church of the aforesaid martyr, and his successors after him, whom we desire, as this document attests, always to be canons in priest's orders and perpetually resident, should forever dispose of the fruits of the church thus appropriated and make distribution of them on the terms listed below: to wit, from the fruits of the aforesaid church, without any reduction whatever, the aforesaid sacristan and his successors after him are to distribute and pay in perpetuity to each vicar ten shillings each year and, on the model of the nine orders of angels, to each canon who makes his personal appearance at the aforesaid solemnity nine pence each year, and to each vicar present on the aforementioned day five pence; and they are to provide solemn lights − like those on Christmas Day − at both vespers and matins and at mass for as long as the aforementioned service lasts. And notwithstanding this, the same sacristan and his successors after him shall, each year on the day of the aforesaid solemnity, expend in perpetuity 60 shillings in bread for the poor and needy on behalf of the souls of ourselves, our successors and benefactors. We desire each and all of these things to be firmly observed and maintained, on pain of excommunication to be incurred *ipso facto* if they should do otherwise. [fo.74] In testimony whereof we have had our seal affixed to the present charter.' Glasney [in the manor of Penryn], 7 September 1276.

1186* TESTIMONIAL. 'To all who see or hear the present letters Walter, by divine compassion bishop of Exeter, eternal greeting in the Lord. Desiring − as is our duty − to bear witness to the truth, we bring to the notice of you all that Master Gerard de Cumerniaco, rector of the church of Madron (*ecc. S.Maderni in Cornub'*), in our diocese, was solvent on the feast of the Nativity of the Blessed Virgin in the year of grace 1276, and in continuous personal residence in the said church as his cure requires. In testimony whereof we have had our seal affixed to the present letters, at the instance of the said Master [Gerard].' Glasney, 8 September 1276.

1187 CHARTER. A sealed letter was issued, stating that, although the bishop had long ago collated, by lapse, Sir Matthew Bacon, priest, to St Michael Penkevel, this was not to prejudice the future rights of the patron, Sir J[ohn de Treiagu], and his heirs concerning the presentation of a suitable person to the diocesan. Cargoll Park, 9 September 1276.

1188 Master Gervase de Crediton, the bishop's clerk, canon of Crediton, made the bishop's commissary-general in the absence of the bishop or his official, with power of canonical coercion. Cargoll Park, 9 September 1276.

1189 Collation of Richard de Dartford, the bishop's clerk, subdeacon, to Lawhitton. Chudleigh, 19 September 1276.

1190 Collation of Master Robert de Penhark, subdeacon, to Lezant. Chudleigh, 19 September 1276.

1191   Inst. of Sir Elias de la Walle, priest, to Gidleigh; patron, William Probus. Chudleigh, 20 September 1276.

1192   Appropriation, with the consent of the dean and chapter, of the parish church of Farringdon and its fruits, the advowson of which the bishop had recently acquired as the free gift of Robert Giffard, the former patron,[166] for the maintenance of two chaplains in the chapel of St Gabriel [fo.74v] which the bishop had recently founded at Bishop's Clyst; an adequate vicarage was to be established. [Bishop's] Clyst, 27 September 1276.

1193   Collation of Master Thomas de Blandford, subdeacon, to Buckerell (*Bokerel*). [Bishop's] Clyst, 30 September 1276.

1194   Inst. of Sir Roger de Hampton, priest, to the vicarage of Tintagel (*ecc. S.Merth' de Tintagel*), presented by Brother William de Veruy, proctor of the abbess of Fontevrault, having a general and particular mandate to make presentations to vacant ecclesiastical benefices in her patronage. London, 21 October 1276.

1195   Inst. of Master Robert de Cumbe, subdeacon, to Moretonhampstead (*Morton*); patron, Sir Richard son of John. London, 27 October 1276.

1196   Inst. of Master Benet de S. Quintino to Holcombe Burnell (*Holecumbe*); patron, the lord R[obert Burnell], the bishop of Bath and Wells. London, 25 October 1276.

1197   A proxy for requesting, challenging and accepting a judge at the papal court was issued to Masters Edmund de Warfield, Nicholas de Honiton, and Richard Carswell, interchangeably, with powers of substitution. All other proxies of any kind at the papal court were expressly revoked, and this proxy was to remain valid until revoked; this proxy was made in duplicate. London, 28 October 1276.

[fo.75] **1198***   MEMORANDUM. 'It is to be recorded that, since a matter of dispute had arisen between the venerable father, the lord Walter, by God's grace bishop of Exeter, on the one part, and the religious men, William, abbot of Ford, and the convent there of the Cistercian Order in the Exeter diocese, on the other part, over various and diverse losses, wrongs, oppressions, contumacies and offences, repeatedly inflicted on the aforesaid bishop and his church by the aforementioned religious, at length the same parties were, at the instance and agency of the said religious, brought before the lord Edward, by God's grace illustrious king of England. The same lord king, being minded to put an end to the matter of the litigation so that the same parties might alike be spared [further] efforts and expenses, and perceiving that such a dispute belonged to the ecclesiastical forum and should be dealt with and brought to a conclusion by churchmen, asked and persuaded the same parties to negotiate amicably for

---

[166] This phrase is a variation on the terms given in Document **B** (fo.1d), to be found in Appendix 1, vol.3.

peace between themselves. On their agreeing to this, provided that the church-men had the capacity and knowledge to negotiate on spiritual matters, the said lord king nominated those prudent men, Master Walter Scammel, dean of Salisbury, and Master Thomas Bek, archdeacon of Dorset, professors of the civil and the canon law, as mediators to negotiate peace between the same parties; this was acceptable to the parties, and they expressly agreed to them as mediators of peace. Before them, on 22 October in the year of grace 1276 at Westminster, the claims, arguments and allegations were put forward on either side, and after the merits of each side's positions were more fully comprehended and weighed, the same abbot, in the name of himself and his aforesaid convent, in the presence of the said mediators and many others, gave to the aforemen-tioned lord bishop, voluntarily and with no power forcing him, 500 pounds sterling as bail into the hands of the said lord bishop, for the losses, wrongs, oppressions, as also the contumacies and offences inflicted on the aforemen-tioned lord bishop and his church by the same [religious]; and he promised that he would in good faith pay, under the regulation of the said dean and archdeacon, at a date or dates to be fixed in advance by them, these 500 pounds in whole or in part as they should think fit to rule on this for the honour of God and his Church, adding to or subtracting from the said sum. The said mediators in fact assigned the following day, in the same place as before, to the said parties for giving judgment on their regulation; when all the parties appeared before them at the said time and place, they deferred giving judgment on their regulation, although the aforesaid bishop appealed urgently for them to do so, but they assigned an excessively protracted date to the parties, although they appear to have no power to do this. The bishop's party did not accept this because by such delay many souls were put at risk. In testimony whereof the venerable father William [de Brouse], by God's grace bishop of Llandaff, Master [fo.75v] Henry de Kilkenny, canon of Chichester, and Master Ralph de Baudoc, canon of London, who had been invited for the foregoing together with many others, affixed their seals to the present letter.' Westminster, 23 October 1276.

1199 INDUCTION. Inst. of Sir Martin de Shaftesbury, chaplain, to a mediety of Petertavy (*Peterestavy*); patrons, the prior and convent of Plympton. *Titing'*, 4 November 1276.

1200 A letter was issued to the official [John de Esse], commanding him, in accordance with the canons of the [Second] Council of Lyons, to cite all the clerks in the city and diocese who held the title of canon, and had not been ordained priest, to appear for ordination on 19 December 1276 in St Stephen's, Launceston, on pain of deprivation; steps would be taken against the con-tumacious. On 16 December all such clerks were to appear in person to show their titles and to submit to examination.[167] [Bishop's] Clyst, 21 November 1276.

1201 Letters of signification of excommunication were sent to the king against Sir John Alet, knight, who had remained excommunicate for 40 days and more. Faringdon, 9 November 1276.

[167] Cf **1092**.

1202 Inst. of John de Forest, subdeacon, to Buckland (*Bocland*) [Monachorum];[168] patron, the lady Amice, countess of Devon. [Bishop's] Clyst, 23 November 1276.

1203 Sir John de Castle, vicar[-choral] in Exeter cathedral, was given custody of the hospital of St John, Exeter, with discretion in the administration of the hospital's property. Crediton [fo.76], 27 November 1276.

1204 Inst. of Sir Matthew de St Minver, chaplain, to the vicarage of St Minver (*ecc. S.Minefreda*); patrons, the prior and convent of Bodmin. Crediton, 30 November 1276.

1205 Inst. of Sir Peter de Dene, priest, to Zeal (*Sele*); patrons, the abbot and convent of Buckfast. [Bishop's] Nympton, 6 December 1276.

1206* 'The abbots of the Cistercian Order beseech the king's excellency and his council, as they besought them previously when they were in parliament at Winchester after the feast of St Hilary. They have an indult from the supreme pontiffs that no bishop or other person, even by reason of a delict, a contract, or a lawsuit, should have the power of promulgating any sentence whatever of excommunication against them, nor of jurisdiction except only in cases concerning matters of faith, and just as the [bishops'] jurisdiction is suspended in respect of the same religious in the spiritual arm, so their authority in the secular arm loses its force, especially since such sentence is in no way *ipso iure*; and the coercive power of the king's majesty ought to enforce only just sentences and not those which are unjust. Since the venerable father, the lord Walter, bishop of Exeter, has unjustly promulgated sentences of excommunication against the abbot of Ford, certain monks of his, and their servants, contrary to their privileges, and has obtained royal letters of caption against them, they humbly beg that the said caption, in whatever way granted, should be revoked.' [No date]

1207* 'Again, the said lord bishop, in person and through his officials, has excommunicated all the proctors and attorneys and servants of the said abbot and convent of Ford, and all who reap their harvests in the autumn, and all who cultivate their land and work in their mills, and he maintains the excommunication from day to day, for which reason the said abbot and convent can find nobody who dares to defend them in either secular or ecclesiastical court, particularly in the diocese of Exeter. For this reason they are suffering great wrongs, losses and injuries in their possessions and property and, unless a remedy is speedily applied, they will suffer to the utmost in future. The aforesaid abbot begs that a remedy for these [ills] be applied through the agency of the lord king and his council, so that it may not come about, through a sentence of such excommunication, that they are cheated of their just defence of their right, that their fields remain uncultivated and that these religious lack the necessities of life. For the aforesaid lord bishop has no other intention, as it appears, but to

[168] As identified by Hingeston-Randolph.

overthrow the said religious entirely and to destroy and overturn their house.'
[No date]

1208 Inst. of James de Mohun, subdeacon, to Walkhampton (*Walchampton*);
patron, the lady Amice, countess of Devon. Lawhitton, 19 December 1276.

1209 Inst. of Sir Solomon de Rochester to Ilfracombe (*Ilfredecumbe*); patron, Sir
H[enry] de Champernowne. Lawhitton, 20 December 1276.

[fo.76v] **1210** Inst. of Master Ralph de Hydon, deacon, to Clayhidon (*Hydon*),
vacant by reason of the Council; patron, Sir John Hydon, knight. Lawhitton,
20 December 1276.

1211 Collation of Master Peter de Exeter,[169] archdeacon of St David's, to the
prebend in Exeter which Sir Henry de Montfort had held. Lawhitton,
20 December 1276.

1212 Inst. of Sir Alan de Sanckeslond, priest, to Merton; patron, Sir John
Wyger, knight, as guardian of the lands and heir of the late Walter de Merton,
knight. St German's, 28 December 1276.

1213[170] Inst. of Brother John, monk of St Martin des Champs, as prior of St
James by Exeter; patrons, the prior (Peter) and convent of St Martin des
Champs, Paris. And Brother John swore obedience to the bishop. Paignton,
6 January 1277.

1214 Collation, by authority of the Council,[171] of Sir Ralph de Kennford,
chaplain, to the vicarage of Bishopsteignton; he was instituted by Sir Peter de
Guildford, the bishop's chaplain, who was then present at that manor, and he
had a charter at the bishop's order. Bishopsteignton, 11 January 1277.

1215* The bishop issued a proxy: 'Let all know that we make, ordain and
appoint Masters John de Pontoise, rector of the church of Tawstock in our
diocese, and Richard de Carswell as our proctors, interchangeably, for the
action or actions which Brother William, abbot of Ford, and his convent of the
Cistercian Order, or also Master William de Ditton have raised against us [fo.77]
or intend to raise before whatsoever judge or auditor of the the papal court is
appointed or will be appointed, [with power] to raise or defend an action, put
forward a defence or a replication, join issue, take oath of calumny and of truth
on our behalf, offer any other kind of oath, advance and reply to *positiones*,
produce witnesses and public documents, and also to oppose charges and prove
defects, seek the benefit of absolution and restoration to original status however
often and whenever there shall be need, appeal and pursue an appeal, substitute
another proctor or proctors in their place, resume the proxy where or when it
shall seem expedient, and do each and all the other things which we could do in

---

[169] This is Peter Quivil, the next bishop.
[170] For some reason, the presentation, dated 20 September 1276, is given in full.
[171] This phrase was added above the line, with no further explanation.

the foregoing cases or business if we were present. We promise to ratify and confirm whatever the same proctors or one of them, or any substitute by one or other of them, shall do on our behalf in the foregoing matters, and we promise to pay, under hypothecation of our property, whatever shall be adjudged on behalf of the same, or one of them, or of a substitute or substitutes for either or both of them. We also ratify whatever has so far been done whether for our benefit or disadvantage by Master Mathias Thiatynus, our permanent attorney (*defensor*) in the papal court, before the venerable Master John de Rocca, papal chaplain, and *auditor causarum* of that palace, in the case which Master William de Ditton has brought or is bringing against us in the aforementioned court. In testimony whereof we have had our seal affixed to the present letters.' Bishopsteignton, 11 January 1277.

1216[172]　　Inst. of Henry de Shonholt, subdeacon, to Portlemouth; patron, Sir Alan son of Roald, knight. Bishopsteignton, 12 January 1277.

1217　　Inst. of Simon de Hydon, deacon, to Hemyock (*Hemioc*), vacant by reason of the Council; patron, Sir John de Hydon, knight. Chudleigh, 19 January 1277.

1218　　Inst. of Robert de Cotton, clerk and deacon, to Clyst Hydon, vacant by reason of the Council; patron, William de Hydon. Crediton, 2 February 1277.

1219　　Inst. of Sir Walter de Torrington, priest, to the vicarage of Dean Prior; patrons, the prior and convent of Plympton. Bishopsteignton, 5 February 1277.

[fo.77v] **1220**　　Inst. of Sir Adam Payne, subdeacon, to Honiton (*Honeton*); patron, the lady Isabella de Forz, countess of Aumale and Devon and Lady of the Isle [of Wight].[173] Fluxton, 16 February 1277.

1221　　Inst. of William de Heanton, subdeacon, to St John's by Antony; patron, Sir William de Alneto, knight. Chudleigh, 10 March 1277.

1222*[174]　　The bishop wrote to [John de Pontoise] the archdeacon of Exeter. 'Among the other anxieties of pastoral care which rest upon us, the reason for the coming of our Redeemer, Who came not only for the sake of the just but for all who had died, unceasingly arouses the duty of our office and diligently summons us to watch over the safety of souls, wholesomely to preserve in health the sheep of the flock entrusted to us, and by the remedy of salvation to lead back those to the path of truth who have strayed in error so that they may be cured, lest — which God forbid — they perish through our dissimulation, and we be punished by God's judgment for our negligence on their account. Indeed, certain of our parishioners through a certain very great ignorance of letters do not know the statutes of the canons and the traditions of the holy fathers, and

---

[172] This entry, but dated 7 January, is repeated, with a *vacat*.
[173] Widow of William de Forz, count of Aumale, and countess of Devon in her own right, 1263–93.
[174] Compare *Councils and Synods* II 1, 33.

have frequently fallen under sentences of excommunication announced by such holy fathers from the days of old, which we relate with sorrow, and unwisely believe that they may do what is unlawful; in order that the snare of such sentences may be with circumspection avoided and the blindness of ignorance shut out, we command you, firmly enjoining you under your duty of obedience and under canonical penalty, that you should have the articles set out below, on account of which sentence of excommunication is incurred *ipso facto*, published by the parish priests in every collegiate and parish church of your archdeaconry on every Sunday and solemnity, and those who fall under the same sentences proclaimed as excommunicate. By our authority you are to enjoin on every rector, vicar and parish priest of such churches that each of them should , within a month, have the contents of the present letter clearly posted up in a prominent place in their churches, under threat of a penalty to be assessed at the judgment of the ordinary. You are to inform us within a month, in letters patent including the content of these letters, as to how you have executed our command.

The content of the articles is as follows:[175] We, Walter, by God's grace bishop of Exeter, proclaim as excommunicate (concerning the Church's privilege) all those who presume maliciously to deprive churches of their rights or through malice strive to infringe or disturb their liberties; (the peace of the realm) all those who presume wrongfully to disturb the tranquillity of the peace of the lord king and of his realm; (false witnesses) all those who knowingly and deliberately bear false witness or arrange for it to be given, and also those who produce such witnesses or suborn them in matrimonial cases where an action is being brought against a marriage or for the disinheritance of anyone; (impediments to marriage) all those who, in matrimonial cases, maliciously raise objections or have them raised whereby true marriages fail to have their due force; (the Great Charter) all those who by any art or device violate, infringe, diminish or alter, secretly or openly, by deed, word or counsel, the long established and approved customs of the realm, and especially the liberties and free customs contained in the charters of common liberties and concerning forests which have been granted by the lord king to the archbishops, bishops and other prelates of the realm of England, and to earls, barons, knights and other free tenants, by rashly contravening them or any of them [fo.78] in any article whatever; (making statutes against the liberties of England) all those who promulgate, or observe when promulgated, statutes against those [liberties] or any of them, or who introduce customs or observe those that have been introduced, including the writers of those statutes as well as those who counselled or put them into effect, or presume to judge in accordance with them; (asylum in church) all those who violently drag away fugitives who seek refuge in a church, graveyard or cloister or forbid them the necessities of life, or carry off, have carried off, or authorise the carrying off of things deposited in the same places, or publicly or secretly offer help, counsel or consent to such persons; (violence to clergy) all who lay violent hands on clerics; (setting fire to churches) those who set fires publicly or break into churches; (laying waste the fields) those who lay waste the fields; (clerical property on farms, etc) all those who presume to waste, carry off or appropriate things from the houses, manors, granges, parks, vineyards, or any other such places belonging to the archbishops, bishops or other ecclesiastical

---

[175] The contents are set out with marginal headings, as underlined.

persons, without the consent of the owners or custodians; (violation of episcopal sequestrations) all those who violate episcopal sequestrations or disturb the jurisdiction of the ordinary, through whom there is no doubt that the liberties of the Church are infringed; all these we proclaim excommunicate.'

1223 Inst. of Sir Robert de la Hope, priest, to the prebend or portion in Chulmleigh (*Caumeleye*) which Master William de Stanford had held; patron, Hugh de Courtenay.

[fo.78v] **1224** A sealed memorandum was issued. To settle the dispute between the bishop and the abbot and convent of Ford, King Edward had appointed as mediators Walter Scammel, dean of Salisbury, and Thomas Bek, archdeacon of Dorset; under their influence the abbot had given a pledge for 50 pounds to the bishop.[176] The mediators appointed a date during the next parliament, to be held at Westminster, after Easter, for giving their award to the parties. On 1 May 1277, during the parliament at Westminster, the parties appeared in person before the mediators and submitted themselves to their arbitration, under penalty of 100 pounds to be paid by the party disobeying the award to the other party; furthermore, the king was to have power to constrain their obedience. However, any dispute concerning the church or manor of Ottery St Mary, or the house which the abbot and convent held near the court of the bishop in the city of Exeter, was to be excluded from the settlement. Westminster, 5 May 1277.

[fo.79] **1225*** 'To all who inspect the present letters, Masters Walter Scammel, dean of Salisbury, and Thomas Bek, archdeacon of Dorset, eternal greeting in the Lord. Let all know that when a matter of dispute had arisen between the venerable father Walter, by God's grace bishop of Exeter, on the one part, and the religious men, brother William, abbot of Ford, and the convent of the same place, on the other, concerning certain sentences of suspension, interdict and excommunication they had passed upon each other, and other wrongs, oppressions, contumacies and personal offences, the same parties, for their own tranquillity and peace regarding the foregoing matters, freely and voluntarily consented to us as their arbiters, definitors, ordainers, award givers or decision makers, submitting themselves totally, high and low, to our arbitration, judgment, ordinance, award and decision, as is more fully contained in the deed, sealed with the seals of the parties, drawn up concerning this. Therefore we, Masters Walter, dean of Salisbury, and Thomas, archdeacon of Dorset, having heard, and quite fully understood, the arguments and allegations of the parties put forward before us concerning all the wrongs, oppressions, contumacies and personal offences arisen between the venerable father Walter, by God's grace bishop of Exeter, on the one part, and the religious men, brother William, abbot of Ford, and the convent of the same place, on the other, and after the merits of each side's positions were weighed, we pronounce:

In the name of the Lord, Amen. We ordain, we command, we award that the aforesaid abbot, on behalf of himself and his convent, for the honour of the lord

---

[176] So far the memorandum is in almost identical terms to **1198**.

bishop of Exeter and his church of Exeter, is publicly and solemnly, and in person in Exeter cathedral, to proclaim in writing and have proclaimed that all sentences of suspension, interdict and excommunication promulgated by the same abbot *de facto* to the prejudice of the lord bishop be null, invalid and void – this before the feast of the Nativity of St John the Baptist (24 June), and in the places where the same abbot had published or arranged to have published such sentences.

The secular officials of the same abbot and convent, who are not exempt from episcopal jurisdiction, are bound by the sentences of suspension and excommunication issued by the authority of the same lord bishop for their crimes and offences; they are, before the aforesaid feast, when told by the same lord [bishop], to appear with bared heads, ungirt and without shoes, to walk humbly and devoutly from the graveyard gate of St Peter's, Exeter, to the main doors of the cathedral, and to receive a single measure of discipline on the spot from the same bishop or someone delegated by him, and, furthermore, be liable to receive any other penance which the same lord [bishop] should think fit to impose on them.

Also, the same abbot, on behalf of himself and his community, is to promise 1,000 marks sterling to the aforementioned bishop for the settlement of all the wrongs, oppressions, contumacies and personal offences fallen on him through the abbot and convent, and to pay them at the mediators' behest; the same abbot, on behalf of himself and his convent, promised that he would, in good faith, pay this 1000 marks to the said lord bishop in accordance with our regulation. Arising from the foregoing, the same abbot and convent are completely to renounce all actions and personal offences competent to the aforesaid abbot and convent against the previously mentioned bishop and any others.

We desire, further, we command and award that the previously mentioned lord bishop, making no difficulties, should relax all sentences of suspension, interdict and excommunication promulgated by authority of the same lord, arising from such wrongs, against the foregoing abbot, his monks, lay-brothers and their exempt officials, [fo.79v] so as to remove even the slightest weight from their consciences. And the lord bishop, after he has touched the 1000 marks, is to remit all but 100 to the aforesaid abbot and convent. But the same lord bishop has voluntarily and freely remitted to the same the aforesaid 1000 marks, all but 100 marks, as a favour to religion and the lord king, and at our request; this 100 marks the same abbot or his successors, on behalf of him and his convent, is to pay in full to the lord bishop or his assign in the said cathedral church, in equal instalments, at next Michaelmas and Easter. If the same lord bishop shall see fit to enjoin any penance on the already mentioned officials, beyond the discipline referred to above, once that discipline has been received, he is, making no difficulty, to remit [such penance].

We also decree that each and all of the foregoing are to be observed inviolably by the aforesaid parties under pain of 100 pounds, and that the party resiling from this, our arbitrament, shall pay in its entirety and without delay the said 100 pounds to the party observing the award. As to this, we reserve to the lord king and to ourselves the power to coerce and compel the party resiling from our decree concerning payment of the aforesaid fine.'
Westminster, 5 May 1277.

1226   A bond was issued under the bishop's seal, admitting a debt of 60 marks sterling to Godfrey [Giffard], bishop of Worcester, arising out of the composition made between the bishop of Worcester and the prior and brothers of the Hospital of Jerusalem in England, which Bronescombe had brought about. The 60 marks would be paid to the bishop of Worcester or his attorney within a fortnight of payment being requested. London, 10 May 1277.

1227   A dispute had arisen between Godfrey [Giffard], bishop of Worcester, and the prior and brothers of the Hospital of Jerusalem in the province of England concerning the church of St Mary, Down Ampney (*Dounhameneye*), in the diocese of Worcester, which the Hospitallers alleged had been appropriated to them by Pope Clement IV, while the aforesaid bishop found their letters suspect and defective; various disputes had been raised before various judges in the matter of this church . . .[177]

[fo.80] **1228**   Inst. of Sir Jordan de Wimborne Minster to Burrington (*Burninton*); patrons, the abbot and convent of Tavistock.[178] Crediton, 21 July 1277.

[fo.80v] **1229**[179]   The bishop wrote to his four archdeacons, of Exeter, of Totnes, of Cornwall and of Barnstaple, and their officials, reminding them of the previous sentences of *ipso facto* excommunication published through all the churches of the city and diocese of Exeter against all those who with malice should presume to deprive churches of their rights or to infringe or disturb their liberties; all those who wrongfully disturbed the rights of the king and his realm and its tranquillity; or obstructed the execution of the king's commands; all those who in any way at all have infringed, diminished or changed the approved customs of the realm or its liberties, as contained in the charters of common liberties and of the forest granted by the king to the archbishops, bishops and other prelates of England, and to the earls, barons, knights and freeholders, or who have introduced new customs. Every one deliberately doing these things was to know that he was *ipso facto* bound by such sentence; if he had done it in ignorance he was to be warned, and to put matters right within a fortnight of such warning, and to make satisfaction as required by his bishop. Careful of his flock ('for there is no excusing the shepherd if the wolf eats the sheep without the shepherd's knowledge' – *cum non sit pastoris excusatio si lupus comedat oves et pastor nesciat*), the bishop ordered the archdeacons to proclaim all this throughout the counties of Devon and Cornwall, in every chapter and congregation. Furthermore, William de Tavistock, Thomas Noel, Osbert Mark, Noel de Trevilla, Peter le Marshal, John de Sackville and John le Portel, in spite of canonical warnings, were continuing to erode what was established to be glebeland at Mylor (*ecc. S.Melori*), to the prejudice of that church, and so had specifically fallen under this excommunication. Glasney, 14 August 1277.

[177] The entry tailed off here, perhaps as not relevant in the register. There is no mention of the affair in Giffard's Register.
[178] Since this entry is repeated on the next folio, and the rest of the page was left blank at this time, it seems likely that this page was meant to be discarded; see Introduction, vol.I, p.x ff.
[179] Compare **1222**.

[fo.81] **1230**[180] Inst. of Sir Jordan de Wimborne, priest, to Burrington (*Berington*); patrons, the abbot and convent of Tavistock. Crediton, 21 July 1277.

1231 Inst. of Sir William de Carnavald, priest, to Ruan Minor (*ecc. de S.Rumano Parvo*) in the manor of Tredevos; patron, Sir Oliver de Dynham, knight, as guardian of the lands and heir of Sir Robert de Carminov. St Germans, 27 July 1277.

1232 Collation of Sir David de St Buryan, priest, to the vicarage of Manaccan; Cargoll Park, 20 August 1277.

1233 Inst. of Master Stephen de Cockington, subdeacon, to Huntsham (*Honesawe*); patron, the lady Joan de Champernowne. Paignton, 18 September 1277.

1234 Inst. of Philip de Bokywis, subdeacon, to East Worlington (*Estwlfrinton*); patron, Robert de Cronthorn, lord of East Worlington. Paignton, 18 September 1277.

1235 Inst of Reginald called le Arceveske, subdeacon, to Poundstock (*Ponntestok'*); patron, Sir William de Bodrugan as guardian of the lands and heir of Sir Roger de Bodrugan. Paignton, 18 September 1277.

1236 Dispensation, at the command of Brother Martin, the papal penitentiary, of William de Crediton, priest, for the irregularity incurred when he had had himself ordained by bishops other than his ordinary without licence. Bishopsteignton, 23 September 1277.

1237 The bishop appointed the treasurer of Exeter cathedral, Sir Richard de Braundesworthy, canon of Exeter, and Brother William, prior of Clive, his commissaries for the cases in progress or to be heard between John de Esse, archdeacon of Cornwall, and Richard, prior of Bodmin, concerning tithes, wrongs and other matters, reserving definitive judgment to himself. Exeter, 2 October 1277.

[fo.81v] **1238** The bishop appointed Master Thomas de Buckland, canon of Crediton, his commissary-general to assist the official in all matters coming before the bishop *ex officio*, enjoying the same jurisdiction as the official but without revoking any other jurisdiction. Fluxton, 14 October 1277.

1239*[181] The bishop wrote to his official [John de Esse]. 'Since it is public and notorious that John de Alet, knight, and Isabella de Albo Monasterio defiled themselves by adultery during the marriage between Isabella and Reginald de Albo Monasterio, her former husband, and, the same Reginald being now dead, the said John and Isabella have lived together in the aforesaid debauchery of the flesh according to the practice of their former life, to the scandal of the whole

---

[180] See note to **1228**.
[181] See O.F. Robinson, 'Canon law and marriage', *JurRev* (1984) 22–40.

Church and to the peril of their souls, and since on this account no small suspicion has arisen that they had fallen under the legal ruling by which an adulterer cannot be joined in marriage to an adulteress even after she is lawfully released from her former husband; and because the same John and Isabella are [allegedly] related to each other in a degree of consanguinity forbidden by law and on this account it was long ago brought to their attention, not without cause on our part, that it was publicly prohibited and forbidden under threat of sanction that they should in any way live together or be joined to each other in marriage until the truth of the matter was investigated more fully; scorning our ban, with ill intent they removed themselves to distant parts, and clandestinely brought about in fact what they could not do in law, the making of mutual promises of marriage. After the perpetration of such a deed, and its being frequently brought to our ears by busy rumour, we could not, and indeed we ought not, without grave scandal to the Church and danger to their souls, allow such an offence to pass under our conniving eyes through negligence. We therefore gave you charge that you should in due form take cognizance of and diligently inquire into these matters; having exercised your jurisdiction in the said affair, you found out the full truth of the story and, after canonical warnings and prohibitions repeatedly made to the parties in canonical form, you lawfully pronounced in writing successive sentences of interdict and the greater excommunication against them on account of their disobedience and many and manifest contumacies. But with hardness of heart they have long persisted under this sentence of excommunication, with gross contempt for the Keys of the Church. Therefore we command you, so ordering lest the Lord's flock suffer ill from their unlawful communion or be infected, that you should see that the said sentence of excommunication, in the form fully written down above, is renewed throughout all our diocese, in the chapters of the archdeacons and in each conventual and parish church, on every Sunday and feast day, with the ringing of bells and the dashing of lit candles to the ground, and that the parties should be publicly proclaimed excommunicate until they should return to the unity of the Church and become worthy to obtain the benefit of absolution in due form.' Faringdon, 24 November 1277.

[fo.82] **1240**   The bishop renewed his sealed letters patent, dated 13 August 1269 at Newlyn, confirming the taxation of the vicarage of St Keverne. Bishop William [Brewer] had appropriated the church to the abbot and convent of Beaulieu, and with the consent of the then abbot, Sir Acius, and the convent, had taxed the vicarage at 15 marks a year, payable, in two instalments, to Benedict, the then vicar and his successors, until the abbot and convent should provide portions of 15 marks value from the property of the church, with the condition that the vicar should bear all the customary burdens of the diocese and the archdeaconry. Bronescombe had admitted William de Portway, priest, to the vicarage, at the presentation of Sir Denis, abbot of Beaulieu, and the convent. The abbot and convent assigned, with the bishop's consent, to the vicar and his successors, in place of the 15 marks a year, all the altarage – except for all the tithes of fish – and also the houses in which the vicars customarily lived, together with the tithes of beans and peas growing in the curtilages, but the tithes of beans and peas and other crops grown in the fields were reserved for the abbot and convent. The vicar was to bear all the ordinary burdens, and also the cost of books and vestments, and the roofing of the chancel. Faringdon, 1 January 1278.

1241   The bishop wrote to [John de Noble], the dean of Exeter, and to [John de Esse], the official, that he had received a letter from John [Chishull], bishop of London, containing a letter from R[obert Kilwardby], archbishop of Canterbury. It ran: 'We recall that, in our common assembly held a little while ago at Northampton,[182] various items of business touching alike the advantage and the honour of the whole English church [fo.82v] were publicly put forward, yet, although by common opinion ways were devised to give them effect, and persons deputed to organize these ways, the outcome of various affairs, or the putting into effect of the same, is still not clear to us, some indeed being completely unaccomplished, and certain new matters have emerged which tend to the overthrow of rights, customs and liberties and to the grave danger of the English church. We therefore command you, my brother, by the present documents, that you should have all your brothers, fellow bishops or suffragans, summoned peremptorily by your letters through our authority to meet with us in their own persons in London on 15 January, together with some senior persons from their chapters, the archdeacons and the proctors of the whole clergy, from each diocese, to deal effectively with the previously mentioned affairs, both past and present, so that a satisfactory end may be put to the same by the mediation of our common counsel, so that things uncertain may be made certain, things incomplete be completed, and matters now arising receive the new help that they ought. And you are to take care to notify us of how you have executed our command through your letters patent, including the contents of these letters. *Setlingdon*, 16 November 1277.' The bishop of London therefore cited Bronescombe to appear in accordance with the archbishop's mandate in letters dated 24 November 1277 at Windsor. Bronescombe, as well as forwarding the citation, ordered the dean to appear at this provincial council in person, with others from the chapter. Horsley, 9 December 1277.

1242*   The bishop issued a letter to [John Noble] the dean of Exeter and [John de Esse] the official: 'The heavier the punishment imposed upon those who abandon the decrees of the canons in any way and are convicted of this, the more strictly the same should be observed. Since therefore at this time in our region a visitation is impending, to be made by the archbishop of Canterbury who has already, it is said, after the example of Him Who sits on the throne and from Whose mouth proceeds the two-edged sword, proceeded in those parts already visited to put into effect the [decrees of] the canons and councils, without regard to persons; because indeed darts seen in advance are said to do less harm, we, wishing rather to anticipate than be anticipated, especially in those matters which have long since come to our ears by the repeated account of trustworthy persons, viz. that our archdeacons, their officials and assistants are not afraid heavily to burden those subject to them by exacting procurations from places they have not visited, contrary to the decrees of the canons, and by other various kinds of oppression which, there is no doubt, contravene the canons as laid down, to the danger of their souls and to the scandal and offence of many; some

---

[182] See *Councils and Synods* II 2, 822–6 at 826.

of them spend what has thus been extorted and other revenues on luxuries outside our diocese and not in the places where they should. And because that which is liable to weakness or disparagement ought, as the canons urge, to be the subject of precautions, we command you, firmly enjoining you by your duty of obedience, that [fo.83] you proclaim and have proclaimed to all our archdeacons, under pain of the canons, that they reside in the places to which they are attached, as they are bound to do, to fulfil their duty according to the terms of the canons, and to make satisfaction concerning those things which are known to have been done up till now by them and their assistants, without forethought and against the canons, as they should wish to escape canonical punishment. You are to proclaim further to all those subject to these archdeacons that when the latter come to them for the purpose of a visitation, they should meet them properly, in accordance with the terms of the Council, without any kind of excess. Further, you are to proclaim and have publicly proclaimed that all those subject to us who hold any cure or administration whatever should study so to conduct themselves in their cure, office or benefice, that they may be fit to render worthy accounts for the same to the one God. You are to inform us before the feast of St Hilary (14 January)' etc. Horsley, 9 December 1277.

1243 A proxy was issued to Ralph de la Pole, clerk, giving him full powers, including accepting any sort of appeal,[183] for all litigation affecting the bishop at the court of Canterbury. London, 21 January 1278.

1244 A proxy was issued in the same terms with the addition of the clause which had been interlined. London, 21 January 1278.

[fo.83v] **1245** A proxy was issued to Master John de Pontoise, rector of Tawstock, giving him full powers to represent the bishop in litigation involving Master William de Ditton at the papal court. The bishop also ratified whatever had been done on his behalf by Matthew Thyatinus, the bishop's permanent attorney at the same court, before the venerable Master John de Rocca, papal chaplain and *auditor causarum* in the papal palace, with regard to William de Ditton.[184] The bishop revoked the proxy issued on 11 January 1277 to Master John [de Pontoise] and Richard de Carswell as far as Richard was concerned. London, 14 January 1278.

1246 A proxy was issued to Masters Edmund de Warefield and Nicholas de Honiton, interchangeably, for the papal court; the bishop revoked all other proxies whatsoever at the papal court.[185] London, 14 January 1278.

---

[183] This clause was added above the line.
[184] See **1215**.
[185] I do not know how to reconcile this with the preceding entry. J.A. Brundage suggests that it was simply a clerical mistake to insert the routine revocation clause, and that the bishop wanted to appoint three proctors under two mandates, one to John alone, one to Edmund and Nicholas jointly.

[fo.84] **1247** The bishop acknowledged, in sealed letters patent, a loan, made to him and his church by Duracius Huberti and Jacobus Scoldi on their own behalf and that of their partners, also citizens and merchants of Florence, of 100 marks sterling – the mark being reckoned at 13 shillings and 4 pence – for the needs of his church. He renounced any defence of the money not having actually been paid over (*pecunia non numerata*), and promised to repay the money to the said merchants, to one of them, or to their messenger bearing the present letters, at the New Temple in London at Pentecost (5 June); if he should fail to repay the money on the said date, he promised to make good to the same merchants all the losses, costs and expenses they had incurred in any way by this failure. The bishop pledged all the property of himself and his church, moveable and heritable, ecclesiastical and secular, present and future as security for the merchants. He further renounced all defences of civil and canon law, and any other delaying tactic, and accepted any forum they should choose. London, 23 January 1278.

[fo.84v] **1248*** The bishop wrote to [Henry de Bollegh], the archdeacon of Totnes: 'The burden of our office presses upon us with so heavy a weight that our care to remain with due diligence on watch both day and night scarcely suffices to lighten the pressure of so great a burden, for as the people grows so grows evil with them in their sins. We have, through you and the local archdeacons, had summoned frequently before us those holding benefices in our diocese that they may receive holy orders as the status of each demands, and further had them canonically warned that they must reside in their benefices as they are required to do. Although we could earlier have imposed punishments more severely for diverse contumacies and offences of this kind, yet humane tenderness compelled us to put off the penalties which the care of our pastoral solicitude, mindful of justice alone, urged us to impose. Because, however, we dare no longer put off imposing, as the law demands, the canonical penalties due for their deserts upon those delinquents – lest perchance the Bridegroom should come and find us sleeping – we order you, firmly enjoining you that you should diligently make inquiry, and have inquiry made, throughout the whole archdeaconry of Cornwall as to which beneficed clergy, having the cure of souls, are not ordained priests, or who, although ordained priest, are not carrying out their office as they are bound to do, thus mocking both their Redeemer and the order of priesthood; who are not personally resident in their benefices; who, while present in body but absent in spirit, know more of earthly and carnal than heavenly matters, receiving their silver penny but not cultivating the Lord's vineyard. And further we suspect that there are some who waste the patrimony of the Crucified, received from our hands and that of our predecessors, because they spend the property of their churches, over and beyond the necessities of their own living, not for the adorning of these churches and the other purposes set out by ecclesiastical canons, but on luxuries, or in business dealings through men of straw, or hand it out to their carnal companions, or purchase temporal possessions, defrauding their churches of such property. Of such as these, as far as is possible, you are to make strict and truthful inquiry. You are also to inquire diligently as to who holds benefices in plurality, contrary to the enactments of the General Council and other canonical decrees, appointing a date for those who are present, and peremptorily citing the absent to appear before our official,

or another acting in our stead, in the chapel of St Michael by Cowick on the day
after *Laetare* Sunday [27 March 1278], to show their papal dispensations, if they
have them, or to do and receive what the course of the law dictates, constraining
any you should find who challenge you or rebel with ecclesiastical censure. For
our part, we will have inviolably observed the sentences of excommunication,
suspension and interdict which you properly impose on the rebels until, God
willing, fitting satisfaction is made. Moreover, because we have entrusted to you
by word of mouth certain matters to be put into effect for the common good
which were recently laid down at the council of prelates and clergy of the
province of Canterbury,[186] concerning which we desire you to show undoubted
fidelity, we make known to all by the content of the present letters that we shall
confirm as right and approved whatever shall be done by you in this affair. You
are to certify to us or our official, at the aforesaid day and place, how you have
carried out this our command as to the appointment of dates and the issuing of
citations, as written above, through your letters patent, including the content of
these letters; over other matters, you are to give a dutiful and faithful report
when so required.' [Bishop's] Clyst, 20 February 1278.

[fo.85] **1249**   An identical letter was sent to [John de Esse] the archdeacon of
Cornwall for the archdeaconry of Exeter.[187] [No date]

1250   An identical letter was sent to Master Thomas de Buckland for the
archdeaconries of Totnes and Barnstaple. [No date]

1251   A letter was issued to [Henry de Bollegh] the archdeacon of Totnes,
requiring him to cite Master Richard de Clifford to appear before the bishop, or
those acting in his stead, in the conventual church of St Nicholas, Exeter, on
4 April, in that he was holding several ecclesiastical benefices without a papal
dispensation, for him to reply to the charges brought against him, and to receive
what the law required. [Bishop's] Clyst, 20 February 1278.

1252   The bishop commended to Sir Adam de Champaus, priest, the custody
of Bondleigh (*Boneleg'*) until next 1 May; patron, Sir Robert de Champaus,
knight. Crediton, 21 February 1278.

1253   Inst. of Master Thomas de Swansea, subdeacon, to South Molton
(*Suthmolton*); patron, Sir Nicholas son of Martin, knight. Crediton, 21 February
1278.

1254   Inst. of Sir William de Winkleigh, priest, to the vicarage of Okehampton
(*Ochampton*); patrons, the prior and convent of Cowick. Crediton, 22 February
1278.

1255*   The bishop wrote to [John Noble], the dean of Exeter. 'Because we
propose, if God disposes, to carry out the duty of visitation, as is incumbent on
us, on the Thursday before the feast of St Gregory, pope, [10 March] and to deal

---

[186] *Councils and Synods* II 2, 824–6.
[187] *Item consimilis litera directa fuit archidiacono Cornub' pro archidiaconatu Exon'.*

with some difficult business concerning that cathedral, we command you to summon or have summoned each and all of the canons of the said church who can conveniently be present to be present in person together with you on the said day in the said place to take part in the duty of such a visitation and to receive what justice shall urge.' The dean was to inform the bishop when he had carried out this task. Plympton, 2 March 1278.

1256 Inst. of Sir Richard de Combe, priest, to the vicarage of Brampford [Speke] (*Braumford*), to be taxed again if the previous taxation was insufficient; patrons, the prior and convent of St Nicholas, Exeter. [Bishops]teignton, 4 March 1278.

1257 Collation of Sir Peter de Guildford, the bishop's chaplain, to the Appledram (*Apeldreham*) prebend of Bosham vacant by the confirmation of Master William de Middleton as bishop-elect of Norwich. Exeter, 18 March 1278 – 'in the twenty-first year of the bishop's consecration'.

[fo.85v] **1258** Inst. of Master Michael, deacon, to Redruth, under pain of the Council; patron, Sir Laurence Basset, knight. Fluxton, 11 March 1278.

1259 Inst. of Sir Roger de Yarcombe, chaplain, to the vicarage of Dunkeswell parish church, to be taxed again if the previous taxation was insufficient; patrons, the abbot and convent of Dunkeswell. Fluxton, 12 March 1278.

1260 Inst. of Gilbert de Rochester, subdeacon, to High Bickington (*Buketon*);[188] patron, the lady Joan de Champernowne. Fluxton, 12 March 1278.

1261 Inst. of Sir Henry son of Warin, chaplain, to Black Torrington (*Blaketorinton*); patron, Sir Roger la Zuche, knight. Exeter, 18 March 1278.

1262* The bishop wrote to the archdeacons of Exeter and Totnes [John de Pontoise and Henry de Bollegh]: 'Because we shall all stand before the judgment seat of our Lord Jesus Christ to receive what accords with our actions in this life, it behoves us to anticipate the day of reaping by works of the utmost charity and, at the prompting of things eternal, to sow upon earth that which we may, on the Lord's return, harvest in heaven with manifold fruit. Therefore, because our beloved in Christ, the prior and convent of Taunton, in the diocese of Bath and Wells, have begun to build a church on a lavish scale, for the completion of which their own resources are insufficient, we admonish and require you, and exhort you in the Lord for the remission of your sins that, when the envoys of the aforementioned church come to you, with copies of the present letter, to seek alms from our parishioners for completing this church, you admit them with kindness and, by word and example alike, grant and arrange for the granting to them of acceptable gifts of charity for the completion of so pious a work – to be valid for one year.' [Bishop's] Clyst, 13 March 1278.

---

[188] So identified by Hingeston-Randolph.

1263   [No name][189] given custody of Sheviock (*ecc. B.Marie de Sevioch'*) until a fortnight after Easter; patron, Sir William de Alneto, knight. [Bishops]teignton, 22 March 1278.

1264   Inst. of Sir William de Frankhill, priest, to Butterleigh (*Boterleg'*); patrons, the prior and convent of St Nicholas, Exeter. [Bishops]teignton, 24 March 1278.

1265   Collation of Master William de Middlewood, deacon, to the vicarage of Pawton. Exeter, 27 March 1278.

1266   Collation of Master Thomas de Buckland to the prebend *de Fonte* of Crediton vacant by the resignation of Sir Peter de Guildford, chaplain. [Bishop's] Clyst, 3 April 1278.

[fo.86] **1267**   Dispensation by papal authority of John de Crediton, clerk, born of a priest and a spinster, from his defect of birth in common form, with the additional clause that if in future he should fall into the aforesaid sin of incontinence and be duly convicted, the dispensation would be invalidated. Crediton, 5 April 1278.

1268   Inst. of William de Heanton, deacon, to Sheviock under penalty of the Council; patron, Sir William de Alneto, knight. Crediton, 5 April 1278.

1269   Inst. of Richard de Dartford, subdeacon, to St John's by Antony in Cornwall; patron, Sir William de Alneto, knight. Crediton, 5 April 1278.

1270   Sir Richard, formerly parson of Buckerell, and Henry, chaplain, had, in accordance with a deed drawn up between them, leased land at *Clisthegen* from Gilbert de Langford; they had granted the same land and lease to the bishop, who had returned the said land and lease to Philip, lord of South Radworthy, on condition that Philip deliver the said land on a six-year lease to Richard de Braundsworthy. The bishop invalidated the deed drawn up between Richard, former parson of Buckerell, and Henry, the chaplain.[190] Exeter, 15 April 1278.

1271[191]   Collation of Master Thomas de Buckland to the prebend at Crediton which Sir Peter de Guildford had held. [Bishop's] Clyst, 3 April 1278.

1272   Collation of Master Henry de Bollegh to the prebend at Exeter which Master William de Middleton[192] had held. [Bishop's] Clyst, 3 April 1278.

[189] Presumably William de Heanton, see **1268**.
[190] It is not at all clear what is going on. Thomas de Blandford was collated to Buckerell in 1276 – **1193**; the previous rector seems to have been John Pycot de Exeter, from June 1272 – **887** – and his predecessor was Nicholas de Honiton. Was this Richard Nicholas' predecessor? Richard de Braundsworthy was a canon of the cathedral, and the bishop's commissary in 1237, and would seem to be a different Richard.
[191] This seems to be a repetition of **1266**; Thomas was apparently exchanging prebends within that church, see **1273**.
[192] Now bishop-elect of Norwich.

1273 Collation of Master Richard Paz to the prebend at Crediton which Master Thomas de Buckland had held. Exeter, 18 April 1278.

1274* The bishop issued a letter: 'With favour and goodwill we carry out the pure petitions of those who, in time of prosperity, give pious thought to the last things. Since therefore our beloved son, Laurence son of Richard, knight, out of zeal for his special attachment [fo.86v], has chosen, as far as in him lies, to be buried in the hospital of St Laurence, Crediton, we, by the content of the present letter and with the lawful consent of the precentor and our canons of Crediton approving this, grant free power to the brothers of the aforesaid hospital to allow the body of the same knight, when he dies, to be buried according to the rites of the Church in the chapel of Blessed Laurence.' The letter was sealed by the bishop and by the precentor and canons. [Bishop's] Clyst, 19 April 1278.

1275 Master Roger le Rus, presented by the true patron,[193] was given custody of Widdecombe in the Moor, saving any other claim in the same. [Bishop's] Clyst, 2 May 1278.

1276 Inst. of Sir William de Frankhill, priest, to the vicarage of [East] Budleigh (*Boddelegh'*); patrons, the lady Marjory, prioress of Polsloe, and the convent. Faringdon, 16 May 1278.

1277* The bishop wrote to the prior and convent of Merton in the diocese of Winchester: 'When you formerly, with our assent and with the consents of our dean and chapter of Exeter, and of the venerable father, the lord bishop of Bayeux, and of the dean and chapter of the same place, thought fit under certain terms, as is set out more fully in the letters then drawn up and notarized, to exchange with the religious men, the abbot and convent of Ste Marie le Val in Normandy, in the diocese of Bayeux, the spiritualities and temporalities of what was then your priory of Caen, in the diocese of Bayeux, for all the spiritual and temporal property depending from what was their priory of Tregony, at the desire of the patrons of each place, and with due observance of legal solemnity; you freely entrusted to our discretion the rule and administration of the said priory of Tregony, which we have for certain periods of time beneficially regulated as we, before God, believed expedient. Since, therefore, you have thought fit, filled with religious zeal, humbly to beseech us that we should deign to grant you that the aforesaid place of Tregony, with all its appurtenances, might be brought under the Rule of St Augustine,[194] as it used to be of old, we, weighing up the adornment of religion and being favourable to your justified petitions, with the consent and agreement of our aforesaid chapter, grant you the free power to present to us one ecclesiastic, a canon of your community, to bear the title of prior, as a fellow brother and canon associated with you in the same, whom you should think fit to choose for service under the Augustinian Rule; on terms that, saving any immunity, the said prior and his successors shall be presented for the future to us and our successors and they shall offer manual obedience, while to you and your successors from the same [priors] and their

[193] In 1280 Sir Ralph son of Richard was patron.
[194] Ste Marie le Val was a Benedictine abbey.

successors is reserved canonical obedience according to the discipline of the Rule, and also the power, when you shall see fit, and with the consent and agrement of us and our successors, of recalling the same priors to your monastery and presenting others in their place in the foregoing manner; [fo.87] the said prior and his successors are to be so far content with all the property which belongs to the said priory of Tregony that they are not in future to claim for themselves anything from the property you have in the diocese of Exeter or, without seeking the consent of you and your successors, presume to occupy it, and they are to employ [Tregony's] goods beneficially and on the spot.' Sealed by the bishop and his chapter, London, 29 May 1278.

1278 An identical letter was issued, except for the consent of the Exeter chapter. London, 29 May 1278.

1279 The bishop entrusted the dean of Chichester and Master Henry de Kilkenny, canon of Exeter, with his investigation of the possession of or rights in certain recently sequestered tithes of the church of Bosham, concerning which the canons were in dispute. They were to report what they found out. London, 1 June 1278.

1280 Collation of Sir William de Pawton to the vicarage of Pawton. London, 30 May 1278.

1281 Collation of Master Andrew de Kilkenny to the prebend at Crediton which Master Richard Paz had held. London, 1 June 1278.

1282 Inst. of Robert de Littlebeare, chaplain, to the prebend of Hayes in Exeter Castle; patron, Hugh de Courtenay. London, 2 June 1278.

1283 Inst. of John de Mettingham, clerk, to Madron; patron, Brother Joseph de Chauncy, prior of the Hospitallers in England. London, 2 June 1278.

1284 The bishop gave his sealed inspeximus to a transcript of a papal privilege given at Lyon, on 31 May in the seventh year of Innocent's pontificate [?31-5-1250]. Papal letters, not withdrawn or cancelled or vitiated in any part, with complete *bulla* and unbroken thread, had been issued to the abbot of Prémontré and his fellow abbots, provosts and all the brothers of the Praemonstratensian Order. Wishing to provide for their peace and tranquillity, and that of their monasteries, the pope granted an indult that no papal letters or letters of papal legates were to be valid against houses of the Order unless they made express mention of the Order and this indult. Anyone who tried to infringe or [fo.87v] rashly go against this privilege should know himself to have incurred the displeasure of Almighty God and of Saints Peter and Paul. London, 1 June 1278.

1285* The bishop wrote to the archdeacon of Barnstaple: 'Although the chapel of Torrington Castle has been vacant for so long that its collation has devolved upon us by reason of the Council, yet because Thomas de Merton has established his title to the advowson of the said chapel in the royal court by the assize of darrein presentment, as we have been informed by the letters addressed to us by the lord king, we, desiring to treat the said Thomas with special grace in this regard, have admitted – at the prompting of charity – our beloved son, Master William de Merton, deacon, to the said chapel at the presentation of the same Thomas. Wherefore we command you that, on receipt of these letters, you induct the said Master William into corporal possession of the said chapel, with its appurtenances, and defend him once inducted.' [Bishop's] Clyst, 10 July 1278.

1286 Inst. of Sir Philip de Bradninch, chaplain, to Butterleigh; patrons, the prior and convent of St Nicholas, Exeter. [Bishop's] Clyst, 11 July 1278.

1287 Richard de Hydon did homage to the bishop for all the lands and holdings which he held of him. [Bishop's] Clyst, 11 July 1278.

1288 Inst. of Sir Henry le Briton, chaplain, to Beaford (*Beauford*); patron, the lady Joan de Champernowne, lord of Beaford. Crediton, 13 July 1278.

1289 Master Gervase de Crediton, canon of Crediton, the bishop's clerk, was made the bishop's proctor at the synod of bishops called in London,[195] which the bishop could not attend personally because he was occupied with various affairs in his diocese. Crediton, 13 July 1278.

1290 Henry de Ponte, clerk, was given custody of St Stephen's by Saltash (*Esse*)[196] until Michaelmas, in the presence of the prior of Barlinch, P[eter] de Guildford, the bishop's chaplain, Hugh de Plympton, Richard de Grangiis, and Sir Roger le Arceveske, knight. [Bishop's] Nympton, 19 July 1278.

[fo.88] **1291** Collation of Sir William de Bodrugan to the prebend at Glasney which Master William de St Just had held. [Bishop's] Nympton, 22 July 1278.

1292 Inst. of William Malerbe, subdeacon, to Alwington (*Alwynton*); patron, Sir Richard Coffin, knight. Pawton, 29 July 1278.

1293 The bishop had granted to Sir William de Egloshayle, knight, and to Mirabelle, his wife, eighteen pounds a year, to be paid, in two instalments at Michaelmas and Easter, from the church of St Thomas at Glasney in the bishop's manor of Penryn, in exchange for his manor of Egloshayle, which he has returned to the bishop, his feudal superior, by charter; William and Mirabelle were to enjoy this pension for life, on condition that, on the decease of one or other of them, the survivor should receive ten pounds, the remainder reverting to the bishop and his successors; when both were dead, the whole sum reverted to the bishop and his successors. The bishop also granted William and Mirabelle his establishment in the village of Penryn with the houses there, with an allowance of wood for a fire for them while they lived there, as his forester

---

[195] *Councils and Synods* II 2, 827–8, where the proxy is printed; the synod was held between July and October, the archbishopric of Canterbury being vacant.
[196] So identified by Hingeston-Randolph, but it could also be Roseash, or even Ashreigny or Ashwater.

from his wood at Penryn allowed, without waste. If the bishop or his successors should fail to pay this pension, the sheriff of Cornwall was to distrain adequately on the bishop's lands and chattels to pay the pension, together with compensation of 100 shillings to be paid to William and Mirabelle and a fine of 100 shillings to the sheriff. Pawton, 28 July [fo.88v] 1278.

1294   Inst. of Sir . . ., priest, to the vicarage of South Tawton; patron, Sir Nicholas de Longespee, the rector. Glasney, 12 August 1278.

1295   Dispensation by papal authority of Harvey de Hellegan, clerk, born of a bachelor and a spinster, from his defect of birth, and he had letters in common form, with the additional clause, etc. Cargoll Park, 19 August 1278.

1296   Collation of Master John de Clifford, the Queen's physician, to the prebend at Exeter which Master Robert de Trillawe had held. Cargoll Park, 20 August 1278.

1297   Appropriation,[197] through sealed letters patent, of St Breward, the advowson of which the bishop had lawfully acquired, to the dean and chapter of Exeter for the purpose of celebrating in perpetuity the feast of St Gabriel [the bishop's patron saint] in the cathedral on the first Monday in September, with similar ceremonies in lights and other things to those used on Christmas Day. Over and above any normal allowance, each canon who made a personal appearance at the feast was to receive two shillings, each vicar[-choral] twelve pence, each clerk in minor orders six pence, and each choirboy two pence, all drawn from this appropriation. On the following day were to be celebrated in perpetuity obits for the souls of the bishop, of his predecessors, William [Brewer] and Richard [Blund], and of his successors as bishops of Exeter, and for the souls of the bishop's father and mother, of his benefactors, and of all the faithful departed; each canon present at this solemn commemoration was to receive two shillings, each vicar twelve pence, each [fo.89] clerk in minor orders six pence, and each choirboy two pence; further, the dean and chapter were each year on the day of this commemoration to feed fifty feeble paupers (*pauperos debiles*) with a pennyworth of food and drink for each of them. The remainder of the revenues from St Breward was to be divided equally among those canons who attended both solemnities, not converted to any other use, except for the establishment of an adequate vicarage at St Breward. This vicarage was to consist of all the altarage and the whole of the glebeland, except for two acres, English measure, on which the dean and chapter might build, together with the greater tithes of the village of Lower Lank and all the hay tithes; the bishop and his successors would collate a vicar who was to bear all the ordinary burdens. Each dean and canon of Exeter was, on his installation, to swear to observe this ordinance together with the other ancient and approved customs of the church of Exeter. Exeter, 5 September 1278.

---

[197] The language is very similar to that used in **1185**.

1298 Collation of Sir Warren de St Teath, priest, to the vicarage of St Breward; he was assigned his portion, as in the previous entry, except that his glebeland was now said to have buildings on it. Tavistock, 11 September 1278.

1299 Induction of Master William de Hococ, deacon, to Denbury (*Devenebyr'*); patrons, the abbot and convent of Tavistock. [Bishop's] Clyst, 24 September 1278.

1300 Collation of a certain priest, 'whose name I do not know, and he did not have letters' to the vicarage of Coldridge;[198] similarly, collation of Sir John de St Keverne to a certain prebend at Crantock, but he did not have letters of induction. Exeter, 5 September 1278.

1301 Induction, on pain of the Council, of Master William Trenchard, deacon, to the vicarage of Marystow (*ecc. S.Marie Stowe*); patrons, the prior and convent of Plympton. Crawley, 27 September 1278.

[fo.89v] **1302** Inst. of Master Nicholas de Leigh, subdeacon, to Otterham (*Oterham*); patron, [the lady] Matilda, lord of Otterham (*ad presentationem Matille, domine de Oterham*). Crawley, 27 September 1278.

1303 Collation of Master Ralph de Pole, subdeacon, to Stockleigh Pomeroy (*Stokel' Pomeray*). Crawley, 27 September 1278.

1304 John de Lardario resigned into the bishop's hands his prebend of Probus, in the presence of Masters Andrew de Kilkenny, Gervase de Crediton, W[illiam] Wancy, P[eter] de Guildford, Reginald le Arceveske, Hugh Splot, and others. Horsley, 4 October 1278.

1305 Collation of John de Lardario to the prebend at Crantock which Sir Peter de Wells had held. Horsley, 4 October 1278.

1306 In sealed letters patent, dated at [Bishop's] Clyst on 21 September 1278, the bishop appointed Ralph de la Pole and William de Essex, clerks, his proctors 'in all causes howsoever touching our person' (*in omnibus causis personam nostram qualitercumque contingentibus*); they could act jointly or severally, and were given full powers; all this was to be signified to any judge or other persons having cognizance as well as any opponents or others having an interest.[199] Horsley, 4 October 1278.

---

[198] *contulit dominus episcopus vicariam de Colrigg' cuidam presbitero cuius nomen ignoro nec habuit literas*.!

[199] *et hec omnia quibuscumque iudicibus seu notionem quamcumque habentibus et adversariis nostris et omnibus quorumcumque interest tenore presentium significamus*. Their powers were almost identical to those given in **976** or **1215**, but they seem to be personal proctors generally appointed – no court is specified – rather than representing the bishop strictly in his official capacity.

1307   Collation of Master Andrew de Kilkenny to Shobrooke (*Schokebrock'*). Horsley, 5 October 1278.

1308   Inst. of Richard de Holywell, subdeacon, to Virginstow; patrons, the abbot and convent of Tavistock. Horsley, 7 October 1278.

1309   Resignation by Richard de Grangiis, clerk, of the rectory of St Michael at Sowton (*ecc. S.Michaelis de Clyst Fomeson*) [fo.90] and his portion in St Teath, renouncing any rights he might have in either benefice.²⁰⁰ Horsley, 11 October 1278.

1310   Inst. of Richard de Grangiis, deacon, to Week St Mary (*Wyk' in Cornubia*); patron, Richard de Albo Monasterio. Horsley, 11 October 1278.

1311   Inst. of Sir Walter de Banton, chaplain, to Huntsham (*Honesham*); patron, Alexander de Vyteri by reason of the dowry of his wife, the lady Ermigade de Ponchardon. London, 27 October 1278.

1312   The bishop issued letters patent, given in September, acknowledging that he owed from his private purse six marks a year at Michaelmas to . . ., rector of . . ., until he should provide him with a richer benefice without the cure of souls. London, 12 November 1278.

1313*   The bishop issued letters patent: 'Let all know that we, being hindered by infirmity of body, by the tenor of the present letters make, appoint and ordain our beloved sons in Christ, Sirs Ralph de Hengham and J[ohn de Pontoise], archdeacon of Exeter, our proctors for reaching an amicable settlement and for fulfilling such settlement between the noble Lord E[dmund], earl of Cornwall, on the one part, and ourselves, on the other, and for doing each and every thing touching the said settlement in the terms pre-arranged by our mutual friends as we should do if we were present, saving in all things the right and honour of the Church and our orders. And we shall ratify whatever the aforesaid proctors of ours shall have thought fit to do in the foregoing.' London, 12 November 1278.

1314*²⁰¹   'It is to be recorded that inasmuch as there were various disputes and disagreements between the noble baron Sir Edmund, earl of Cornwall, and Sir Walter, by the grace of God bishop of Exeter, all have now been resolved by their mutual friends, in these terms: That the bishop releases the people of Cornwall from the obligations imposed on them against their will and by his jurisdiction; That, at the same time, [the earl] demands of the bishop that, since he imposed an obligation on him against his will and by force, on that account he should undertake that he will never demand any of these things of him in a

²⁰⁰   The sealed letter of resignation is given in full.
²⁰¹   This entry was written in French, uniquely in this register. My thanks to Dr Alison Adams for translating it. It was presumably written in French because it gives the earl's side of the story, and he would have been fluent in French, but probably not in Latin. Again, a layman's dating is by the regnal year – the sixth year of the reign of King Edward.

court of law; That he should revoke the sworn statements he had made against him by force, and they should be absolved and declared free of them; and that William de Monkton should be absolved according to the rites of Holy Church and the bishop should repeal everything [ie, his excommunication], out of respect for the earl; and if there are any others who were excommunicated or declared excommunicate for temporal offences, they should be absolved on the same terms. [fo.90v] And moreover, [the earl] demands that as to the sandpits of Mylor it should be arranged that three knights of good standing representing the earl, and three others representing the bishop, meet at the site, and on oath make certain treaties concerning what is settled on the church of Mylor and what belongs to the community, so that nobody henceforth should take from the settled part without asking permission of the priest of Mylor, and the rest should remain for the community. And if the bishop has taken ransoms, fines or requisitions unlawfully from the people of Cornwall, let them be returned to those from whom he has taken them under the supervision of a clerk representing the earl and another representing the bishop. And if the two cannot reach an agreement they should elect a third clerk. And all this should be accomplished between now and Pentecost, such that the bishop's representative should be taken under the reasonable protection of the earl, and none of the earl's friends, clerical or otherwise, who have been involved in these disputes, nor any of his people of Cornwall, should be harassed or brought to court by the bishop or any of his supporters on this account at any time, or in respect of any article alleged by the bishop against William de Monkton for the distress that he has done in the king's name, or in respect of defamation of any cause or action that the bishop had or might have up to this day. And the aforementioned bishop promises in good faith that this undertaking will be observed loyally and without default, and he submits himself to the jurisdiction of the archbishop of Canterbury or the official of Canterbury in any matters pertaining to spirituality, and matters pertaining to the earl and his followers, which may or must be tried, determined and settled in the king's courts, should be entered on the roll of the chief justices of the king in such a way that they could distrain him without complaint or dispute to do and observe all these things faithfully. And in witness of the aforesaid matters the bishop has appended his seal to this document, together with the seals of Master John de Pontoise, archdeacon of Exeter, and of Sir Ralf de Engham, king's justice.' London, 12 November 1278.

1315 Inst. of Robert de Chester, clerk, to Combpyne (*Cumbe*); patron, Sir Thomas de Pyne, knight. [Bishop's] Clyst, 21 December 1278.

1316 Inst. of John de Exeter, subdeacon, to Affeton;[202] patrons, the prior and convent of St Nicholas, Exeter. [Bishop's] Clyst, 21 December 1278.

1317 Inst. of Sir Nicholas de Castello, chaplain, to the church or chapel of St Mary, Truro (*Triueru*). [Bishops]teignton, 9 January 1279.

[202] Nowadays in West Worlington, but a separate parish until the fifteenth century, as N. Orme informs me.

1318   Collation of William de Nympton [fo.91] to the prebend of Probus which John de Lardario had held. [Bishops]teignton, 6 January 1279.

1319   Inst. of Sir Roger de Kynemanesdun, chaplain, to Gidleigh (*Gyddelegh'*); patron, Sir William de Pruz. [Bishops]teignton, 10 January 1279.

1320   Inst. of Sir William, chaplain, to the vicarage of Ashburton (*Asperton'*) parish church; patrons, the dean and chapter of Exeter. Exeter, 21 January 1279.

1321   Inst. of John de Jacobstow, chaplain, to the vicarage of Dawlish (*Douliz*) parish church; patrons, the dean and chapter of Exeter. Exeter, 21 January 1279.

1322   Inst. of Richard de Cerne, subdeacon, to Willand (*Wylond*); patrons, the prior and convent of Taunton. Exeter, 21 January 1279.

1323   Collation of Sir William de Meeth, chaplain, to the vicarage of St Teath. Exeter, 21 January 1279.

1324*[203]   The bishop wrote to the earl of Cornwall. 'We have reverently received your lordship's recent letters, [saying] that you are about to send a special clerk and messenger to Cornwall in the near future, to complete and perfect the terms of the peace recently drawn up between us, and we rejoice at this since we are similarly minded. However, so that nothing may happen which might with good reason be an impediment to peace or stir up matters which have been laid to rest, may it please your lordship to send such clerk to some safe and well-known place outside the county of Cornwall, which is, as you know, with reason mistrusted by us and ours on various grounds, so that he may not be a stirrer-up of discord but may rather love and cherish your and my tranquillity, in mutual charity, than bind himself to our discords and losses. For our part, we propose to observe this to the best of our ability. If, however, it seems useful and expedient that such business be postponed until after Easter so that, after we have had a discussion together face to face, the terms of the peace begun between us may reach a happy outcome by unanimous agreement, please reply to us, by the bearer of this letter, as to what your will is on this.' [No date]

1325   Inst. of Sir Roger de Brightwell, chaplain, to Landewednack (*ecc. S. Wynewali de Landewenesek*); patron, John son of Sir John de Reviers. [Bishop's] Clyst, 19 February 1279.

1326   Inst. of Sir Nicholas de St Olave, chaplain, to Poughill (*Poghell*), Devon; patrons, the prior and convent of St Nicholas, Exeter. [Bishop's] Clyst, 2 February 1279.

1327   Inst. of Master William de Middlewood, priest, to the vicarage of Altarnun (*Alternon*); patrons, the dean and chapter of Exeter. Chudleigh, 24 February 1279.

[203]   This actually reads like a real letter.

1328   Inst. of Richard de Bath, subdeacon, to Sampford Peverel; patron, Sir Hugh de Sampford Peverel. Chudleigh, 25 February 1279.

1329   The bishop wrote to the official of Canterbury. Master Clement de Liskeard, clerk and subdeacon, had appeared before the bishop at his manor of Bishopsteignton, showing letters of presentation and inquisition to the church of Roche, but the bishop had not admitted him. Master Clement appealed to the see of Canterbury on the grounds that, despite having been presented by the true patron,[204] he had, without any just impediment, not been admitted as rector to Roche. The bishop duly referred the appeal to Canterbury.[205] [Bishops]teignton, 1 March 1279.

[fo.92] **1330**   Collation of Master John de Worlington to the prebend of Crantock which John de Lardario had held. Newenham, 25 March 1279.

1331   Collation of Master David de Molton, clerk and subdeacon, to Lawhitton, which Richard de Dartford had held. Newenham, 25 March 1279.

1332   Inst. of Master William de Northover, priest, to the vicarage of Bovey Tracy (*Bovy Tracy*); patrons, the master and brothers of the Hospital of St John the Baptist at Bridgewater. [Bishop's] Clyst, 28 March 1279.

1333   Inst. of William de Aldsworth, subdeacon, to St Mawgan in Pydar (*ecc. de la Herne*); patrons, Sir Guy de Nonant, knight, and the prior and convent of Plympton, saving in all things any right of the bishop and his church. [Bishop's] Clyst, 6 April 1279.

1334   Inst. of Sir Robert de la Hope, chaplain, to Dolton (*Dewelton*); patron, Sir Hugh de Courtenay, knight. Newenham, 12 April 1279.

1335   Inst. of Master Clement de Liskeard, subdeacon, to Roche; patrons, Sir Robert de la Roche, knight, and the lady Agnes de la Roche. Horsley, 13 May 1279.

1336   Collation of Master Richard Paz to the treasurership of Crediton. Mitcham, 7 June 1279.

1337   Inst. of Hamund de Pipewell, subdeacon, to Philleigh (*Eglosros*); patron, Sir Oliver de Dynham, knight. Chidham, 23 June 1279.

1338   Richard de Grangiis was given custody of Chawleigh (*Chalveleg'*), at the bishop's pleasure. Chidham, 23 June 1279.

1339   Inst. of Sir John de Exeter, treasurer of Exeter cathedral, to Alphington (*Alfinton*); patron, Sir John de Neville, knight. Chidham, 29 June 1279.

---

[204]   Feminine, so presumably Agnes de la Roche; see **1335**.
[205]   See **1335**; perhaps the exact patronage was in doubt.

1340   Hamund de Pipewell resigned his claims to the churches of Philleigh and Bicton (*Buketon*),[206] and was admitted to Chawleigh (*Chauueleg'*); patron, Sir Hugh de Courtenay. Overton, 3 August 1279.

[fo.92v] **1341**[207]   'Brother J[ohn Peckham], by God's mercy archbishop of Canterbury, primate of all England, to his beloved in Christ the chancellor and university of masters and scholars of Oxford in the diocese of Lincoln, greeting, grace and benediction. We rightly use whatever influence we can to further those who seek the pearl of knowledge in the field of scholarly discipline, and freely grant to them those things whereby their material distress may be removed and their status prosper in tranquillity. Hence, lending an ear to your devout prayers, we are taking under our protection your persons, together with all the property you hold in common which you possess in due form at present or which you may acquire by lawful means in future – if the Lord so grant. We confirm especially by the authority of the present letters, and corroborate by the patronage of the present document, the liberties and immunities duly granted, so that you hold them all lawfully and in due form, by bishops, kings, magnates, and others of Christ's faithful, to you and through you to your successors, with the unanimous and express consent of our brethren. Furthermore, we understand that certain persons, unmindful of their own salvation, when they have been bound by sentences of suspension or excommunication for crimes committed against the university of Oxford imposed by the chancellor of the same university or by his judges-delegate or by the same chancellor, sometimes together with the regent scholars, sometimes with [both] regents and non-regents, are withdrawing from you and your jurisdiction, rashly holding the keys of the Church in contempt. In order that the said sentences may be confirmed in their rigour, we grant you leave by the tenor of the present letter, with the express and unanimous consent of our brethren, whenever we or our brethren shall lawfully be called upon by you in this regard, that they may be handed over for the enforcement [of the sentence] by the agency of us or our brethren or of their officials in our province. Furthermore, desiring to provide more fully for your tranquillity so that your community may in the future be prosperously and quietly governed, we grant to you and, with the express and unanimous consent of our brethren, ordain and lay down that if any beneficed clergy of our province are found, by day or by night, bearing arms to the disturbance of the peace or disturbing the tranquillity of this university by any other means, and are lawfully convicted thereof, or presumptively convicted by their flight, their benefices are to be sequestrated for a period of three years by their prelates on the chancellor's denunciation being made to the said bishops under the common seal of this university, and lawful satisfaction shall for the time being be made to the person or persons injured by those who have been convicted, confessed or fled, from the fruits – receivable or received – of such benefices. If [the offenders] do not hold an ecclesiastical benefice, they are to be held

---

[206]   Identified thus by Hingeston-Randolph; it could alternatively be High Bickington.
[207]   This letter is printed in *Councils and Synods* II 2, 851–3, and Archbishop Peckham's *Register*, I, *ep*.23, p.30; it is mentioned by J.I. Catto, *The History of the University of Oxford*, I (Clarendon Press, 1984), 107 & 139.

incompetent to receive such benefices for a period of five years, unless due satisfaction be made meanwhile by the same to the injured persons and they thus return to the university's favour; their reputation is to be held intact once satisfaction is made. In testimony of all of which our seal, together with the seals of those of our brethren present, is affixed to this document. Given in our synod at Reading', 31 July 1279.

[fo.93] **1342*** The bishop wrote to the [rural] dean of St Germans in Cornwall. 'The priory of St Germans with the possessions and rights which belong to the same priory, both temporal and spiritual, together with the custody of the same priory when it shall fall vacant, belong to us and our church of Exeter by full title. We and our predecessors, by reason of our aforesaid church of Exeter, have been from time immemorial and still are in peaceful possession of the same. All of this is common knowledge in the regions of Cornwall and throughout our whole diocese of Exeter, but certain minions of Satan, unmindful of their own salvation, have by force expelled or ejected our officers who had custody in our name of the said priory, the same being vacant through the death of Richard, the former prior, or have maliciously disturbed or interfered with the same to prevent their peaceful custody of the said priory in our name, and moreover are still not ceasing to disturb or interefere with the same, thus infringing or disturbing ecclesiastical liberty to our manifest detriment and the substantial prejudice and oppression of our church of Exeter and the overthrow of ecclesiastical liberty; on this account there is no doubt that these men have, with risk of damnation, *ipso facto* fallen under the sentence of the greater excommunication. We therefore command you, firmly enjoining you in virtue of your obedience, that you should go in person to the aforesaid priory, taking with you six rectors, vicars or chaplains from the neighbourhood, and announce publicly that all the aforesaid malefactors have generally incurred the aforesaid sentence of the greater excommunication. If you should find there any malefactors of this sort disturbing or in any way molesting our officers having custody of the aforesaid priory as regards the custody of the same priory, its possessions, rights or anything belonging to it, you are to warn them to desist completely from such disturbance or obstruction; failing this you are publicly to announce and have announced, throughout your deanery and wherever else you shall see fit, on Sundays and feast days, with ringing of bells and lit candles, that each and every one of them, particularly and by name, has fallen under the said sentence of excommunication, until they shall deserve to obtain the benefit of absolution in legal form. And you are to inform us . . .' etc. [Bishop's] Nympton, 11 August 1279.

1343 Two days later the bishop wrote again to the dean of St Germans; if, despite his denunciations, the offenders refused to desist, the dean was publicly to place the church of St Germans and the whole place under ecclesiastical interdict for as long as the malefactors remained there or obstructed the bishop's officers, as well as following up the individual sentences of excommunication. [fo.93v] And he was to inform the bishop etc. [Bishop's] Nympton, 13 August 1279.

1344 Collation of Master John de Worlington, chaplain, to the prebend at Crantock vacant by the voluntary resignation of Sir Solomon de Rochester. Canonsleigh, 8 August 1279.

1345 Sir Richard le Deneis, chaplain was given custody of the vicarage of Tamerton at the bishop's pleasure. [Bishop's] Clyst, 22 August 1279.

1346 Collation of Master Philip de Exeter, chaplain, to the archdeaconry of Barnstaple. Exeter, 28 August 1279.

1347 Collation of Sir Robert de Torrington, chaplain, to the vicarage of Paignton. Exeter, 28 August 1279.

1348 Dispensation of Henry de Stockleigh, acolyte, from his defect of birth, and he had letters in common form, with the additional clause, etc. [Bishops]teignton, 30 August 1279.

1349 Inst. of Sir Robert de Cockley, chaplain, to Churchstanton (*Churistanton*); patron, Sir John de Todenham, knight. [Bishop's] Clyst, 20 September 1279.

1350 Inst. of John de la Tor, subdeacon, to Stokeinteignhead (*Stokes in Tinhyde*); patrons, the prior and convent of Plympton. [Bishop's] Clyst, 24 September 1279.

1351 Inst. of Master Hamund Parleben, subdeacon, to Ladock; patron, the earl of Cornwall. [Bishop's] Clyst, 24 September 1279.

1352 Inst. of Sir Jordan de Ashwater, chaplain, to Coryton; patron, Sir Henry de Champernowne, knight. [Bishop's] Clyst, 24 September 1279.

1353 Inst. of Sir . . . de Widdecombe, priest, to Gittisham (*Gidesham*); patron, Sir Richard de Loman, knight. Fluxton, 25 September 1279.

1354 Inst. of Walter de Ferrars, subdeacon, to Bere Ferrars; patron, Sir Reginald de Ferrars, knight. Fluxton, 25 September 1279.

1355 Inst. of Herbert de Ferrars, subdeacon, to Newton Ferrars (*Newinton*); patron, the lady Yseude de Ferrars. Fluxton, 25 September 1279.

1356 Collation by lapse of Sir Walter [fo.94] de Denton, priest, to the vicarage of Buckland [Brewer].[208] Fluxton, 26 September 1279.

1357 Letter commending Geoffrey de Poolhampton, priest, to Buckerell, in accordance with Pope Gregory's decree published at the recent Council of Lyons [c.14]. Fluxton, 26 September 1279.

---

[208] See footnote to **790**.

1358 Collation of Master Robert de Ros to the prebend at Crantock which Master John de Worlington had held. Horsley, 12 October 1279.

1359 Inst. of Master Vincent de Acland, deacon, to Molland; patrons, the abbot and convent of Hartland. London, 29 October 1279.

1360 Collation of Sir William de Totnes, chaplain, to the vicarage of St Neot (*ecc. S.Neoti in Cornubia*). London, 6 November 1279.

1361 Collation of Sir Nicholas called Strang, deacon, to Sowton (*Clyst Fomechun*), on his resignation of Knowstone (*Cnodston*). Horsley, 25 November 1279.

1362 Richard de Bath, subdeacon, was given custody of North Lew (*Northlyw*) at the bishop's pleasure. Faringdon, 17 December 1279.

1363 Jordan de Spineto, William de Aldsworth, William Brown and John de Coleshill granted letters dimissory; Richard de Shoghtebyr' had received them in October. Faringdon, 17 December 1279.

1364 Be it noted that . . . was publicly denounced in full consistory at Exeter . . .[209]

1365 Inst. of John de Coleshill, subdeacon, to North Bovey (*Northbovy*); patron, Sir Thomas Pippard, knight. Faringdon, 24 December 1279.

1366 Collation of Sir Gilbert de Tyting, chaplain, to Bishopsteignton. Faringdon, 24 December 1279.

[fo.94v] **1367** Inst. of Master William Brown, subdeacon, to Michaelstow (*ecc. S.Michaelis de Hellesbir'*); patron, the earl of Cornwall. Faringdon, 25 December 1279.

1368 Inst. of Master Andrew de Kilkenny, subdeacon, to Bridestowe (*Brichtestowe*); patrons, the prior and convent of Plympton. Faringdon, 30 December 1279.

1369 Collation of Edmund de Mandeville to the prebend at Bosham vacant by the voluntary resignation of Anthony Bek. Faringdon, 30 December 1279.

1370 Inst. of Sir John Prig', priest, to the vicarage of Ashburton; patrons, the dean and chapter of Exeter. Faringdon, 31 December 1279.

1371 Letters patent recording the institution of Master Andrew de Kilkenny, subdeacon, to Bridestowe, vacant by the resignation of Sir Gilbert de Tyting, at the presentation of the prior and convent of Plympton, to whom the customary pension was reserved. Faringdon, 30 December 1279.

[209] Several lines were left blank.

1372   The bishop wrote to the bishop of Bath and Wells, sending him a clerk — unnamed — from his diocese who had been presented to Rockbeare, in the diocese of Exeter, to be dealt with 'as you should wish or we be able to do' (*pro ipso faciatis quod vos facere velletis seu nos facere possemus*). Winchester, 31 December 1279.

1373   Walter de Baunton granted letters dimissory. Merton, 23 January 1280.

1374   Inst. of Sir Nicholas de Totnes, priest, to Rewe; patron, Sir John de Exeter, clerk. Alresford, 28 January 1280.

[fo.95] **1375**   The bishop wrote to . . ., his official. The church of St Cleer (*ecc. S.Clari in Cornubia*) had been sequestered because the rector had failed to attend for ordination or to keep residence; the bishop had relaxed the sequestration and ordered the official to see to this and not re-impose it, as long as the said church was not defrauded of the due services. Henley, 31 January 1280.

1376   Inst. of Sir Andrew de Caynes, chaplain, to the vicarage of Stratton; patrons, the prior and convent of Launceston. Charlton, 1 February 1280.

1377   Inst. of Adam de Segrave, clerk, to the prebend or portion in Chulmleigh (*Culmelegh*) which Sir Robert de la Hope had held; patron, Sir Hugh de Courtenay. Frampton, 5 February 1280.

1378   At the entreaty of the most serene lady, Queen Eleanor of England, the bishop ordered his official . . . to lift the sentences of suspension or interdict imposed on the monks of Buckland, of the Cistercian Order, or their lands, because they had presumed to celebrate the divine offices in the diocese of Exeter without authority or licence; they were to be permitted such celebration until Pentecost or the bishop's having speech with the Queen. Charlton, 5 February 1280.

1379   Inst. of Sir John de Deneworthy, priest, to Kenn; patron, Sir Oliver de Dynham. [Bishop's] Clyst, 10 February 1280.

1380   Inst. of Sir William de Monk Okehampton, priest, to Virginstow; patrons, the abbot and convent of Tavistock. [Bishop's] Clyst, 10 February 1280.

1381   Inst. of Ralph de Ferrrars, clerk, to Thurlestone (*Thorleston*); patron, Sir Hugh de Ferrars. Plympton, 17 February 1280.

[fo.95v] **1382**   Collation of Master Henry de Sackville to the prebend at Crediton which Sir Henry de Ashcombe had held. Palston [in South Brent], 18 February 1280.

1383   Sir J[ohn] Pycot resigned his prebend at Crediton into the bishop's hands. Chudleigh, 21 February 1280.

1384 Collation of Sir John [Pycot] to the prebend at Exeter which Master Thomas de la Knolle had held. Chudleigh, 21 February 1280.

1385 Collation of Sir Clement de Langford to the chancellorship of Exeter cathedral, on his resigning Instow (*Yeonestowe*) into the bishop's hands. Chudleigh, 21 February 1280.

1386 Inst. of Ralph de Do, priest, to Moreleigh (*Morleg'*); patron, Sir Peter de Fishacre, knight. Chudleigh, 22 February 1280.

1387 Inst. of David Martin to Ermington (*Ermynton*); patron, Sir John Peverel, knight. Chudleigh, 23 February 1280.

1388 Collation of Master Andrew de Kilkenny to the prebend at Crediton which Sir John Pycot had voluntarily resigned; Andrew resigned the prebend he had previously held there. Fluxton, 4 April 1280.

1389 Master William Brown granted letters dimissory, allowing him to be ordained deacon before Easter by any bishop in the province of Canterbury. Fluxton, 6 April 1280.

1390 Inst. of Thomas de Ferrars to St Mellion; patron, Reginald de Ferrars. Fluxton, 6 March 1280.

1391 Inst. of Sir Robert, chaplain, to the vicarage of St Austell; patrons, the prior and convent of Tywardreath. [Bishop's] Clyst, 12 March 1280.

1392 The bishop issued an inspeximus, because of the fragility of the seal, of Sir Roger de Dartford's commendation in perpetuity to the rectory of St Columb Major, dated 14 August 1266 [**632**]; patron, Sir Ralph de Arundel, knight. [Bishop's] Clyst, 12 March 1280.

[fo.96] **1393** Inst. of William de Braunton, subdeacon, to Charles (*Charnes*); patron, Sir John de Ponchardon, knight. [Bishops]teignton, 16 March 1280.

1394 Dispensation of Sir Geoffrey, canon of St Germans, born of a deacon and a spinster, from his defect of birth. [Bishops]teignton, 16 March 1280.

1395 The bishop held an ordination; the names of the ordinands were held by Master Andrew de Kilkenny, official of Exeter. [Bishops]teignton, 16 March 1280.

1396 Inst. of Sir Adam de Leake, priest, to St Olave's, Exeter; patrons, the prior and convent of St Nicholas, Exeter. [Bishop's] Nympton, 1 April 1280.

1397 The bishop held an ordination; the names of the ordinands were held by [Master Andrew de Kilkenny] the official of Exeter. Crediton, 7 April 1280.

1398   Inst. of Jordan de Spineto, subdeacon, to Landulph (*Landylp'*); patron, Sir Herbert de Spineto, knight. [Bishop's] Clyst, 7 April 1280.

1399   Inst. of Henry, priest, to the vicarage of St Anthony in Meneage; patrons, the prior and convent of Tywardreath. [Bishop's] Clyst, 16 April 1280.

1400   Inst. of Sir John de Christow, chaplain, to the vicarage of Heavitree (*Hevetre*); patrons, the dean and chapter of Exeter. [Bishops]teignton, 17 April 1280.

1401   Inst. of John son of Richard, deacon, to Widdecombe in the Moor; patron, Sir Ralph son of Richard, knight. [Bishop's] Clyst, 22 April 1280.

1402   Inst. of Sir John de Gatepath, priest, to the vicarage of Colaton Raleigh (*Colleton*); patron, Sir John [Noble], dean of Exeter. [Bishop's] Clyst, 22 April 1280.

1403   Inst. of Adam de Morchard, priest, to Washford Pyne (*Wasford*); patron, Sir Herbert de Pyne, knight. [Bishop's] Clyst, 3 May 1280.

1404   Inst. of Sir William de Thelbridge, priest, to Thelbridge (*Telebrigg'*); patron, Sir John de Charteray, knight. [Bishop's] Clyst, 3 May 1280.

1405   Inst. of Sir John de Shipton, priest, to the vicarage of Christow, vacant by the voluntary resignation of Sir John de Christow, the former vicar; patrons, the prior and convent of Cowick. [Bishop's] Clyst, 1 May 1280.

[fo.96v] **1406**   The bishop had given the administration of the priory of St Germans, canons of the Augustinian Rule, to Sir Geoffrey de St Germans, priest, a canon of the priory; he therefore required the canons to obey Sir Geoffrey as their prior in both temporal and spiritual matters. [Bishops]teignton, 16 March 1280.

1407[210]   A proxy was issued for Master Andrew de Kilkenny, the official, and addressed to J[ohn Peckham], the archbishop of Canterbury, for the synod of bishops to be held in London three weeks after Easter (12 May). The bishop was unable to attend, 'being repeatedly afflicted by ill-health of body, weakening of powers and other blows of fortune'. Master Andrew was given powers to act for the bishop in whatever was agreed and laid down for the honour of God and the benefit of the Church. [Bishop's] Clyst, 4 May 1280.

1408   Inst. of Sir Luke de Tywardreath, priest, to the vicarage of St Andrew's, Tywardreath (*Tywardreit*); patrons, the prior and convent of Tywardreath. London, 20 May 1280.

1409   The bishop wrote to [Andrew de Kilkenny], his official. At the petition of the Lady Eleanor, Queen of England, he had ordered the official to relax the

---

[210] Only known from this text, printed in *Councils and Synods* II 2, 870; cf **573**.

sentences of suspension or interdict imposed on the monks of Buckland, of the Cistercian Order, or their lands, for having celebrated the divine office without licence, either until Pentecost (19 June) or until the bishop had spoken with the Queen; now, at her further request, this period was to be extended until 17 October, and he was not meanwhile to cause them any annoyance or hindrance. London, 27 May 1280.

1410 Inst. of John de Warmington, subdeacon, to Poughill (*Poghehull*), Devon; patrons, the prior and convent of St Nicholas, Exeter. Canonsleigh, 24 March 1280.

[fo.97] **1411** Collation of Sir Robert de Scarborough, deacon, to the prebend at Crediton vacant by the voluntary resignation of Master Henry de Sackville. Horsley, 20 May 1280.

1412 The bishop wrote to [Philip de Exeter] the archdeacon of Barnstaple, ordering him to admit Sir Peter de Guildford, the bishop's chaplain, or his proctor, by title of commendation to Bratton [Fleming]; patron, John de la Torre. Horsley, 31 May 1280.

1413 Inst. of Sir Gilbert, chaplain, to Ashcombe (*Ascumbe*); patrons, the prior and convent of Merton. Horsley, 2 June 1280.

1414 The bishop in letters patent made Duracius, a citizen and merchant of Florence, his proctor or attorney, with power of substitution, for receiving the one hundred pounds sterling which the earl of Cornwall was due to pay the bishop on 24 June in accordance with the settlement made by Queen Eleanor and [Robert Burnell], the bishop of Bath and Wells. Horsley, 11 June 1280.

1415 Collation of Sir Solomon de Rochester to the prebend at Crediton vacant by the voluntary resignation of Sir Robert de Scarborough. Faringdon, 16 June 1280.

1416 Sir G[ilbert] de Tyting resigned his prebend at Crediton into the bishop's hands. [Bishop's] Clyst, 29 June, 1280.

1417 Collation of Sir Gilbert [de Tyting] to the prebend at Exeter which Master Henry de Kilkenny had held. [Bishop's] Clyst, 29 June, 1280.

1418 Inst. of Nicholas de Gatcombe, subdeacon, to Ashwater (*Assewat'*); patron, Sir Walter de Dunheved, knight. [Bishop's] Clyst, 29 June, 1280.

1419 Inst. of Robert Caveneye of Rockingham, clerk, to Bicton (*Bugeton*); patron, King Edward, as guardian of the heirs of Reginald Arblaster. [Bishop's] Clyst, 30 June, 1280.

[fo.97v] **1420** Inst. of Sir Robert de Esse of Okehampton, priest, to the chapel of Sticklepath (*Stikelepath*) [in Sampford Courtenay]; patron, Sir Hugh de Courtenay. Chudleigh, 8 July 1280.

1421   Brother Robert, abbot of Buckfast, received a blessing and was put into possession.²¹¹ Chudleigh, 3 July 1280.

1422   Collation of Richard de Dartford, deacon, to Shobrooke, vacant by the voluntary resignation of Master Andrew de Kilkenny. [Bishops]teignton, 20 July 1280.

1423   Collation of Sir Hugh de Plympton, priest, to the prebend at Crediton which Sir Gilbert de Tyting had held. [Bishops]teignton, 20 July 1280.

1424   Collation of Sir Richard de Teignton, priest, to a portion in Gerrans. [Bishops]teignton, 20 July 1280.

1425   The bishop gave to Sir Roger called le Arceveske, knight, the guardianship and marriage of the heir or heirs of Walter de Bath. [Bishops]teignton, 20 July 1280.

1426*²¹²The bishop issued sealed letters patent: 'Let all know that we, considering the end of all worldly vanity and with our mind upon the last things, have been moved, at the prompting of divine charity and for the salvation of our soul, to grant and confer upon the dean and chapter of Exeter the church of Buckerell (*Bukerel*), of which we are the patron, with all its rights, offerings and all other appurtenances to be appropriated to the aforesaid dean and chapter to be lawfully held in perpetuity, for the maintenance of two chaplains in the almost completed chapel [of St Gabriel] next to the chapel of St Mary, on the south side of our cathedral of Exeter, where we have chosen the site of our tomb. The chaplains are to celebrate Mass in perpetuity for our soul, the souls of our benefactors and of all the faithful departed. We reserve an adequate vicarage in the same church of Buckerell, to be taxed by us or our successors, to which the same dean and chapter shall be bound to present [a vicar] to us and our successors, on condition that the said dean and chapter should in perpetuity pay annually to the said chaplains for their support twelve marks sterling, in equal instalments at Michaelmas and Easter.' [Bishops]teignton, 20 July 1280.

1427   Inst. of Sir Walter de Guildford, chaplain, to Knowstone (*Scnodston*), vacant by the voluntary resignation of Sir Nicholas le Strong; patrons, the abbot and convent of Hartland. [Bishops]teignton, 22 July 1280.

1428*   The bishop issued sealed letters patent: 'We wish it to be known to all of you by the tenor of these presents that, we, by the content of the present letter, relax the interdict imposed on the abbey of Buckland [fo.98] of our diocese, which has been re-founded, and we grant that the abbot and monks of the Cistercian Order dwelling there may lawfully celebrate the divine office there, and may in perpetuity freely perform what pertains to the Cistercian Order in accordance with the Rule of St Benedict, saving always in all things the right,

²¹¹ The entry promised to give the terms more fully at the bottom of the folio, but this was not done.
²¹² Bronescombe died two days after this appropriation.

honour and dignity of the bishop and of the church of Exeter.' [Bishops]teignton, 22 July 1280.

1429*[213]   LETTER OF THE SAME BISHOP AGAINST THE HOUSEHOLD MEMBERS OF THE LORD EDMUND, EARL OF CORNWALL, WRONGDOERS TO THE BISHOP. The bishop wrote to [Roger de Torridge], the dean, [John Noble or John de Esse[214]], the archdeacon, and [Ralph de Hengham], the precentor of Exeter: 'The bride of Christ, the Church our mother, which has been ground down by various pressures in these days, groans sorrowfully, saying with the prophet "See, O Lord, and consider how I am made wretched; see my affliction because my enemy is uplifted".'[215] Recently out of duty we sent men tried and chosen and ecclesiastics in priest's orders, to St Allen in Cornwall to warn by our authority, in a spirit of gentleness and peace, certain nobles, knights, bailiffs, free men and common folk of the county of Cornwall, and certain of the intimate household of the noble Lord Edmund, earl of Cornwall, armigerous persons forsooth, and others sent from his side or at his command, as is alleged, [to warn them] to cease and desist, desist and cease from their planned and malicious aspiration against the Church of God and its liberties before proceeding to put it into action, and to bring to their attention the salvation of their souls and the dangers which they would incur *ipso facto* from such a plan if it were put into effect.

Certain of these aforementioned lay persons, being armed in order to execute this sort of conspiracy, calling boldness to their aid, gathered a mob and, like the savagest of executioners, seized by a spirit of madness, rushed out with drawn swords and other weapons against the aforesaid ecclesiastics wherever they could find them, in the church, the holy places, the sanctuary, and outside; others, whether bowed before the altars or fleeing in all directions, they atrociously wounded, flogged, and hurled to the ground; they dragged them at their horses' tails, and treated them inhumanly and basely; they spilled blood in the church of God, carried out other atrocities and wrongs, and put the fear of death in them; they foully defiled the priestly garments they were wearing by cutting off the tips of their cowls almost to the midpoint and the upper parts of the hoods which they were wearing – in mockery of a tonsure; they turned their madness upon the dumb animals, that is, their palfreys and other horses, for from some of them they cut the ears, tails and upper lips clean off, others they actually killed, others they mutilated and wounded so as to lay bare the bone; further, they committed sacrilege, rapine, and other enormities, which it would take too long to enumerate, in contumely of the Creator, contempt of the Church, and subversion of ecclesiastical liberty.

Although, therefore, on the evidence of a deed which is manifest, notorious, and incapable of being hidden by any tergiversation, we would be able to proceed with very great severity against the aforesaid sacrilegious persons, their prompters and accomplices, as justice recommends, yet by reason of our respect

---

[213] This entry was added later to fill in the blank lower half of the folio. It has been numbered in continuation because its subject and date do fit within the register.

[214] Depending on whether the archdeacon of Exeter or Cornwall is meant; cf **1012** & **1013**.

[215] *Lamentations* 1, 11 & 9.

for the personal absence of the lord king, and the belief — which we dare not banish totally from our mind — that such transgressors and their accomplices may, God willing, return to their senses and make worthy satisfaction, we defer temporarily the execution of the law, etc.

We command you, by virtue of your obedience and under canonical pains, that you should publicly and solemnly denounce and have denounced, in our cathedral church and in every collegiate and parochial church in our diocese, on every Sunday, with candles lit and bells rung, all the aforementioned sacrilegious persons with their prompters and accomplices, and all those offering them help, aid and counsel and also reckless companionship with malignant intent, as falling or having fallen under the canons *ipso facto*, until such time as you shall receive other commands from us. And the content and effect of these letters is to be published without delay in the cathedral church of Exeter in the presence of the archdeacons, after summoning together as many of the clergy as can conveniently be present. We do not wish this denunciation in any way to extend to the persons of Richard of Almain, son of the king of Germany, and Guy de Nonant, knights, or John [fo.98v] de Insula, John Heyron, Maurice Caperon and Richard Garron, who, returning to the bosom of the Church, have taken a corporal oath to abide by the commands of the Church, to make satisfaction to those injured, and to undertake fitting penance.' The recipients were to inform the bishop in letters patent of what they had done. Ospringe, 9 May 1273.